A CLOUD OF WITNESSES FROM THE HEART OF THE CITY

First Presbyterian Church, Raleigh,

1816–2016

MERCER UNIVERSITY

MERCER UNIVERSITY PRESS

Endowed by

TOM WATSON BROWN
and
THE WATSON-BROWN FOUNDATION, INC.

A CLOUD OF WITNESSES FROM THE HEART OF THE CITY

First Presbyterian Church, Raleigh,

1816–2016

W. GLENN JONAS JR.

MERCER UNIVERSITY PRESS | Macon, Georgia

2016

MUP/ H925

Published by Mercer University Press
1501 Mercer University Drive
Macon, Georgia 31207

9 8 7 6 5 4 3 2 1

Books published by Mercer University Press are printed on acid-free paper that meets the requirements of the American National Standard for Information Sciences—Permanence of Paper for Printed Library Materials.

ISBN 978-0-88146-591-4
Cataloging-in-Publication Data is available from the Library of Congress

Contents

Acknowledgments vii
Foreword by Merrill C. Hawkins xi
1. Who Are the Presbyterians? 1
2. Establishing a Presence 17
3. Growing in Prominence 39
4. Leading the Way 70
5. Surviving Dissension 100
6. Poised for a New Century 132
7. Growing into a New Century 157
8. Strengthening the Legacy 180
9. Building a Heritage 206
10. Facing a New Century 230
Conclusion: Serving Christ for Two Centuries 255
Appendix 1: God, the Giver of Victory and Peace: A Thanksgiving Sermon 265
Appendix 2: Casting Our Burden on the Lord 279
Index 287

This book is dedicated to William P. McPherson. I never had the privilege of knowing him personally. However, I do know that he loved his church and particularly cared about preserving its history. Now one of the "cloud of witnesses," he awaits the final consummation of all things.

Acknowledgments

There is great value in chronicling the history of a local congregation. Church historian Buddy Shurden speaking of the value of writing local congregational history, once wrote, "I believe that one of the most urgent and neediest areas in…[historical work] is that we learn to do serious, in-depth, scholarly work on local churches."[1]

Local congregational history allows for a particular community of faith to see its story set in the broader context of local, state, and national history. That is what I have sought to do in this book. The first chapter provides the reader with a general overview of the Presbyterian tradition from its beginning and development until the nineteenth century when First Presbyterian Church was established. Each successive chapter begins with the American historical context for the time period covered by that chapter. The national scene then transitions to the local Raleigh setting against which the church's history is told. I hope the reader will not find this arrangement tedious and unimportant. I believe the best way to tell the church's history is within its broader historical context.

Edward Hallett Carr once observed that history is a "process of interaction, a dialogue between the historian in the present and the facts of the past."[2] Primary sources are foundational to the work that historians do. The historian, working in the present to interpret the past, is always limited by the sources that are available. Fortunately, the primary sources for writing the history of First Presbyterian Church have been preserved very well over the years. The church is to be commended for its careful attention to preserving and protecting these priceless records, an effort that extends back into the nineteenth century. Without these sources,

---

[1]Walter B. Shurden, "Microscopic Baptist History," *The Baptist Studies Bulletin* 3 (March 2004): 2.

[2]Edward Hallett Carr, *What is History?* (New York: Alfred A. Knopf, 1963) 5. For Ranke's influence on the discipline of history in the nineteenth century, see Georg G. Iggers, "The Image of Ranke in American and German Historical Thought," *History and Theory* 2/1 (1962): 42.

this book could not have been written. I could not have completed it in a timely manner had I not been trusted by the church with these sources. I extend both my gratitude and appreciation to the church for their careful attention to these documents.

It should be noted that since I am not a member of First Presbyterian Church, my telling of the story may differ in detail from the way someone who is a longtime member may tell it. Writing history involves reading the sources and then making decisions about what to include and what to exclude. I take full responsibility for these decisions. Some may read this book and be frustrated or disappointed that a particular person or anecdotal story is missing. If so, I apologize and assure the reader that there was no intended malice on my part.

I am grateful to numerous people for their help in this project. First, I am very grateful to the Session of the First Presbyterian Church. I appreciate the confidence that they had in selecting and entrusting to me the responsibility of writing the church's bicentennial history. Second, I appreciate the help given to me by Drs. Edwin Stock and Ed McLeod. They were quite helpful in providing information that was included in chapters 10 and 11.

Here at Campbell University, I am very grateful to the staff of Wiggins Memorial Library. The library provided to me a study carrel, which became a quiet refuge for research and writing. The librarians were also quite helpful, especially in securing interlibrary loan materials. I am also grateful to my colleagues in the Department of Christian Studies at Campbell University. For several years now, they have heard probably more about this project more than they wanted. Thank you for your patience and helpful suggestions. Dr. Adam English, chair of the Department of Christian Studies here at Campbell and my good friend, made some very helpful suggestions to me throughout the process. I am also grateful to Dr. Michael Wells, the dean of the College of Arts and Sciences, and Dr. Mark Hammond, our vice president for academic affairs and provost, for their support and patient encouragement throughout my work on this project.

I extend gratitude to Dr. Merrill Hawkins, professor of religion at Carson-Newman University, for providing a gracious foreword to this book. Mel and I have been close friends for many years, and I appreciate his willingness to read the manuscript. Numerous telephone conversations over the last four years have revolved around this project, and I am grateful for his advice.

I express my appreciation to Mercer University Press and its editor, Dr. Marc Jolley. This is now the fifth project that we have worked on together, and I continue to be impressed by your professionalism and how easy it is to work with you. Thank you again for your willingness to accept this project.

A special word of thanks needs to be extended to Mr. Dave Permar, a longtime member at First Presbyterian Church. I don't think this project could have happened without his involvement. Special thanks for the many, many phone calls and meetings at the church, where he graciously provided everything I needed to expedite my work. Dave served as my liaison to the church. He made it possible for me to have access to all of the church's records. He also served as my primary contact for questions, background information, and suggestions. It has truly been a pleasure getting to know him and working with him.

I am greatly indebted to Jonathan Lee for his editorial help with this book. Jonathan is very gifted in a number of areas, none more so than his editorial skill. He provided excellent proofreading, caught my errors, and made some helpful suggestions throughout the book. If the reader finds this book to be enjoyable, a great deal of credit needs to go to Jonathan.

Finally, thanks to my family for the many nights and weekends you allowed me to come back up to the office and work when the building was quiet. Thanks for your encouragement and support!

There is a famous New Testament text from the anonymous writer of Hebrews that declares, "Therefore, since we are surrounded by so great a cloud of witnesses, let us also lay aside every weight and the sin that clings so closely, and let us run with perseverance the race that is set before us."[3] The "cloud of witnesses" refers to the heroes of the faith named in the previous chapter envisioned as encouragers to the faithful in the writer's era. I have pondered this text as I have gotten to know the "cloud of witnesses" through the years at First Presbyterian Church while

---

[3]Hebrews 12:1 (NRSV)

reading the church's records. Their witness in the past serves as an encouragement to the present generation to persevere in faith.

In November 2000, First Presbyterian Church adopted as its mission statement, "Serving Christ from the Heart of the City to the Ends of the Earth, with Love, Faith, and Action."[4] The chapters that follow tell the story of how a local cloud of witnesses served Christ from the heart of the city to the ends of the earth.

—W. Glenn Jonas Jr.
Epiphany, 2016

[4]Minutes of the Session, 15 November 2000.

Foreword

Raleigh's First Presbyterian Church has a rich and full history as a leading community of faith in North Carolina's capital city. Present in the city from its earliest history, First Presbyterian Church has grown up with the city of Raleigh and the state of North Carolina during their shared history. From that Sunday so many years ago on 21 January 1816, when Reverend William McPheeters gathered several "professors of the religion of Jesus Christ" to form the congregation to the Capital Campaign of the late 1990s, First Presbyterian Church has been in the center of the spiritual lives of many citizens of Raleigh. Historian Glenn Jonas has captured the story of this congregation, providing a detailed narrative of everything, to paraphrase the words of beloved former pastor Edwin Stock, on the right and the left of the church.

Readers of this thoroughly researched history will find an exhaustive account of the life of First Presbyterian grounded in the primary documents of the congregation. Church minutes, session records, and denominational publications have all been consulted. Many congregational histories consist of little more than a narrative of persons from the past, with no connection to the wider history of the church's context. This volume possesses no such weaknesses. Jonas has placed the story of First Presbyterian within the wider context of Reformation history, as well as early American religious history and the history of North Carolina. Institutions and the people who lead them always stand in multiple contexts. Readers of this account of the story of First Presbyterian will have at their hands a narrative that links the congregation to wider currents of human activity.

Local histories crafted by professional historians make several important contributions, and this volume is no exception. First and foremost, this volume brings together the scattered records that contain the life of First Presbyterian Church into a single story for the congregants to have for many years to come. This local interest, which rightly motivated the congregation to commission the study, does not exhaust all the benefits of its writing. Second, the history will provide a local study of an expression of American religious history in general and Southern religion in particular. Historical scholarship increasingly looks to examine how national and regional trends find expression in local communities. This magnificent study of this gifted congregation will provide such a local study that will serve the interests of professional historians and other critical readers for quite a few years to come.

First Presbyterian is to be commended for commissioning the history of the congregation. Glenn Jonas provides a detailed accounting of the institution and the stories of the people who are part of the institution that has graced the city of Raleigh since its early days.

—Merrill Hawkins
Professor of Religion
Carson-Newman University
Jefferson City, Tennessee

First State House completed and occupied in 1794.

This painting of the First State House was painted by Jacob Marling in 1818. The brick building in the background was the first branch of the Bank of New Bern, located at the south west corner of Fayetteville and Morgan Street. On Sunday, January 21, 1816, Rev. William McPheeters organized the Presbyterian Church at a church service in the State House. The church soon purchased a lot at the south west corner of Morgan and Salisbury and began building the first brick church in Raleigh.

The Raleigh Academy

In 1801, a group of Raleigh citizens petitioned the legislature to allow them to use Burke Square (where the Governor's mansion is now located) for the Raleigh Academy. In 1804, the building was competed and a French Huguenot Minister, Rev. Marin DeTargny was hired as Principal. After a few months he went to Charleston, S.C. and become the minister of the French Protestant Church. In 1806, the Reverend William Leftwich Turner was hired as Principal of the school and Pastor of the City. As Pastor of the City, the Reverend Turner conducted services in the State House on a regular basis and the Academy grew to overflowing. In 1809, Turner accepted a call to be minister of the Fayetteville Presbyterian Church. Turner was formerly employed as Professor of Language at Washington College in Lexington, Va. In 1810, William McPheeters was hired as Principal of The Raleigh Academy and Pastor of the City.

First Sanctuary

The Presbyterian Church was the first brick church in Raleigh. Construction began in July, 1816. The building was dedicated in February 1818 and torn down in 1898.

Session House, completed in 1825.

Session House and First Sanctuary

Rev. William McPheeters, D.D.

Served as founding pastor of the Raleigh Presbyterian Church from January 21, 1816 through 1830. The above portrait of Dr. McPheeters was made by Jacob Marling.

Believed to be Mrs. William McPheeters

Sylvania Williams (Easton) Potter and Henry Potter

Henry Potter was a Federal District Court Judge, was a charter member, Elder and Trustee of First Presbyterian Church.

Rev. Drury Lacy, D.D., 1837–1855

Mrs. Drury Lacy (Mary Rice)

First President of first Missionary Society, 1875–1880

Leopold Heartt home built in 1855 on Hargett Street.

Heartt was Raleigh's first Fire Chief and an Elder at First Presbyterian.

Susan McPheeter's home on Dawson Street.

Rev. J.E. Atkinson D.D., 1855–1875

Rev. John S. Watkins, D.D., 1878–1892

Rev. Eugene Daniel, D.D., 1893–1902

Dr. Alfred H. Moment, D.D., 1903–1907

Peace Institute, opened 1872

Old Main, Peace College

Second Sanctuary, completed 1900, photo taken ca. 1920

The Second Sanctuary interior as it appeared from1900–1956.

Rev. William McC White, D.D., 1908–1934

Edmund Burwell Crow, 1874–1945

Founder and teacher of The Vanguard Class

Christian Education Building, completed ca. 1925

Interior of Vanguard Room, as renovated, ca. 1925

First Vanguard Church

Located at the southeat corner of Martin of Swain Streets, ca. 1920

E. E. Moffitt, 1836–1930

Leader of Foreign Missionary Society

Primary Sunday School Class in front of Christian Education Building, ca. 1930

Middle Sunday School Class

Mary Bates Sherwood (second row, far right), ca. 1930

Rev. P. D. Miller, D.D., 1934–1941

Rev. Maurice O. Sommers, D.D., 1941–1949

New Kate Sprunt Library, opened 1953

Norman Acker, organist; Martha McCorkle and William McCorkle (right to left) in basement dining room, Christian Education Building

Rev. James Sprunt, D.D., 1951–1957

Rev. Albert George Edwards, 1958–1986

Chancel renovation, ca. 1956

Mrs. B. H. Bunch (left), honored at a Christmas Party in Fellowship Hall, in basement of Christian Education Building

First Presbyterian Church member,
David Fox wins a gold medal at the 1996 Olympics.

Rev. Edwin W. Stock, Jr., D. Min., leads a fundraising campaign
for a new child development center; a family life center, and mission outreach

Rev. Edwin W. Stock Jr., D. Min., 1988–2002

Rev. Edward A. McLeod, D.D., 2004–

First Presbyterian Church Session during the 1990's

First Presbyterian Diaconate during the 1990's

Dedication of renovated Second Sanctuary, September 30, 2012

1

Who Are the Presbyterians?

The moniker "frozen chosen" is often used to describe the Presbyterian denomination. The term conjures up images of formal, buttoned-down worship coupled with the notion of God's eternal decrees of election. Whereas many Presbyterian churches today do have a formalized, liturgical style of worship, and while the denomination is rooted in the Reformed tradition, the nickname is not accurate. In the United States, much of the Presbyterian tradition experienced significant growth from the revival fires of the First and Second Great Awakenings, which were influential in American religious history in the eighteenth and nineteenth centuries. At first glance, it may be easy to stereotype the Presbyterians, but in reality, there is much more to the story.

For the last five hundred years, at least three types of ecclesiastical polity have guided various Christian traditions. An "episcopal" type of polity, prevalent in Roman Catholic, Episcopal (Anglican), and Methodist traditions, employs bishops who hold authority over the various churches in their dioceses. The "congregational" style of polity, utilized by Baptist, Congregationalist, and non-denominational churches, centralizes authority within a local congregation. "Presbyterian" polity is a representative form of church governance. Each local Presbyterian congregation is governed by a "session." The members of the congregation elect the "elders" who make up the session, and aid in teaching, worship, and discipline matters within the church. A second group of officers, called "deacons" comprises the "diaconate" and is elected to serve the physical needs of the church, such as caring for the poor or ministering to the grieving. The "presbytery" governs local Presbyterian congregations in a geographical area and is made up of elected representatives from each of the congregations it governs. The "synod," made up of elected representatives from each presbytery, governs a larger geographical area, typically several states. The General Assembly, which meets annually, caps off the entire system.[1]

The Beginning of the Presbyterian Tradition

The story of Presbyterianism began in the sixteenth century, one of the significant centuries in Western Christianity. Spurred by the Renaissance, the Roman Catholic Church encountered significant internal challenges during this century, resulting in the movement known as the Reformation. Rather than a unified movement, the Reformation was instead a series of various movements that simultaneously broke out in different locations throughout Western Europe. Presbyterianism is rooted in the Swiss wing of the Reformation.

The first reform efforts in Switzerland began with Ulrich Zwingli in Zurich, where in 1518 he became priest of the largest church in the city. By the time of his arrival in Zurich, he had already embraced Protestant theology, having been prompted to do so by his study of the Greek New Testament. He gained the support of the city council, which cooperated to pass laws purging from the city any trace of Roman Catholic practices or traditions. Zwingli's reform efforts in Zurich lasted until 1531. During that year, the five Catholic cantons in Switzerland launched a military attack on the city. Zwingli joined the effort to defend the city but was killed in the Battle of Koppel. Within a month of his death, the Peace of Koppel was signed with the result that each canton in Switzerland would have the freedom to choose between Catholicism and Protestantism.

Following the death of Zwingli, John Calvin became the most important name associated with the Reformation in Switzerland. Calvin was born in 1509 in Noyon, France. His father had an important job as secretary to the bishop of Noyon. The position paid well and provided the necessary funds for Calvin's schooling. He studied for a career in law at the Universities of Paris, Orléans, and Bourges. During his schooling, like Zwingli before him, he became thoroughly influenced by the spirit

[1]Randall Balmer and John R. Fitzmier, *The Presbyterians* (Westport, CT: Greenwood Press, 1993) 15–16. This is a very good and brief history of the Presbyterian tradition. It uniquely includes a biographical dictionary of significant Presbyterian leaders throughout the denomination's history.

of humanism and its attention to ancient culture. It is not known when Calvin made his formal break with the Roman Catholic Church. It is clear that he was Protestant by 1534 because in that year he fled from France due to persecution of Protestants. He finally settled in Basel, Switzerland.

In 1536, Calvin wrote the first edition of the *Institutes of the Christian Religion*. One of the most important theological works in Christian history, it brought him immediate attention and fame. Originally published as a manual that could be easily concealed in one's pocket, it went through a number of revisions. The final edition, which occupied four volumes, was published in 1559. Reading the different editions of the *Institutes* provides an interesting picture of how Calvin's theology grew and developed from 1536 until 1559.

A significant turning point in Calvin's life came in 1536 when he visited Geneva. There he met William Farel, who had initiated Protestant reforms in the city. Farel, needing help, requested that Calvin stay in Geneva and join the reform movement. Calvin agreed to stay and remained there for two years, but it was a turbulent period. Almost immediately, Calvin began writing laws that he expected the city council to endorse. He sought to establish a "theocracy" in Geneva that would be governed by the same laws as the ancient Hebrews in the Old Testament. His vision included such things as "blue laws" (which forbid any business dealings on Sundays), forced church attendance, a confession of faith to which all citizens of Geneva were expected to assent, training of children in Protestant ideas, and a system of lay inspectors who would observe the conduct of the citizens and report any moral problems to Calvin. The laws proved so unpopular that the people initiated a riot against the city government. Although the annual election of 1537 favored Calvin and his supporters, a year later the opposition won and took over the council. Calvin and Farel fled to nearby Strasbourg.

Calvin spent three years in Strasbourg, which proved to be his happiest and most peaceful. Though he turned his attention to writing, he always yearned to return to Geneva to complete the experiment with theocracy he started there. That opportunity came in 1541. The political situation with the city government changed once again, and Calvin was invited to return. This time he was assured that there would be support for his reform efforts. Following his return in 1541, he remained there until his death in 1564. During those years, his dream of creating a theocracy was realized although, by modern democratic standards, it was an oppressive, restrictive place to live. Nevertheless, Calvin should be regarded as one of the greatest reformers of the Reformation era, especially because of his keen theological insights and writing.[2]

Following Calvin's death in 1564, his followers began to organize his theology around the core principle of predestination, an emphasis that differed from his own approach in *The Institutes of the Christian Religion*. Predestination subsequently became the defining characteristic of Reformed theology during the last quarter of the sixteenth century, largely due to the efforts of Calvin's later adherents. Those efforts eventually drew opposition from Jacob Arminius, a Dutch pastor and professor at the University of Leyden. Arminius began to speak out against the logical determinism of Calvinism as it was portrayed by the Calvinists. Reaction to Arminius came swiftly in the form of heresy charges. Although eventually acquitted, Arminius spent his last few years in controversy. He died in 1609.

In 1610, Arminius's loyalists issued the *Remonstrance,* a document that encompassed the main points of his opposition to Calvinist theology built around predestination. The *Remonstrance* had five points: (1) God's salvation is available to all; (2) Christ died for all people; (3) apart from the Holy Spirit no one can acquire salvation; (4) it is possible to resist the grace of God; (5) it is possible to fall from grace or lose one's salvation. The *Remonstrance* represents a clear articulation of what is known today as Arminian theology. As one might expect, since Holland was dominated by Calvinists in the early seventeenth century, those loyal to Calvinism convened the Synod of Dort in 1618 and formally rejected each point of the *Remonstrance.* The canons of Dort have been remembered by students through the years by the acrostic TULIP: (1) total depravity; (2) unconditional election; (3) limited atonement; (4) irresistible grace; (5)

[2]Information about John Calvin in the preceding paragraphs was first published by the author in Kathryn Muller Lopez, Donald N. Penny, W. Glenn Jonas, Jr., and Adam C. English, *Christianity: A Biblical, Historical, and Theological Guide for Students* (Macon, GA: Mercer University Press, 2010) 199–201.

perseverance of the saints. Thus, a century after the Reformation began, the stage was set for the division of Protestantism between Calvinism (known as "Reformed theology") and Arminianism.

Prior to the debate in the seventeenth century in Holland between the Calvinists and Arminians, major political and religious changes occurred in England and Scotland. Protestantism was initiated in England during the reign of Henry VIII. It progressed further under the rule of Henry's successor and only male heir, Edward VI, who had assumed the throne as a child. Edward's untimely death in 1553 brought to the throne Mary Tudor, the firstborn child to Henry VIII and his first wife, Catherine of Aragon. Mary was determined to restore the connection between England and Rome. During her reign, she earned the nickname "Bloody Mary" from her persecution and the martyrdom of more than three hundred Protestants. Mary died after reigning for only five years, and the throne was assumed by her half-sister Elizabeth I, who finally provided political stability with a reign that lasted for forty-five years.

Elizabeth was politically shrewd and understood that she needed to formulate a *via media* in matters of religion lest England descend into civil war between Protestants and Catholics. By retaining the episcopal form of ecclesiology on the one hand and freedom from Rome on the other, she was able to organize the Anglican Church in such a way that moderates from both the Catholic and Protestant persuasions could be accommodated. Not everyone was satisfied. Protestants who fled to the Continent during Mary's persecutions returned when Elizabeth assumed power, hopeful that she would continue the Protestant cause. Their disappointment in her unwillingness to "purify" the English church any further (in the direction of Protestantism) served as the genesis of the Puritan movement, which developed in the last few decades of the sixteenth century.

The Reformation in Scotland, led by John Knox, was most significant for Presbyterian history. Knox received his education from the University of Glasgow and became involved in the political conflicts of the day between Scotland and France. The French took him prisoner and forced him into slave labor rowing aboard a galley. He was released in 1551, went to England, and became chaplain to Edward VI. With the ascension of Mary to the throne, he joined other Marian exiles and fled

England for Geneva, where he came under the tutelage of John Calvin. Under Calvin's influence, he aided in the translation of the Geneva Bible (1560) and wrote *The First Blast of the Trumpet against the Monstrous Regiment of Women*, aimed at the reigns of the queens of England and Scotland, Mary Tudor and Mary Guise, respectively. Knox was primarily agitated by their Catholicism, but he also opposed women rulers in general. When Elizabeth I ascended to the throne, she took offense to the book also. In the meantime, Knox returned to Scotland as both the English and French were withdrawing. This left him with the freedom to create the Scottish Church (called the "Kirk" in Scotland) in a thoroughly Calvinist image.[3] According to Balmer and Fitzmier, Knox's "chief contribution to Presbyterianism lay in his efforts to establish a Presbyterian polity distinct from the English episcopacy and to develop Reformed liturgical forms for the Kirk."[4]

As Puritanism developed in England during the early seventeenth century, so did different forms of church polity. Most Puritans opposed the episcopal system but were divided between the congregational and presbyterial ecclesiastical polities. Presbyterianism in Scotland proved to be successful, and some in England began to champion that system for the English church. In 1643, Parliament called into session the Westminster Assembly of Divines for the purpose of reforming the English church government and theology. While the assembly never achieved its full goal of ecclesiastical reform in England, it was successful in producing several creedal statements that were instrumental to the Presbyterian tradition: *The Form of Presbyterial Church Government* (1644), *The Directory of Public Worship* (1644), *The Westminster Confession of Faith* (1647), *The Larger Catechism* (1647), and *The Shorter Catechism* (1647).[5]

The Presbyterian Tradition in the United States

As early as the 1640s, Scottish immigrants, though not great in number, had trickled into New England, bringing their Presbyterian

---

[3]James H. Smylie, *A Brief History of the Presbyterians* (Louisville, KY: Geneva Press, 1996) 30.

[4]Balmer and Fitzmier, *Presbyterians*, 17.

[5]Ibid., 18.

faith with them. Presbyterian growth in the New World is mostly attributed, however, to the migration of the Scotch-Irish, beginning in the late seventeenth century. Middle colonies, such as New Jersey and Pennsylvania, were most frequently their destination because the religious pluralism there afforded more freedom than the colonies to the north and south. These two colonies became the center of Presbyterianism in colonial America.

The most important person associated with the development of Presbyterianism in the New World was Francis Makemie, often called the "father of American Presbyterianism."[6] Born in 1658 in Ireland and educated in Scotland, in 1681 he was commissioned in Northern Ireland to serve as a missionary in the American colonies. In 1684, Makemie established America's first Presbyterian congregation, located in Snow Hill, Maryland. His greatest work, however, was his success in establishing in 1706 the Presbytery of Philadelphia, the first such organization of Presbyterians in America. The new presbytery successfully unified diverse Presbyterians from England, Wales, Scotland, New England, and the Scotch-Irish.[7]

Makemie was also an early voice for the cause of religious freedom in the colonies. In 1707, the colonial governor of New York, Lord Cornbury, had Makemie and a colleague, John Hampden, arrested for preaching without a civil license. Cornbury frequently used this tactic to discourage those who dissented from the colony's established religion, the

---

[6]Ibid., 194.

[7]See Ibid., 24–25. The charter members of the Philadelphia Presbytery came from remarkably diverse backgrounds. Samuel Davis was a merchant as well as a minister in Lewes, Delaware. He originally came to the colonies from Ireland. George McNish, from Scotland, and John Hampden, a Scotch-Irishman, originally came to the colonies, representing the Moravian tradition. Three were originally from New England: Nathaniel Taylor, Jedediah Andrews, and John Wilson. And Makemie himself was originally from Ireland and educated in Scotland and had solid connections in both England and New England. See also Smylie, *Brief History*, 43. According to Smylie, within ten years the presbytery had grown into the Synod of Philadelphia, which was divided into four presbyteries: Philadelphia, New Castle, Long Island, and Snow Hill (the Snow Hill Presbytery never achieved organizational structure).

Church of England. Although Hampden was released shortly after his imprisonment, Makemie remained in prison for six weeks. When he came to trial, he successfully argued that he was not a dissenter and that his theology fully complied with the Act of Toleration passed by Parliament in 1689. Nevertheless, he was held responsible for the court costs of the proceedings against him. Following his acquittal, he wrote and published *A Narrative of a New and Unusual American Imprisonment of Two Presbyterian Ministers and Prosecution of Mr. Francis Makemie*, which embarrassed Cornbury and subsequently led to his recall to England.[8] Historian Mark Noll noted that "this event solidified the image of Presbyterians as defenders of freedom in the public mind and won new respect for the denomination in America."[9] Makemie died the following year (1708) in Virginia.

As the eighteenth century progressed, so did the organization of the Presbyterians in colonial America. The Subscription Controversy became the denomination's first major dispute. The disagreement centered on issues related to ordination and whether candidates should be required to subscribe to the *Westminster Confession of Faith* and catechisms. Those who advocated subscription argued that formally subscribing to the *Confession* was necessary to insure doctrinal purity. Opposition came from those who believed that while the *Confession* and other statements were helpful tools, they nevertheless were devised by humans and therefore inferior to Scripture. The controversy first surfaced in the Philadelphia Synod in the 1720s. The controversy generally reflected cultural and theological differences between the Scotch-Irish, who favored subscription and tended to be more conservative, and those from England and New England, who descended from the Puritan tradition and tended to be more concerned about spiritual piety. The Adopting Act of 1729 at-

---

[8]Balmer and Fitzmier, *Presbyterians*, 194.

[9]Mark A. Noll, *A History of Christianity in the United States and Canada* (Grand Rapids: Eerdmans, 1992) 69. For information about Makemie's life and writings see Isaac Marshall Page, *The Life Story of Rev. Francis Makemie* (Grand Rapids: Eerdmans, 1938); B. S. Schlenther, ed., *The Life and Writings of Francis Makemie* (Philadelphia: Presbyterian Historical Society, 1971); and J. H. Smylie, "Francis Makemie: Tradition and Challenge," *Journal of Presbyterian History* 61/2 (Summer 1983): 197–209.

tempted to bring compromise to the two sides. It provided that any minister or candidate for ordination who differed with, or objected to, any of the particulars of the *Westminster Confession of Faith* was to be judged by the appropriate presbytery as to whether or not the objection could theologically be justified according to the broader parameters of the *Confession*.[10]

No religious movement was more important to the American colonies than the First Great Awakening, a series of revivals that erupted throughout the eastern seaboard. The Awakening dawned just as Presbyterianism was beginning to experience growth, and it to be both a blessing and a curse to Presbyterians. The denomination experienced substantial growth prior to the American Revolution as a result of the Awakening, but the Awakening also exacerbated the growing division between the New England-influenced Presbyterians and the more conservative, traditional Presbyterian style of the Scotch-Irish.

Presbyterian growth created a need for ministers that far exceeded the supply of duly educated clergy who could be transplanted from England and Scotland. Aware of the need, Will Tennent Sr. organized a small school for training ministers in his home. Called "Log College" (originally a term of derision), Tennent began the process of educating ministers with an emphasis on piety. His three sons were among the earliest students, but his son Gilbert became the most ardent supporter of the revivalist fervor and champion of what became "New Side" Presbyterianism. Gilbert became so enthused about "experimental" religion that he wrote a sermon called "The Danger of an Unconverted Ministry." The sermon was published and quickly became a source of controversy in Presbyterian circles because it was regarded as a direct affront to Presbyterian ministers who did not support the pietistic enthusiasm of the revivals. Using the words of Jesus in Mark 6:34, Tennent attacked the ministers who opposed the revivals, declaring that their church members were like "sheep not having a shepherd." He compared these ministers to the Pharisees who opposed Jesus, claiming that they had "no experience

---

[10]Balmer and Fitzmier, *Presbyterians*, 23–25. See also *Dictionary of Christianity in America*, ed. Daniel G. Reid et al. (Downers Grove, IL: InterVarsity Press, 1990) s.v. "Subscription Controversy."

of a special work of the Holy Ghost upon their own souls, [and] are neither inclined to nor fitted for discoursing frequently, clearly, and pathetically upon such important subjects." Toward the conclusion of the sermon, he called for "those who live under the ministry of dead men…repair to the living where they may be edified," an obvious attempt to encourage laity to leave the churches of those ministers who opposed the Awakening.[11]

The "Old Side" ministers, on the other hand, were troubled by numerous issues raised by the Awakening. The excessive emotionalism of the revivals troubled many Presbyterians, particularly as they heard reports of crying, shouting, involuntary bodily convulsions, and many other such expressions. They also condemned the contemptuous attitudes of many New Side ministers toward their more reserved counterparts. The practice of using itinerant clergy also became an issue for the Old Side Presbyterians because it seemed to disrupt proper order and, more importantly, presbyterial control over the clergy. These differences between Old Side and New Side led in 1741 to a split between the two parties in the Synod of Philadelphia.[12] The Old Side Presbyterians remained with the Synod of Philadelphia while the New Side formed the Synod of New York.

Despite the Old Side/New Side division, Presbyterianism continued to grow in the eighteenth century. In the four decades between 1740 and 1780, the number of congregations grew from ninety-five to almost 500.[13] The need for properly educated clergy led to the chartering of the College of New Jersey in 1746, from which both Princeton University and Princeton Theological Seminary would eventually emerge. As might be predicted, during the years of the split between the old and new sides, the number of Old Side ministers dwindled from twenty-seven to twen-

---

[11]Gilbert Tennent, "The Danger of an Unconverted Ministry," in *Sermons of the Log College*, ed. Archibald Alexander (Ligonier, PA: Soli Deo Gloria Publications, 1993), http://www.sounddoctrine.net/Classic_Sermons/Gilbert%20 Tennent/danger_of_unconverted.pdf.

[12]See Balmer and Fitzmier, *Presbyterians*, 30; Smylie, *Brief History*, 49.

[13]Edwin S. Gaustad, *Historical Atlas of Religion in America*, rev. ed. (New York: Harper and Row, 1976), as cited by Balmer and Fitzmier, *Presbyterians*, 31.

ty-three while the number of New Side clergy increased from twenty-two to seventy-three. Despite their apparent strength, the New Side made the most effort for reunification with the Old Side, a reunification eventually brought about in 1758. Thus was born the Synod of New York and Philadelphia, organized upon a compromise. Both sides endorsed the Awakening as a legitimate work of God while also recognizing that there were emotional excesses that were not healthy. The compromise also granted a certain measure of liberty regarding interpretation and acceptance of the Westminster standards and, perhaps most importantly, gave the power of ordination to the presbyteries.[14]

In May 1789, American Presbyterians held the organizational meeting of the first General Assembly of the Presbyterian Church of the United States of America. The meeting occurred at the Second Presbyterian Church in Philadelphia. The new General Assembly was divided into four synods: New York and New Jersey, Philadelphia, Virginia, and the Carolinas. The General Assembly encompassed sixteen presbyteries, 177 ministers, 111 probationers, and 419 churches.[15]

The Presbyterian Tradition in North Carolina

Francis Makemie was the first Presbyterian minister to conduct services in North Carolina. Records show that he came to the state in 1683 and again in 1684 although most of his ministry centered in the Middle colonies.[16] The great period of Presbyterian growth in North Carolina came in the middle decades of the eighteenth century from two sources. Scotch-Irish settlers began to migrate from Pennsylvania into the Piedmont region in the 1730s. During the next decade, Scottish Highlanders began to arrive from Scotland through the port in Wilmington. They

---

[14]Balmer and Fitzmier, *Presbyterians*, 32.

[15]Lefferts A. Loetscher, *A Brief History of the Presbyterians*, 3rd ed. (Philadelphia: Westminster Press, 1978) 77, as cited by Balmer and Fitzmier, *Presbyterians*, 38.

[16]Walter H. Conser and Robert J. Cain, *Presbyterians in North Carolina: Race, Politics, and Religious Identity in Historical Perspective* (Knoxville: University of Tennessee Press, 2012) 3; *Encyclopedia of North Carolina*, ed. William S. Powell et al. (Chapel Hill: University of North Carolina Press, 2006) s.v. "Presbyterian Church."

settled first in Bladen County, eventually spreading to the neighboring counties of Cumberland, Sampson, Moore, Robeson, Richmond, and Anson.[17]

Most of the Presbyterian preaching among the Scottish settlers in North Carolina was done by missionaries making their way through the colony. Such missionaries included William Robinson and John Thompson, both sympathetic with the Old Side perspective during the years of the First Great Awakening. Hugh McAden was one of the first New Side missionaries to labor in North Carolina. McAden was a graduate of Princeton College and was licensed by New Castle Presbytery in 1755. According to his own account, there were very few organized churches, if any, and no regular ministers. Most of McAden's preaching was in open-air assemblies or in private homes. McAden attempted to preach to the Gaelic-speaking Scottish Highlanders who had settled along the Cape Fear River, but his inability to speak the language presented a barrier that prohibited effective ministry. McAden convinced James Campbell, a Presbyterian minister in Pennsylvania, to settle among Highlanders along the Cape Fear and minister to them.[18]

James Campbell was the most important Presbyterian minister in North Carolina in the decades prior to the American Revolution. An early historian of North Carolina Presbyterianism, William Henry Foote, spoke of the importance of Campbell's ministry: "The wonder is that in the circumstances of these colonists the sense of religion was so well maintained under the ministrations and labors of one solitary preacher, James Campbell, who pursued his laborious course alone among the out-spreading neighborhoods in what is now Cumberland and Robeson, from 1757 to 1770."[19]

Campbell was born in Scotland around 1700 and migrated to the American colonies around 1730 and arrived in Philadelphia as a licensed

---

[17]Guion Griffis Johnson, *Ante-bellum North Carolina: A Social History* (Chapel Hill: University of North Carolina Press, 1937) 349.

[18]Ernest Trice Thompson, *Presbyterians in the South,* 3 vols. (Richmond, VA: John Knox Press, 1963–1973) 1:62.

[19]William Henry Foote, *Sketches of North Carolina: Historical and Biographical Illustrative of a Portion of Her Early Settlers* (New York: Robert Carter, 1846) 131.

Presbyterian preacher. He began to minister to the Scottish immigrants in Pennsylvania until a crisis of faith caused him to doubt his salvation and call to ministry. An encounter with the great George Whitefield helped bring Campbell to a restoration of his faith. Whitefield recalled conversing with several ministers, including Campbell, in his journal:

> A third minister was a Mr. Camel [*sic*], who has been a preacher of the doctrines of grace for these four years; was a regular and moral liver, and accounted a very good man. But within these last few years, being convinced of sin, and that he knew nothing experimentally of Jesus Christ, (though he had pretended to preach Him so long), after many struggles with himself, told the Synod he was unconverted, and therefore dare not preach until he was; accordingly, he has left off preaching these two months, and has labored under unspeakable anguish and distress of soul. By some he is looked upon as melancholy, and beside himself; but I had much discourse with him, and really believe these humiliations will prepare him for great and eminent services in the Church of God.... At our persuasion, Mr. Camel [*sic*] promised to preach next Sunday, and I believe, will be instrumental in convicting many heart hypocrites among the Dissenting ministers.[20]

By all accounts, the counsel from Whitefield dispelled Campbell's doubts. He returned to preaching in the Lancaster area of Pennsylvania and then, in 1757, made his way south into North Carolina, where he settled a few miles north of Fayetteville on the Cape Fear River.[21]

Campbell became the first regular minister among the Scottish Highlanders although many had been in the state for several decades. It is noteworthy that these Scots were able to maintain their Presbyterian faith without formal church organization and ministerial leadership. One historian explained,

> [t]he fact that most of the Highlanders spoke only Gaelic protected them from the near-by Baptist missionaries at Sandy Creek and kept them faithful to Presbyterianism Calvinism during the many years when they were without the ministrations of a regular pastor. Their custom of family worship also kept their faith alive. Children learned the catechism from their elders and the church officers examined them

[20]George Whitefield, *George Whitefield's Journals* (Lafayette, IN: Sovereign Grace Publishers, 2000) 222.

[21]Foote, *Sketches*, 132.

> frequently on it. Before each hearth where there was reverence for the forms of the Scotch church the whole family read the Bible aloud every day and repeated the Shorter Catechism.[22]

The Highlanders contracted with Campbell in October 1758 to be their minister and offered him a salary of "a hundred pounds in good and lawful money of North Carolina."[23] Because the Anglican Church was the established religion in the North Carolina colony, before he began his ministerial duties, Campbell first had to swear an oath before the court in Cumberland County: "I James Campbell, do declare that I do believe that there is not any transubstantiation in the sacrament of the Lord's Supper, in the elements of the bread and wine at or after the consecration thereof by any person whatsoever."[24]

Campbell's ability to speak the Gaelic language along with English helped make his ministry successful along the regions of the upper Cape Fear. Reportedly, he preached in three locations regularly: the home of Roger McNeill (located along Tranthams Creek), the home of Archibald McKay (located on Yadkin Road and called "Long Street" then), and

---

[22]Johnson, *Ante-bellum*, 349.

[23]Quoted in Duane Meyer, *The Highland Scots of North Carolina, 1732–1776* (Chapel Hill: University of North Carolina Press, 1957) 114. According to Meyer's research, twelve men in the community signed the contract with Campbell promising payment: Hector McNeill, Gilbert Clark, Thomas Gibson, Alexander McAlister, Malcolm Smith, Archibald McKay, John Patterson, Dushee Shaw, Neill McNeill, Archibald Buie, and Anguish McPherson. Archibald McNeill and Archibald Clark are listed as witnesses to the contract's signing. The full contract is reprinted in *Colorful Heritage: An Informal History of Barbecue and Bluff Presbyterian Churches*, ed. Victor E. Clark and Louise Davis Curry (Dallas: Argyll Printing Center, 1989) 110. Clark and Curry edited together histories of these three churches written by different individuals and also reprinted a number of primary sources related to the three churches. Although only published as a typewritten manuscript, it is a valuable source of information about the early years of these three Presbyterian churches.

[24]Meyer, *Highland Scots*, 114–15. Dissenting ministers could not perform marriages legally until 1762, and even after that, the fee for service had to be surrendered to the Anglican minister in the parish. The Anglican Church was disestablished in North Carolina in 1776 when the state wrote its first constitution.

John Dobbin's Ordinary (located on Barbecue Creek). According to sources, he preached two sermons each week in a rotation between the three locations, one sermon in English and one in Gaelic. He used the opportunity of the open fourth Sunday to preach in other surrounding communities. These three congregations were eventually constituted as the Bluff, Long Street, and Barbecue Presbyterian churches.[25]

Campbell continued his ministerial labors until 1770, when Rev. John McLeod came with a new group of Scottish immigrants to the area. The two men ministered among the people together, but as the American Revolution began, politics divided them. McLeod, new to the colonies, was understandably a Loyalist. A number of the recent immigrants were loyal to the Crown also. McLeod left the Cape Fear region and joined the British army. He was captured by the Patriots, jailed in Halifax, and eventually released on the promise that he should leave the North Carolina colony. His ship left from Charleston and was presumably lost at sea. Conversely, Campbell and many of the Scots who had been in the colonies for much longer were more acquainted with and sympathetic to the Patriot cause. According to reports, the two groups, Loyalist and Patriot, came to worship armed. One can only surmise how tense the atmosphere must have been. Campbell encountered hostility from Loyalists at the Barbecue Church one Sunday morning, from a man in the church named McAlpin Munn, following a prayer he prayed publicly supporting the Patriot cause against the British. Because of such hostility encountered from Loyalists, Campbell fled for Guilford County but returned to the Cape Fear region in 1780, where he died shortly thereafter.[26]

An important milestone for the further expansion of Presbyterian-

---

[25]"The Reverend James Campbell (1705–1780)," accessed 8 February 2013, http://www.phcmontreat.org/bios/Campbell-James.htm. See *Colorful Heritage*, ed. Clark and Curry, for a full history of these three churches.

[26]See *Colorful Heritage*, ed. Clark and Curry, 40–41. The writer of the Barbecue Presbyterian Church history reports the legend that Munn said to his pastor in words similar to these: "Meenister, if ever ye pray again as ye did the day, the bullet is molded and the powder is in my horn to blow it through your head! By the way, I enjoyed your sermon this morning. You sure lambasted those sinners" (see page 40).

ism in North Carolina came with the organization of the Orange Presbytery in 1770. It was carved out of the Hanover Presbytery, which had been organized in 1755 with a boundary that included "Virginia and Southward."[27] The 24 May 1770 meeting of the Synod of New York and Philadelphia provided the authorization for the organization of the new presbytery:

> A petition from some members of the Hanover Presbytery requesting that they may be erected into a distinct Presbytery was brought in and read. The Synod agree to grant this prayer of the said petition, and the Reverend Mr. Hugh McAden, Henry Pattillo, James Creswell, Joseph Alexander, Hezekiah James Balch and Hezekiah Balch are erected into a Presbytery, to be known by the name of the Presbytery of Orange, and their first meeting to be at the Hawfields the first Wednesday of September next, and that Reverend Henry Pattillo open the Presbytery with a sermon. But the vacancies in these parts are allowed the same liberty of applying to the Synod for supplies as they have had in several cases heretofore.[28]

Orange Presbytery became the first presbytery to be organized entirely within the boundary of the colony of North Carolina. It had jurisdictional authority over South Carolina and Georgia in its early years, but that eventually changed in 1784 with the organization of the Presbytery of South Carolina. The Orange Presbytery began with six members, but within a decade, it included nineteen ordained minsters and five candidates for ordination.[29]

The eighteenth century was a good century for Presbyterianism in America. Despite divisions caused by theological disputes and the religious fervor of the First Great Awakening, the future of the movement looked bright, especially following the organization of the General Assembly in 1789. The nineteenth century would bring unique challenges but also new opportunities for growth. This was the environment within which the First Presbyterian Church of Raleigh came to be organized in 1816.

---

[27]Robert Hamlin Stone, *A History of the Orange Presbytery, 1770–1970* (Charlotte, NC: Heritage Printers, 1970) 5.

[28]Ibid., 5–6.

[29]Conser and Cain, *Presbyterians in North Carolina*, 39.

2

Establishing a Presence

The Context

The world in 1800 was a very different place than it is today.[1] The population of the planet that year was 978 million, and it would be four years before it topped one billion. The population of North America was only seven million.[2] The most important news in Europe was centered in France, where the French Revolution had settled, and Napoleon Bonaparte was coming to power. Under his leadership, France would be the major military/political player in Western Europe until his defeat at Waterloo in 1815.

The United States was still in its infancy in 1800. Twenty-one of the fifty-six signers of the Declaration of Independence were still alive. The nation was in the midst of grieving the leader of the Continental Army and first president, George Washington, who had died just a few weeks before the dawning of the new century. The Constitution had been ratified for only twelve years. Washington, D.C., succeeded New York City as the capital of the United States, and the nation's second president, John Adams, became the first to occupy the White House that year.

During the first three decades of the nineteenth century, several important events happened that brought tremendous change to the young

---

[1]Throughout this book I will be telling the story of the First Presbyterian Church in Raleigh, North Carolina, within the context of American history and local Raleigh history. Much of the historical contextual information will be the same that I used in the chapters of my book *Nurturing the Vision: First Baptist Church Raleigh, 1812–2012* (Macon, GA: Mercer University Press, 2012). I am grateful to Mercer University Press for allowing me to use this information.

[2]United Nations Population Division, "Table 2. Population of the World and its Major Areas, 1750–2150," in *The World at Six Billion*, 6, last modified 19 September 2001, accessed 3 March 2013, http://www.un.org/esa/population/publications/sixbillion/sixbilpart1.pdf.

nation. Thomas Jefferson defeated John Adams for the presidency in the election of 1800, spelling the demise of the Federalist Party and giving rise to the Democratic-Republican Party, which would dominate American politics for the next several decades.[3] One of Jefferson's most important accomplishments was the Louisiana Purchase in 1803, which doubled the land size of the United States and represented a foreign policy victory over France. Several years later, the American victory over the British in the War of 1812 finalized America's complete break from Great Britain. Then in 1823, the United States further declared its sovereignty when James Monroe's address to Congress intoned the famous "Monroe Doctrine," a claim that has since been the bedrock of American foreign policy. The young nation was clearly in the process of maturing in the first third of the nineteenth century.

The most important religious development as the nineteenth century emerged was the Second Great Awakening. Historians differ over the exact dates for the Awakening, but the general consensus is that the movement began sometime after the American Revolution and continued until the 1840s. Characterized by fervency and great emotionalism, the Second Great Awakening challenged religious Americans to implement moral reforms in numerous areas of society. In that regard, the Second Great Awakening awakened concern among American Christians for domestic ills such as slavery, alcohol abuse, and low literacy rates, which eventually mobilized them to work for a better society. Subsequently, the later decades of the nineteenth century witnessed the organization of new colleges, as well as the creation of a public school system, abolitionist organizations, and temperance societies. In addition to prompting general moral concern, it also motivated American Christians to think about carrying the gospel beyond the borders of the United States to other nations in the world through foreign missions.[4] The

[3]See David McCullough, *John Adams* (New York: Simon & Schuster, 2001) 543–67, for a more in-depth account of the election of 1800.

[4]For a good discussion of the Second Great Awakening, see Sydney E. Ahlstrom, *A Religious History of the American People* (New Haven: Yale University Press, 1972) 415–509; Mark A. Noll, *A History of Christianity in the United States and Canada* (Grand Rapids: Eerdmans, 1992) 165–245; Whitney R. Cross, *The Burned-over District: The Social and Intellectual History of Enthusiastic*

Awakening exploded in three areas: New England, the Cumberland Valley, and western New York. Camp meetings were a unique phenomenon that developed in the western revivals. They typically ran for several weeks, attracted sometimes thousands of people at a time, and were characterized by tremendous emotional outbursts. From North Carolina, a fiery Presbyterian preacher named James McGready moved westward in 1796 after being frustrated by opposition he received to his New Side revivalism. He eventually settled in the Cumberland Valley and helped spark the Gaspar River and Cane Ridge camp meetings.[5]

Not everyone was happy about the emotional revivals. The same debate between Old Side and New Side erupted once again among Presbyterians as the revivals and camp meetings proceeded. The emotionalism was a cause for concern as was the theology portrayed by Presbyterian New Side evangelists, which seemed to many to reflect disdain for the *Westminster Confession* by leaning too heavily in the direction of Arminian free will. Furthermore, on the frontier, the dearth of properly educated Presbyterian clergy forced some presbyteries to ordain ministers without the requisite educational credentials. In 1810, the Synod of Kentucky attempted to force its ministers to toe the line on Reformed doctrine with the result that the Cumberland Presbytery withdrew from the synod to form the Cumberland Presbyterian Church, which was devoted to the New Side ideology.[6]

The most famous evangelist of the Second Great Awakening was Charles Grandison Finney. Finney's career exemplifies the frustration that many Presbyterians felt about the New Side theology and revivalism.

Religion in Western New York, 1800–1850 (Ithaca, NY: Cornell University Press, 1950); William G. McLoughlin, *Revivals, Awakenings and Reform: An Essay on Religion and Social Change in America, 1607–1977* (Chicago: University of Chicago Press, 1978) 98–140; William G. McLoughlin, *Modern Revivalism: Charles Grandison Finney to Billy Graham* (New York: The Ronald Press Co., 1959) 3–165.

[5]Randall Balmer and John R. Fitzmier, *The Presbyterians* (Westport, CT: Greenwood Press, 1993) 45. Western New York was nicknamed the "Burned-over District" because of the religious enthusiasm that captivated the area. For the classic study of that area and era, see Cross, *Burned-over District.*

[6]Balmer and Fitzmier, *Presbyterians*, 46.

Educated as an attorney, Finney had a profound conversion experience and calling to ministry. The St. Lawrence Presbytery ordained him to the ministry on 1 July 1824 even though he admitted that he had never read the *Westminster Confession of Faith*. Finney's revivals reflected a perspective different from the more Calvinist-oriented revivals of the First Great Awakening. During the First Great Awakening, Jonathan Edwards wrote the classic definition of a revival from the Calvinist perspective in his *Narrative of a Surprising Work of God*. Edwards believed that revivals were the result of prayer and God's providence. Finney disagreed. He believed that if the evangelist used the proper techniques, "new measures" as he called them, a revival would be the result. His *Lectures on Revivals of Religion* (1835) articulated how to bring about a revival with such "new measures" as publicity, using women to pray in the meetings, protracted meetings, and of course the famous "anxious bench," where the unconverted were brought to sit at the front during the services. Finney's skills as an orator brought him great success in the Burned-over District of western New York. In his later years he became the president of Oberlin College in Ohio.[7]

The City of Raleigh and the Raleigh Academy

As the new nation looked forward to a century of promise, the young city of Raleigh, North Carolina, also looked to the coming century with optimism. The first mayor of Raleigh, John Haywood, was selected in 1795. Beginning in 1799, two newspapers were published weekly in the city: *The Minerva*, which was published by New Jersey native William Boylan until 1810, and the *Raleigh Register*, which was published by Joseph Gales. Gales, originally from England, came to Raleigh by way of Philadelphia. The *Raleigh Register* lasted as the major newspaper for the city from its inception in 1799 until 1863.[8]

---

[7]Ibid., 46–47.

[8]Elizabeth Reid Murray, *Prehistory Through Centennial*, vol. 1 of *Wake: Capital County of North Carolina* (Raleigh: Capital County Publishing Co.,1983) 112–13. Although Murray's history of Wake County is the most comprehensive, there are several histories of the city of Raleigh that should be noted: Marshall Lancaster, *Raleigh: An Unorthodox History of North Carolina's Capital* (Asheboro,

Urban problems developed early in the life of the new city. Maintenance of roads was one example. In 1795, the General Assembly passed a law that any free male resident of the city of Raleigh would be required to work on the road in the city or supply three male slaves to do so in his place. That law was applicable to all free male residents of the city, whether they were property owners or renters.[9] A suitable location for a cemetery created another urban concern for the young city. In 1798, the city commissioners set aside four acres of state-owned land, near the city limit, which became Raleigh's City Cemetery.[10]

Educational opportunities for families in the young city of Raleigh were very limited in the city's first couple of years. Families who could afford it employed private tutors or sent their children to a neighboring county or state for schooling. As the city grew, it became apparent that a need for a school existed. In 1801, the General Assembly granted permission to use Burke Square for the location of a school given the name of the Raleigh Academy. The school opened on 2 July 1804 with a faculty comprising Rev. Martin Detargny, principal; Miss Charlotte Brodie, teacher of needlework; and Chesley Daniel, teacher of reading and writing. By the end of the first term, Detargny was replaced as principal by the much more youthful Daniel, a recent graduate of the University of North Carolina.[11]

By all accounts, the first year of the Raleigh Academy was an "eminent success."[12] Students who did not live in the city boarded with local

---

NC: Down Home Press, 1992); David Perkins, ed., *The News and Observer's Raleigh: A Living History of North Carolina's Capital* (Winston-Salem, NC: John F. Blair, 1994); Steve Solpen, *Raleigh: A Pictorial History* (Norfolk, VA: Donning Company Publishers, 1977); and James Vickers, *Raleigh, City of Oaks: An Illustrated History* (Woodland Hills, CA: Windsor Publications, 1982). For a history of the *Raleigh Register*, see Robert Neal Elliott, Jr., *The Raleigh Register, 1799–1863* (Chapel Hill: University of North Carolina Press, 1955).

[9]Murray, *Prehistory*, 111.

[10]Ibid., 112.

[11]Ibid., 183–84. Detargny served for one month as principal, and Daniel served in the position until the end of 1805.

[12]Kemp P. Battle, *Early History of Raleigh, The Capital City of North Carolina: A Centennial Address, October 18, 1892* (Raleigh: Edwards and Broughton, 1893) 67; the complete text is available through Google Books. See also Murray,

families while some stayed in rooming houses.[13] Kemp P. Battle commented upon the different curricula for boys and girls:

> It will be noticed that great stress is laid on Latin in the training of boys, while the girls were confined to the English branches. Further, it is observable that the principle of practical training...was introduced for the benefit of the girls, while the boys had none at all. The boys were instructed as if they were designed for one of the learned professions. The girls were educated to be good spellers and readers, to be well acquainted with geography, and their hands were trained to be able to use deftly the needle. Many of them...learned to play on a piano or guitar under a music teacher of reputation, an Englishman named Thomas Sambourne.... They were not stuffed with the classics and higher mathematics and other "ologies," but they were taught to be graceful and agreeable companions and excellent housewives.[14]

Public examinations were held semiannually in the statehouse, where examples of the students' work were also displayed.[15]

Chesley Daniel served as principal of the school until the end of 1805 and was succeeded by Aaron F. McGready, who died before completion of a year in the position. Atlas Jones, professor of languages at the University of North Carolina, acted as an interim principal until a permanent replacement could be secured. At this point, the city's leaders decided that since there was no permanent minister in the city, the school should hire a principal who would also be qualified to serve as "Pastor of the City." In November 1806, Rev. William Leftwich Turner, a Presbyterian minister from Lexington, Virginia, was hired to fill that dual role. Joseph Gales, editor of the *Raleigh Register*, trustee of the Raleigh Academy, and secretary of its board, later spoke about Turner's hiring:

> It happened during the Commencement week of our University that the Rev. Wm. Turner and another young clergyman, from Virginia, paid a visit to the city as missionaries, and sent round a notice that a

---

Prehistory, 184. Murray indicates that the enrollment approached sixty students from several North Carolina counties by the end of the first year.

[13]Murray, *Prehistory*, 184.

[14]Battle, *Early History*, 68.

[15]Murray, *Prehistory*, 184.

> sermon would be preached at the Statehouse at a certain hour. Most of our principal inhabitants were attending the commencement; but a respectable number of hearers attended. Amongst others, I attended, and was pleased with the service.[16]

Gales communicated his pleasure with Turner to the other board members, who acted to hire the young minister. Turner remained in the position until moving to Fayetteville, North Carolina, in 1809. At the conclusion of his tenure, the school had 150 students. New teachers were employed with the expansion of the student body. A new building for the female students was constructed, and a library was established. New classes were added, and by all accounts, fundraising had been successful.[17] Because of the success to the academy that Turner brought, and his service as the city's only permanent pastor, his departure in 1809 must have been a blow to the young school as well as to the city. Turner served as the pastor of the First Presbyterian Church in Fayetteville until his death in 1813 at the young age of thirty.[18]

Turner's successor, William McPheeters, became the most instrumental figure for the advancement of the Presbyterian denomination in the nascent city of Raleigh. McPheeters was born on 28 September 1778 near Staunton, Virginia, to William and Rachel Moore McPheeters. His father was a magistrate in Augusta County, where the family resided. Fortunately, the McPheeters had means to provide their son with a good education. He graduated from Liberty Hall Academy (known today as Washington and Lee University), having studied under the tutelage of Rev. William Graham, a prominent Presbyterian minister. In 1797,

---

[16]Joseph and Winifred Marshall Gales, "Recollections of Joseph and Winifred Gales," 152, Gales Family Papers, Southern Historical Collection, University of North Carolina, Chapel Hill, as cited by Murray, *Prehistory*, 174.

[17]Charles Lee Coon, *North Carolina Schools and Academies, 1790–1840* (Raleigh: Edwards and Broughton, 1915) 396–416. The complete text is available through Google Books.

[18]William P. McPherson, ed., *The History of First Presbyterian Church, Raleigh, North Carolina: 1816–1991* (Raleigh: Commercial Printing, 1991) 12.

McPheeters traveled to Cynthiana, Kentucky, to study medicine with his older brother James, who was a practicing physician in the town.[19]

Through involvement with the local Presbyterian church in Cynthiana, McPheeters felt a calling to pastoral ministry. Late in the year of 1799, he returned to Virginia, where he was received under the care of the Lexington Presbytery as a candidate for ministry. He pursued theological training under Rev. Samuel Brown, pastor of New Providence Presbyterian Church in Rockbridge, Virginia. On 19 April 1802, New Providence Church licensed McPheeters to the ministry. Then, after returning to Kentucky and preaching in numerous churches, by March 1803, he assumed charge of a very small church in Danville and taught school to supplement his income. On 25 September 1804, he married Elizabeth McDowell, and one month later, with his new bride, he returned to Virginia, where he continued to preach in various churches. The following year, he began to preach at his home church, the Bethel Presbyterian Church. The church called him to be pastor in 1806, and he received full ordination on 21 April 1806.[20]

Tragedy struck later in the year with the untimely death of his wife. In McPheeters's own account of his life, he does not describe the cause of her death, other than saying it was the result of a "lingering illness," but it must have been a difficult experience for the young minister.[21] Three years later, he married Lavinia Moore on 18 March 1809. On 30 December of that year, she gave birth to McPheeters's first child, a girl whom the couple named Lavinia after her mother. Tragedy then struck again on 15 January 1810 as his second wife died. Again, McPheeters does not give the cause of death, but one can speculate that so close to the birth of their child, the death may have been due to complications from giving birth.[22]

---

[19]John S. Grasty, *Memoir of Samuel B. McPheeters, D. D.* (St. Louis: Southwestern Book and Publishing Company, 1871) 26; the complete text is available through Google Books. Samuel McPheeters, also a Presbyterian clergyman, was the son of William.

[20]Grasty, *Memoir*, 27.

[21]Ibid., 28.

[22]Ibid.

At this time, McPheeters entered into discussions with the Raleigh Academy. Having tragedy strike twice in four years might have given him the impression that he needed a change of scenery, but he offers no such hint in his account. He only indicates that the trustees of the academy contacted him "by special messenger." There is no information about how the trustees knew of McPheeters. Possibly, the young minister had developed a reputation that extended beyond his town of Bethel, Virginia. Nevertheless, McPheeters writes that following a visit to Raleigh in February 1810, he "was pleased with the prospect," returned to Virginia to prepare for the move, arrived back in Raleigh on 22 May 1810, and began his duties as principal of the academy and minister to the city in June.[23]

Soon after McPheeters assumed his duties at the Raleigh Academy, the trustees contracted with Raleigh builder William Jones to build a house for the principal. An editorial in the *Raleigh Star* from 31 May 1810 provides a clue about the state of the other building on the academy property at the time: "We think this will be a handsome specimen of the chaste, elegant and correct style of building, and hope it will contribute somewhat to eradicate the vandalism that so generally pervades our architecture."[24] McPheeters's first year at the academy was successful. Enrollment reached between 130 and 140 students.[25] The trustees declared: "We cannot close this report without giving credit to the Rev. Mr. McPheeters, which his assiduity and uncommon attention to the welfare of the institution merits."[26]

Another important development that came to the academy during McPheeters's first year was an emphasis upon discipline. A particular issue related to discipline surfaced in 1812. On 2 October, the *Raleigh Register* reported that the administrators of the school were concerned about two issues related to the students. The first involved money. The

---

[23]Ibid., 28–29.

[24]*Raleigh* (NC) *Star*, 31 May 1810, 87, as cited by Coon, *North Carolina Schools*, 419.

[25]*Raleigh Star*, 5 April 1811, 55, as cited by Coon, *North Carolina Schools*, 423.

[26]*Raleigh Star*, 15 November 1811, 3, as cited by Coon, *North Carolina Schools*, 428.

trustees recommended to the parents that they not "put any considerable sum of money in the disposal of such students, nor allow them to contract a debt at any store in the city." Instead, the parents were instructed to "authorize some respectable resident to allow their children or wards small sums of pocket money at stated periods, and, in all cases, to authorize the purchase of any articles of clothing, books, etc., which it may be necessary for them to obtain on credit during their stay at the Academy." It is difficult to tell exactly what the problem was, but it would seem that there were complaints from local businesses related to unpaid debts.[27]

Another disciplinary issue concerned students leaving their agreed-upon boarding houses, where parents or guardians had placed them for the year, and moving to other dwellings "abruptly and without notice, without the knowledge of their said parents or guardians." As might be imagined, there were some families in the city who supplemented the family income by renting out rooms to Raleigh Academy students. The boarding problem posed the risk of inhibiting "respectable families from taking students to board," which, it was deemed, would "greatly injure the interests of the Institution." To correct the problem, the trustees made a rule that if a student leaves the living arrangement originally agreed upon for another dwelling, the parents or guardian of that student would still be liable to pay for the original room arrangement for the remainder of the school session, and the student would be "dealt with accordingly" for having violated a rule.[28]

A report in the *Raleigh Star* boasted,

> The parents and guardians of students at the Raleigh Academy, and the friends of the institution and literature in general, may be gratified...that the business of education was never more prosperously conducted than at present. The students are numerous and industrious, and are well attended by efficient instructors.... Every exertion is made

---

[27]*Raleigh* (NC) *Register*, 2 October 1812, 4, as cited by Coon, *North Carolina Schools*, 436.

[28]Ibid.

> by the trustees to sustain and increase the reputation which the Raleigh Academy has deservedly acquired.[29]

Clearly, McPheeters's leadership had paid dividends. The school was growing and the future looked bright. On a personal note for McPheeters, he was married to Margaret Ann McDaniel on 10 March. Professionally and personally, 1812 was a favorable year for McPheeters.[30]

In terms of pedagogy, the Raleigh Academy provides various examples of how education was conducted in the early nineteenth century. For example, at the end of each session, the academy held public examinations in the statehouse, where the trustees, faculty, students, and other interested parties gathered to hear the students give recitations, demonstrate their mastery of various subjects, or give public readings. On occasion, the students performed plays or gave musical performances. These events were always reported in the local newspapers in the city along with the various subjects taught for the session by the academy faculty. Those reports provide an interesting window into the subjects studied by students in that era. For example, the *Raleigh Star* reported in 1813 that during the spring session, the preparatory school of the academy provided instruction in the following areas: "Murray's Introduction," "Sampson's Beauties of the Bible," "English Grammar," and "Arithmetic." The Male Department provided these classes: "Spelling," "English Grammar," "Latin Grammar," "Corderii," "Esop and Erasmus," "*Selectae e. Viteri* and *Profanis*," "Caesar and Sallust," "Caesar and Virgil," "Do 2nd Class," "Virgil," "Cicero," "Greek Testament," "Arithmetic," "Euclid and Chymistry [*sic*]," (there is a notation here that says, "the Chymical [*sic*] experiments afforded much entertainment"), and "Geography." The Female Department provided these classes: "Spelling," "Murray's Introduction," "English Reader," "Murray's Sequel," "Osian," "Cowper's Task," "Milton's Paradise Lost," "English Grammar," "English Grammar (Parsing)," "Murray's Exercises," "Geography," "Blair's Rhetoric," "Ferguson's

---

[29]*Raleigh Star*, 24 April 1812, 67, as cited by Coon, *North Carolina Schools*, 432.

[30]*Raleigh Register*, 27 March 1812, as cited by Coon, *North Carolina Schools*, 432.

Astronomy," "Blair's Natural Philosophy and Astronomy," "Arithmetic," "French Grammar (2 classes)," "Telemaque," "*Selectae e. Viteri*."[31] The modern reader might find interest in the attention given to classical literature, particularly the Latin classics. Also, it is worth noting that Greek was taught as a subject and that the boys and girls had separate curricula and emphases although there were common subjects.

In 1814, McPheeters led the Raleigh Academy trustees to approve the Lancasterian system of education for a portion of the school, a major step that provided the opportunity for many students, especially those from poor families, to be educated at the school.[32] The system was originally developed by Joseph Lancaster (1778–1838), a British pioneer in the efforts to develop public education. The method allowed the brighter students in the academy to teach other children, all under the direction of an adult teacher. Lancaster envisioned a system where 200 to 1,000 students would be seated in a large room in rows that contained ten students each. The adult teacher taught a "monitor" on each row, usually the brightest of the students, who, in turn, taught each of the other students on his or her row. The system also used student monitors who kept attendance, examined the students, and distributed the supplies necessary for the learning process. The classroom was conducted with very strict rules so that order was maintained at all times.[33]

The following year, the Lancasterian system became fully implemented at the school. The *Raleigh Register* reported that the system allowed for a teacher to instruct many more pupils in the classroom. Furthermore, it allowed the children to be taught "the rudiments of learning in a much shorter time than in the usual way." According to the report, the Lancasterian method proved to be more economically advantageous

---

[31]*Raleigh Star*, 25 June 1813, 104, as cited by Coon, *North Carolina Schools*, 441.

[32]*Raleigh Register*, 1 April 1814, as cited by Coon, *North Carolina Schools*, 441.

[33]*Encyclopaedia Britannica Online*, s.v. "Lancaster, Joseph," accessed 23 April 2013, http://www.britannica.com/EBchecked/topic/329001/Joseph-Lancaster; see also "The Lancasterian Monitorial System of Education," accessed 23 April 2013, http://constitution.org/lanc/monitorial.htm, for more information about this educational philosophy.

than the academy's old system, in that no books were required. Finally, the trustees offered, "free of expense," training to any child whose family could not afford to pay for education.[34] The academy created a separate division that employed the system while the other tuition-paying students continued as before. By June 1815, Raleigh Academy reported that between seventy and eighty students were being educated through the Lancasterian method and that it proved to be highly successful:

> The trustees cannot pass over the Lancaster school without expressing their particular approbation of the manner in which it has been conducted during the short period it has been in operation. Though this school has had an existence of a few months only, the trustees find that children, who before they entered it, did not know a letter in the book, can read, write, have some knowledge of figures, and can repeat by heart a number of moral verses. Some, indeed have obtained a considerable knowledge of English grammar and geography.[35]

McPheeters presided over the Raleigh Academy during its peak years. By late 1815, the trustees reported an enrollment that approached 200 students, many of whom came from outside of North Carolina.[36] In 1817, the campus consisted of four buildings occupying four acres with a total value of $2,750 [$49,700].[37] By 1820, the trustees recognized McPheeters's tenth anniversary with a simple statement that under his leadership the school had "flourished."[38]

---

[34]*Raleigh Register*, 17 March 1815, 3, as cited by Coon, *North Carolina Schools*, 444.

[35]*Raleigh Star*, 16 June 1815, 3, as cited by Coon, *North Carolina Schools*, 445.

[36]*Raleigh Star*, 17 November 1815, 3, as cited by Coon, *North Carolina Schools*, 446.

[37]Coon, *North Carolina Schools*, 451. The bracketed monetary amounts in this book represent the amount of money needed in 2013 to have the same purchasing power as the initial amount for the corresponding year. See Samuel H. Williamson, "Purchasing Power of Money in the United States from 1774 to Present," accessed 18 August 2014, https://www.measuringworth.com/ppowerus/.

[38]*Raleigh Register*, 22 December 1820, 3, as cited by Coon, *North Carolina Schools*, 458.

McPheeters remained at the helm of the Raleigh Academy until 1826. At age forty-eight, he had devoted sixteen years to the academy. Originally hired as "Principal of the Academy and Pastor of the City," the eventual establishment of the First Presbyterian Church of Raleigh no doubt added to his work load. One can only speculate about his reason for resigning as principal of the academy. He may have just needed to rest, to back away from what must have been a stressful period in his life in the dual role. A clue may be found in a short reference printed in the *Raleigh Register* on 23 December 1825: "The Institution having heretofore been subjected to considerable trouble and loss from the lax and irregular way in which the tuition money has been paid to the Treasurer, it must be understood, that a certificate will in future be required of every pupil at the commencement of each session."[39] Was the reason for his resignation related to the academy's financial problems?[40] McPheeters gives no reason himself, saying only that "I continued my connection with the Academy until I handed in my resignation, in the year 1826."[41]

First Presbyterian Church of Raleigh

The religious climate in the city of Raleigh developed slowly. During the years 1802–1804, a series of revivals swept through Wake County that captured first the Presbyterians and Methodists and eventually the Baptists. Small Baptist churches began to spring up throughout Wake County as a result of the religious awakening. After 1810, Methodists held revivals on the John and Samuel Whitaker plantation, off of Fayetteville Road and south of the city. Those events usually lasted for five or six days and brought a variety of people and commerce to the outskirts of the city.[42]

Despite the revivalist fervor within the county, more than a decade passed after the founding of the city of Raleigh before there were any

---

[39]*Raleigh Register*, 23 December 1825, 3, as cited by Coon, *North Carolina Schools*, 482.

[40]See Murray, *Prehistory*, 186, for information about the academy's financial problems at the end of the 1820s.

[41]Grasty, *Memoir*, 29.

[42]Murray, *Prehistory*, 168–73.

church buildings or regular worship services. The worship services that did take place usually were led by itinerant preachers in the courthouse. After its completion in 1794, the statehouse served as the location for most of the worship services and funerals in the city. In 1801, the General Assembly passed a resolution "that all regular Ministers of the Gospel, of any denomination whatever, should in the recess of the General Assembly, have the privilege and liberty of performing divine service, in either the Senate Chamber or Commons Hall, until the citizens of Raleigh have their church prepared."[43] The citizens of the city had earlier petitioned the General Assembly for a lot and sufficient funds to build a church building. The committee that dealt with the petition refused to allow the funds but did grant a parcel of land for such use with the stipulation that when the church building was completed it "shall be free and open to all ministers of every denomination."[44] Though the church building was never built, the property located at Moore Square was eventually used by the Baptists and later by the Christian Church ("Campbellites").

The first church building in the city continued the nondenominational tradition and was built in 1808 between Morgan and Hargett streets. Instrumental in the building of the church named "Bethel" was Rev. William Glendinning, an eccentric man who donated the lot upon which the church was built.[45] The earliest denominational group in the city to organize was the Methodists. Bishop Francis Asbury reportedly preached in the statehouse on 6 March 1800.

By the time McPheeters arrived on the scene in 1810, the city's religious life was emerging rapidly. The Methodists and Baptists organized churches in 1811 and 1812, respectively.[46] The Presbyterians formally organized the First Presbyterian Church on 21 January 1816 although there had been a thriving Presbyterian presence in the city for several years. William Turner and William McPheeters, both "Pastors of the

---

[43]*Raleigh Register,* December 22, 1801, as cited by Murray, *Prehistory*, 173.

[44]*Raleigh Register,* February 23, 1802, as cited by Murray, *Prehistory*, 174.

[45]Murray, *Prehistory*, 175; see also Vickers, *Raleigh,* for information about Glendinning. Apparently, Glendinning was prone to apocalyptic visions and was considered quite bizarre until his death in 1816.

[46]Murray, *Prehistory*, 176; see also Jonas, *Nurturing the Vision*, 20–21.

City," were Presbyterian. The Raleigh Academy had strong ties to the Presbyterians. Joseph Caldwell, the first president of the University of North Carolina, was ordained to the Presbyterian ministry in the statehouse in 1811. The Orange Presbytery met in the city in 1809 and 1813. Why did it take until 1816 for the Presbyterians to formalize into a constituted church? Although it is only speculation, it could be that since Turner and McPheeters were leading the services in the statehouse, when the Methodists and Baptists left to organize their congregations, the majority of those remaining were Presbyterians and so the organization of the group into a Presbyterian congregation would have been the natural thing to do.

Although the earliest records currently in possession of the church date back only to 1831, there is evidence that a book of sessional minutes existed at one time that may have contained the church's earliest records. The church archives also contain an early membership registry with the names of charter members dating back to 1816. The following notation is also included in this registry:

> (Copy) Raleigh July 23rd 1816
>
> On Sabbath January 21st 1816 a Presbyterian Church was organized in the city of Raleigh, by the Reverend William McPheeters. Mr. Wm. Shaw, Thos. Emonds, William Peace, and John Smith were solemnly set apart to the office of ruling elders, by prayers and imposition of hands.
>
> The underwritten persons, professors of the religion of Jesus Christ are regarded as composing, at this date (July 23 1816) the Presbyterian Church in the city of Raleigh.[47]

---

[47]Church Registry, 23 July 1816, 18. This registry is the oldest registry in the church archives. The church has an impressive archival collection composed of minutes of the Session dating back to 1831. There are also minutes of the Diaconate dating back to the late nineteenth century although these records are not as complete as the minutes of the Session. Finally, there are other records related to various organizations in the church. There appears to have been the organizational meeting on 21 January 1816, followed a few months later on 23 July with a second meeting whereby McPheeters was requested to author a church covenant. See "The Church in Raleigh," *North Carolina Presbyterian* (Fayetteville, NC), 1 January 1859, 1. The meetings occurred in the statehouse.

The account continues by listing the following names: William McPheeters (pastor); William Shaw, Thomas Emonds, William Peace, and John Smith (ruling elders); John Hinton, Henry Potter, Benjamin Rounseville, Robert Harrison, Ruth, Emonds, Rabeteau,[48] Mary Birch, Margaret Capa, Pricilla Shaw,[49] Sylvia Potter, Elizabeth Haywood, Rebecca Goodwise, Thisbe Stigbie, Margaret McPheeters, Sarah Birch, Elizabeth Hinton, Nancy Holmes (woman of color).[50] The account also lists several "Occasional Members": Alfred Wright, S. Saunders, Susan D. Nye, Dorcas J. Alexander, Mary Alexander, and Sarah Saunders. The provenance of the information is explained in the final paragraph: "The above is copied from a book of Sessional Records begun as dated above [23 July 1816]. The names hereinafter recorded are gathered from the old book of Sessional Records mentioned on previous page and from a list furnished by Jesse Broom, Elder, former clerk of session and such other sources as are available at this date (July 21, 1874)."[51] It appears, therefore, that the earlier copy of the minutes of the session, though lost, did contain information about the formal constitution of the church in 1816 and that vital information was reconstructed at a later date to preserve the accuracy of the information.

Almost immediately following the organization of the congregation, the members began the process of constructing a building, first by securing the purchase of a lot on the corner of West Morgan and South Salis-

---

[48]Church Registry, 23 July 1816, 18–19. The account includes the dashes in front of the names "Ruth," "Emonds," and "Rabeteau." On the next page of the registry, the charter member names are listed and the first names of these three women were added in at a later date. The full names are therefore: "Mary" Ruth, "Jane" Emonds, and "Susannah" Rabeteau.

[49]See Murray, *Prehistory*, 179. Mrs. William Shaw (Pricilla) lived the latter years of her life and died in Milton, NC. On her tombstone in the Milton town cemetery are the following words: "She was the first Presbyterian who resided in the City of Raleigh."

[50]"Nancy Holmes" is referenced as a "woman of color," which may indicate that she was a free black.

[51]Church Registry, 23 July 1816, 18; see also Battle, *Early History*, 67. Kemp Battle in his 1892 address at the Raleigh Centennial celebration indicated that the First Presbyterian Church was organized in 1806. The evidence from the church's records suggests that he was mistaken.

bury Streets. The church advertised for construction bids from "the best workmen," with the intention of building a brick church "66 feet by 44—26 feet pitch, with a steeple."[52] On 4 July 1816, the church laid the cornerstone with "religious solemnity," perhaps as part of Raleigh's Fourth of July celebration that year.[53]

Two years later, the new building was completed with dedication services held over two days (7 and 8 February 1818) to celebrate. The *Raleigh Register* published the church's report of the grand event: "On Saturday, last, our new church was opened and dedicated to the service of the Supreme Being, by the Rev. Wm. McPheeters, Pastor of the congregation, who delivered a very appropriate discourse on the occasion." Present as well were the reverends Jesse Turner and John Knox Witherspoon from Fayetteville and Hillsboro (Hillsborough), respectively.[54] Jesse Turner was the brother of William Leftwich Turner, Raleigh's first "Pastor of the City" and principal of the Raleigh Academy, who had left Raleigh in 1809 to become the pastor of Fayetteville's First Presbyterian Church until his untimely death in 1813. Jesse Turner succeeded his brother, becoming the Fayetteville church's fifth pastor.[55] John Knox Witherspoon was the founding pastor of the Hillsboro (Hillsborough) Presbyterian Church. Witherspoon also held the distinction of being the grandson of Rev. John Witherspoon of New Jersey, one of the signers of the Declaration of Independence.[56] The dedication celebration continued the next day with a sermon by Turner, followed by observance of the Lord's Supper. During the afternoon service, Witherspoon preached, and

---

[52]*Raleigh Register*, 17 February 1816, 3. See also Murray, *Prehistory*, 178–79.

[53]*Raleigh Register*, 5 July 1816, 3.

[54]*Raleigh Register*, 13 February 1818, 3.

[55] A. L. Phillips, *An Historical Sketch of the Presbyterian Church of Fayetteville, N.C.* (Fayetteville, NC: J. E. Garrettt, 1889), 14, 16, reprinted in *History of First Presbyterian Church*, ed. Harriot Sutton Rankin (n.p., 1928), https://digital.lib.ecu.edu/16995.

[56]See "Hillsborough Presbyterian Church (1816)," accessed 16 May 2013, http://www.visithillsboroughnc.com/content/hillsborough-presbyterian-church-1816; see also "The History of Hillsborough Presbyterian Church," accessed 16 May 2013, http://www.hillsboroughpres.org/history.php.

Turner performed the ordinance of baptism. Finally, the weekend events concluded with an evening service by candlelight featuring another sermon by Turner.[57]

How to pay for the new building became the next matter of concern for the young congregation. The total cost of the structure was approximately $17,000 [$321,000]. The church raised most of the cost by the sale of pews. On 27 February 1818, the *Raleigh Register* carried an announcement that forty-five pews were purchased with prices ranging from $125 [$2,360] to $590 [$11,100], depending upon the location and size of the pew. The purchase netted $14,400 [$272,000] in total. The church also determined that an annual "tax" on the pews should be levied in order to support the pastor's salary. Fourteen pews remained along with a "piece of vacant ground purchased with the church lot," giving the church confidence that when all would finally be sold, "it is presumed that a handsome surplus will remain, to be applied to the contingent expenses of the church, or for the purchase of a clock or an organ…as the pew holders may hereafter determine."[58]

While the church raises money in different ways today, the sale of pews provides excellent insight into how the process took place in the early nineteenth century. It proved to be an efficient way to provide for the financial needs of the church. Each transaction was documented legally. Within the church archives are several copies of such transactions. One example begins:

> Made the 28th day of February in the year of our Lord one thousand eight hundred and eighteen, between Calvin Jones, William Peace, and Henry Potter of the City of Raleigh, County of Wake, and State of North Carolina, Trustees, to the use of the Society owning the brick Presbyterian Church in said City, and Lot No. 164 on which it stands, on the one part and William Shaw of the same city on the other part, witnesseth THAT for and in consideration of the sum of three hun-

---

[57]*Raleigh Register*, 13 February 1818, 3. It is curious that the account makes no mention of McPheeters being involved in any of the services on Sunday (8 February) although there is no mention of him being absent. The most eye-catching part of the account is that Turner, rather than the church's pastor, administered the ordinance of baptism.

[58]*Raleigh Register*, 27 February 1818, 3.

> dred and seventy five dollars,...we,...have bargained, sold, alien, eufeoffed and confirmed, and by these presents do bargain, sell, alien, eufeoff and confirm unto the said William Shaw, his heirs and assigns, one pew in the said Presbyterian Church on the lower floor, known and designated by No. 43 (Forth-three), which number is at present painted on the door of said pew, together with so much of the undivided use of the ground which has been set apart for the said church by the deed bearing the date February 21, 1816.[59][end block]

The document further indicates that "There shall be no interment, entombing, or depositing of any human corpse in the said church or in or on the ground set apart for the church." Finally, it spells out that an "annuity" would be regularly collected, determined by the price of the pew, for the salary of the minister and that in matters of business, which may come before the church, such as selection of a pastor, "who shall in every instance be of the Presbyterian order," each pew owner is entitled one vote for every $50 [$945] worth of pew or pews that he possesses.[60] Eugene Daniel concluded that the document demonstrates that the church property was owned by a "quasi joint stock company called the Church 'Society.'"[61] Although by today's standards, the modern reader and church member might consider the legal jargon to be stilted and much too formal, it does reflect the era, and as previously mentioned, the system proved to be a highly effective means by which to raise the necessary funds for the building and its upkeep and for the support of the pastor.

The first church building stood for almost eighty years, replaced by a new structure in 1898. Of the thirty-four other Presbyterian church buildings in the Orange Presbytery at the time, it was the most expensive and one of only five that was constructed with brick.[62] Although the Methodists and the Baptists had organized their churches earlier, the Presbyterians could have been proud that their church building was the best at the time. In addition, the building served the Raleigh community.

---

[59]The document quoted above is reproduced in Daniel, "Years 1816–1855," 19. The original contract and several others like it (with buyers' names changed) exist in the church archives.

[60]Ibid.

[61]Ibid., 21.

[62]Murray, *Prehistory*, 179.

For instance, the Raleigh Academy began conducting its public examinations in the building. Furthermore, the North Carolina Bible Society held its meetings there. Fourth of July celebrations were also conducted in the building, and most importantly, when fire destroyed the statehouse in 1831, the legislature and supreme court used the property to carry on the functions of the state government until the present capitol building was completed in 1840.[63]

In 1825, the church added another structure to its campus: the "Session House." A simple structure measuring about fifty feet by thirty-five, it stood adjacent to the church building until 1898. The Session House served a variety of purposes through the years. For example, meetings of the session occurred there, in addition to the meetings of Sunday school classes and the functions of other church organizations. Alexander B. Stronach recalled his impressions of the building from boyhood memories. He remembered a "railed platform 'two steps up from the floor,' [which] provided a rostrum for the session moderator, and on Sunday for the teachers of the 'small fry classes.'"[64]

William McPheeters served as pastor of Raleigh's First Presbyterian Church until 1824, when he resigned his formal pastoral responsibility. He nevertheless remained in the city and continued to preach at the church for several years afterward.[65] After severing his ties with the Raleigh Academy in 1826, McPheeters, along with Joseph Gales, editor of the *Raleigh Register*, became involved the following year with the incorporation of the North Carolina Institution for the Instruction of the Deaf and Dumb, a project for which he would devote almost a decade of work.[66] In 1836, the church invited McPheeters to resume his pastorate there on a fulltime basis, but he declined. He chose instead to move to Fayetteville to serve as an administrator and teacher at a female school in

---

[63]Daniel, "Years 1816–1855," 21–22.

[64](Raleigh, NC) *News and Observer*, 15 and 22 March 1908, as cited by Murray, *Prehistory*, 179.

[65]See William Henry Foote, *Sketches of Virginia: Historical and Biographical,* 2nd ed. (Philadelphia: J. P. Lippincott, 1856) 213. This source indicates that Rev. Thomas P. Hunt became the church's pastor in 1828 and remained for two years, whereupon Rev. Michael Osborne ministered for a few years.

[66]Murray, *Prehistory*, 326.

that city, but he remained only one year before returning to Raleigh. He then became a representative for the Board of Domestic Missions of the General Assembly of the Presbyterian Church, a position he held until 1839. Davidson College offered him the presidency of the school in 1840, but his health had declined by that time, and he was forced to decline the offer. He died on 7 November 1842.[67]

McPheeters is best remembered as both a pastor and an educator. He left a large footprint in the city of Raleigh when he died in 1842. The city's grief was evidenced at his funeral on 9 November 1842, which reportedly drew an estimated 1,000 mourners. The city's businesses were closed, and "the quiet of the Sabbath seemed to pervade the streets."[68] The First Presbyterian Church was draped in black to indicate mourning. Rev. Drury Lacy, the church's pastor, delivered the funeral sermon. Several tributes were published extoling McPheeters's character and virtues. One of the most glowing tributes declared: "That stern integrity, that uncompromising adherence to truth and right, that modesty that kept him from pride and vanity, and that piety which clung to Christ as his Lord, that amiable deportment in his intercourse with man, which had been the crown of his life, seemed brighter when contemplated from the grave."[69]

The resignation of McPheeters from the pastorate of First Presbyterian Church and his subsequent death serve as a transition to the next era in the church's history. During the decade of the 1830s, the church continued to grow and become stronger due to good pastoral and lay leadership. For that part of the story, we turn to the next chapter.

---

[67]*Dictionary of North Carolina Biography,* ed. William S. Powell (Chapel Hill: University of North Carolina Press, 1979–1996) s.v. "McPheeters, William." McPheeters's cause of death was reported to be a "calculus affection," a reference to either kidney stones or gall bladder stones. One report indicates that a surgical procedure ("lithotomy") was performed but to no avail. See *Raleigh Register,* 8 November 1842, 3.

[68](Raleigh) *North Carolina Standard*, 16 November 1842, 3.

[69]Foote, *Sketches*, 216.

3

Growing in Prominence

The Context

The election of Andrew Jackson to the presidency in 1828 signaled a political shift away from Jeffersonian Democracy to what came to be termed "Jacksonian Democracy." In addition to emphasizing a strong executive branch, Jackson's presidency marked the first time the "common man" gained political power. The electorate was extended during that time to include all white, adult males regardless of whether they owned land.

The Jacksonian era was also the age of "Manifest Destiny"—the belief that God had divinely ordained white Americans to expand across the North American continent. While the westward movement was positive for many Americans and ultimately good for the nation as a whole, for the Native Americans it was disastrous. As whites moved westward, Native Americans were forcibly removed from their territorial lands. In 1830, Congress passed the Indian Removal Act. During the next eight years, the peaceful, "civilized" tribes of the Southeast (Chickasaw, Creek, Choctaw, Seminole, and Cherokee) were forced westward to Oklahoma. The journey of the Cherokee, which commenced in 1838, was particularly tragic since the tribe had worked so hard to become "civilized" in the eyes of white settlers. During their journey westward, more than one-quarter of the Cherokee nation died from disease and other hardships.[1]

Ultimately, the doctrine of Manifest Destiny and its application by the United States in the annexation of Texas led to war between the United States and Mexico from 1846 to 1848. A decade earlier, Texas had won its independence from Mexico and existed as an autonomous

[1]For a fuller discussion about the plight of the Native Americans in the middle decades of the nineteenth century see Samuel Eliot Morison, *The Oxford History of the American People* (New York: Oxford University Press, 1965) 445–52.

republic although most Texans desired annexation with the United States. The Treaty of Guadalupe Hidalgo ended the conflict between Mexico and the United States and increased the territorial holdings of the United States. Specifically, the treaty forced Mexico to cede control of Texas along with the present-day states of California, Nevada, and Utah and parts of Colorado, Arizona, New Mexico, and Wyoming.[2]

The middle decades of the nineteenth century in America brought great advances in the areas of commerce. In 1830, a blacksmith from Illinois named John Deere invented the steel plow, which began to revolutionize farming. By 1858, Deere was manufacturing 13,000 plows per year. Cyrus McCormick and Obed Hussey invented reapers in 1831, which further increased agricultural growth as they began to be mass produced. The garment industry became modernized after Isaac Singer began to mass produce the sewing machine in 1851. That era also marked the beginning of collective bargaining with the formation of the National Trades Union in 1834.[3]

New frontiers in communications were emerging as well. For instance, in 1844, Samuel Morse developed the electronic telegraph and a system of codes so that messages could be communicated over great distances. Just fourteen years later, the transatlantic cable was completed between the United States and Europe, allowing for instant communication between the two continents.[4] Transportation also saw great advances. For instance, the development of the clipper ship (the fastest sailing vessel on the seas in that day) significantly reduced the travel time between the Atlantic and Pacific Oceans. This and other advances of its kind contributed to increased trade between the United States and other nations. In addition to the impact of advances in transportation on foreign trade, steam ships began to utilize waterways in the nation's interior, fostering trade between different regions of the country. Yet the most important advance in transportation during those decades was the devel-

---

[2]Ibid., 550–65.

[3]Rebecca Brooks Gruver, *An American History* (New York: Alfred A. Knopf, 1985) 286–310.

[4]Ibid.

opment of the railroad, which eventually led to a system of tracks that spread across the country.

The middle of the century was also an era of great social change. Industrialism provided a promise of a new life and steady income that brought millions of immigrants to America from Northern and Western Europe before the American Civil War. Between 1815 and 1820, more than a hundred thousand immigrants flooded into the United States. The numbers grew from there. In the 1830s, more than half a million arrived at America's shores. During the 1840s, one and a half million immigrants made the difficult six-week ocean voyage to America. Finally, during the decade of the 1850s, the number of immigrants who came to America was two and a half million. By 1860, more than 8 percent of all Americans were foreign born.[5]

This period also marked the beginning of the struggle for women's rights. Opportunities for women to be educated began to be more plentiful by the 1830s. Oberlin College in Ohio became the first institution of higher education in America to allow women to matriculate as students. Shortly thereafter, in 1836, Wesleyan College was founded in Georgia as a college exclusively for women. In 1837, Mount Holyoke College was established in Massachusetts.[6] As women became better educated, many also began to speak out about social ills in society. Two women who were important and early pioneers in the movements for the abolition of slavery and women's rights were Sarah and Angelina Grimké. These two sisters, daughters of a prominent slave-holding family in Charleston, South Carolina, eventually rejected their family's racial views and became important voices for social change.[7] Other examples of early women activists include Lucretia Mott and Elizabeth Cady Stanton, whose advocacy for the rights of women eventually led to the first Women's Rights Convention, which met in 1848 in Seneca Falls, New York. While the work of these women was important in drawing attention to the rights of

---

[5]Ibid., 294.

[6]Ibid., 329.

[7]See Pamela R. Durso, *The Power of Woman: The Life and Writings of Sarah Moore Grimké* (Macon: Mercer University Press, 2004).

women, it would not be until the twentieth century that women would win full suffrage and an equal place in American society.[8]

While the women's rights movement brought important social change to America in the nineteenth century, the institution of slavery proved to be the most significant, and ultimately divisive, issue of the century. There had been opponents of slavery since the colonial era, most notably the Quakers. But by the 1830s, slavery became the dominant issue of the day and remained so until the Civil War. The abolition movement began to gather support in the 1830s, largely through the efforts of William Lloyd Garrison, a journalist from Massachusetts and publisher of *The Liberator*. Garrison was tireless in his efforts to denounce slavery, not only as a social evil but also as a sin, and his writings helped to generate a movement composed of Northern intellectuals and other notable reformers. The strength of the abolition movement in the middle of the nineteenth century eventually exacerbated sectional tensions between the North and South, which ultimately drove a wedge in the Union and led to the Civil War.[9]

Along with economic and social changes in the middle of the nineteenth century came significant religious developments. The large waves of immigrants, many of whom were Roman Catholic, spurred an intense anti-Catholic sentiment among many Protestants. Such competition between denominations led to the rise of certain indigenous religious traditions, including the Church of Jesus Christ of Latter Day Saints (begun by Joseph Smith in western New York) and the Campbellite movement (founded by Thomas Campbell and his son Alexander). Both of those traditions gained large numbers of members and grew into important traditions within American religion.[10]

---

[8]Ibid., 329–32.

[9]Winthrop D. Jordan and Leon F. Litwack, *The United States* 7th ed. (Englewood Cliffs, NJ: Prentice Hall, 1991) 261–63.

[10]For a good discussion of the indigenous religious traditions that began in the famed "Burned-over District" of western New York see Whitney R. Cross, *The Burned-over District: The Social and Intellectual History of Enthusiastic Religion in Western New York, 1800–1850* (Ithaca, NY: Cornell University Press, 1950). This work is quite dated but is a classic interpretation of new religious traditions in America in the first half of the nineteenth century.

The City of Raleigh in the Antebellum Years and the Story of John Chavis

The Jacksonian era also brought change and growth to the city of Raleigh. The 1830s saw the development of the railroad extended to Raleigh and greater Wake County. By 1833, a rail line had been completed between Weldon, North Carolina, and Petersburg, Virginia, which brought connections with lines further north. Support for the railroad could be found in the editorials from the period. For instance, in 1835, the editor of the *Raleigh Register* encouraged citizens to support efforts to build more lines, arguing that the railroad would increase the value of real estate and ensure the general prosperity of the city. Furthermore, he argued, it would bring new citizens to the city and would prevent others from moving west in order to find better agricultural prospects. In other words, the railroad would "give you a certain market at your doors."[11] Eventually, a charter for a line from Raleigh to Gaston near Weldon was secured by 1836, and within four years, passengers (and freight) were able to travel from Raleigh to Baltimore (338 miles) in thirty-two hours, including the stops.[12]

Religious diversity also characterized the city of Raleigh during the antebellum years. A special census of the city taken in 1858 indicated that 962 residents of Raleigh were church members. The individual groups were categorized as follows:

Christian Church—130
Baptists—240
Methodists—226
Presbyterians—180
Episcopalians—126
Roman Catholics—60[13]

---

[11]*Raleigh* (NC) *Register*, 22 September and 29 December 1835, as cited by Elizabeth Reid Murray, *Prehistory Through Centennial*, vol. 1 of *Wake: Capital County of North Carolina* (Raleigh: Capital County Publishing Co., 1983) 245–46.

[12]Murray, *Prehistory*, 246–49.

[13]Ibid., 386. The census was taken by John Spelman for the city commissioners the year following the city's extension of the city limits in 1857.

The U.S. Census from 1860 reported a total of fifty-two churches in Wake County: twenty-nine Baptist, fourteen Methodist, four Presbyterian, two Episcopalian, one Lutheran, one Roman Catholic, and one "Free Church." The census failed, however, to include some of the county's churches, such as those affiliated with the Christian Church denomination.[14]

Among the antebellum Presbyterians in Raleigh, the story of John Chavis, a "free black," is inspiring and yet illustrative of the strict limitations placed on black Americans in the South. Many of the details of his life are not known, but it is believed that he was born in 1763 and died in 1838.[15] Sources indicate that he was born either in the West Indies or near Oxford, North Carolina. He served in the 5th Virginia Regiment for three years during the American Revolution, the requisite service to earn him a bounty warrant issued by Captain Mayo Carington, stating that he had "faithfully fulfilled [his duties] and is thereby entitled to all immunities granted to three year soldiers."[16] The 1789 tax records in Mecklenburg County, Virginia, list him as a "free black whose property consisted of a single horse."[17]

Following his military service, Chavis sought a formal education. Legend has it that Chavis enrolled at the College of New Jersey (now Princeton University), the result of a wager by two of his white neighbors that a black man could not attain a college education. Reportedly, he was tutored privately by the school's president, John Witherspoon. Although

---

[14]Murray, *Prehistory*, 386.

[15]Helen Chavis Othow, *John Chavis: African American Patriot, Preacher, Teacher, and Mentor, 1763–1838* (Jefferson, NC: McFarland and Company, 2001) 9. This is the only book-length study of Chavis's life. See also W. Sherman Savage, "The Influence of John Chavis and Lunsford Lane on the History of North Carolina," *Journal of Negro History* 25/1 (January 1940): 14–24. Two good encyclopedia articles on Chavis are *Dictionary of North Carolina Biography*, ed. William S. Powell (Chapel Hill: University of North Carolina Press, 1979–1996) s.v. "Chavis, John" and *Dictionary of American Biography*, ed. Allen Johnson and Dumas Malone (New York: Charles Scribner's Sons, 1929) s.v. "Chavis, John."

[16]*Dictionary of North Carolina Biography*, s.v. "Chavis, John"; Othow, *John Chavis*, 40.

[17]*Dictionary of North Carolina Biography*, s.v. "Chavis, John."

there is no formal record of a degree completion at Princeton, his name is mentioned in the University's trustee minutes for 29 September 1792 with a recommendation that he be received for study at the school.[18] Othow argues that the legend about the wager is not accurate. Records reveal that other blacks were tutored by Witherspoon and that Chavis had the intellectual skills that would have easily won him acceptance to the school. Furthermore, Chavis had expressed interest in the Presbyterian ministry, and Princeton would have been the natural location for him to seek such training.[19]

Having received only private tutoring at Princeton, Chavis enrolled in the Liberty Hall Academy (now Washington and Lee University) and completed his educational training there prior to 1802. From the previous chapter, the reader will recall that William McPheeters attended the same school at approximately the same time. It is reasonable then to believe that the two men would have become acquainted during that time.[20]

On 19 November 1800, Chavis was licensed as a minister in the Presbytery of Lexington, Virginia. For the next seven years, he served as a missionary to slaves in Maryland, Virginia, and North Carolina. He preached to white congregations as well and seemed to move freely among both whites and blacks at the beginning of the nineteenth century. The Orange Presbytery in North Carolina became his base in 1809. The presbytery appointed William McPheeters and Samuel Smith Downey to oversee his work. Though never ordained or assigned a permanent pastorate, Chavis had a thriving itinerate ministry until 1832, when repercussions from the Nat Turner Rebellion the previous year prompted North Carolina to pass a law forbidding blacks from preaching. That law effectively ended Chavis's preaching.[21]

The Nat Turner Rebellion instilled fear among white citizens in Raleigh. Fearful whites took measures to provide for the safety of the city in the case of a slave rebellion in Raleigh by organizing men exempt from

---

[18]Othow, *John Chavis*, 41; *Dictionary of North Carolina Biography,* s.v. "Chavis, John"; *Dictionary of American Biography*, s.v. "Chavis, John."

[19]Othow, *John Chavis*, 41–47.

[20]See chapter 2.

[21]*Dictionary of North Carolina Biography,* s.v. "Chavis, John."

military service into a Senior Volunteer Association, with Thomas G. Scott as commander. In the event of an emergency, the bell in the belfry at First Presbyterian Church would be rung, summoning women and children to the church building for safety. Interestingly, the bell was also used as a fire alarm in the city, and one evening shortly after the organization of the Senior Volunteer Association there was a fire in a blacksmith shop. As the bell from the church rang out the fire alarm, James D. Royster recalled the "frantic rush for the church by night-clothed families only to learn the alarm had been sounded because of a fire."[22]

Chavis is best remembered for his work in education during his years in Raleigh and Wake County. Recognized for his knowledge of Greek and Latin, Chavis soon developed a reputation as an effective educator. He began teaching in Raleigh around 1805. Originally, his school was integrated, but when the white parents complained, he was forced to teach the black and white children separately. In late summer 1808, he placed ads in the *Raleigh Register* announcing that his school would instruct white children during the day and free black children in the evenings.[23] Chavis taught in other areas of Wake County, and it was reported that he also taught in Granville, Chatham, and Cumberland counties from time to time.[24] Numerous important North Carolinians were counted among his pupils, including Governor Charles Manly, Archibald and John L. Henderson (sons of Leonard Henderson, chief justice of the North Carolina Supreme Court), U.S. congressman Abraham Rencher, Priestly Hinton and his brother, and U.S. senator Willie Person Mangum.[25] During his years in the Senate, Mangum frequently corresponded with Chavis, the latter offering his opinion on the issues of

---

[22]Kemp P. Battle, *Early History of Raleigh, The Capital City of North Carolina: A Centennial Address, October 18, 1892* (Raleigh: Edwards and Broughton, 1893) 48; cited in Murray, *Prehistory*, 166. The text of Battle's book is available through Google Books.

[23]Murray, *Prehistory*, 189.

[24]Othow, *John Chavis*, 64–65; Murray, *Prehistory*, 189.

[25]Murray, *Prehistory*, 189.

the day. Upon Chavis's death in 1838, he was buried in the Mangum family cemetery in Durham.[26]

Chavis represents an inspiring, if tragic, story of a free black in Raleigh's antebellum years. The story of Lunsford Lane is one of the most inspiring slave narratives from the period. Lunsford Lane was born in 1803 into slavery on the Sherwood Haywood estate in Wake County. Lane became an astute businessman and possessed a remarkable entrepreneurial spirit. His owner allowed him to earn money through extra work, and with help from his father, he developed a particular blend of smoking tobacco for which a local demand soon developed. Lane ultimately accumulated enough money to purchase his own freedom and move to the North. There he continued his business and amassed enough money to return to Raleigh, where he sought to purchase freedom for his wife and children. When he returned to the city, a local mob of whites, angry about his success, abducted, tarred, and feathered Lane. With the aid of whites, Lane and his family boarded a train for Philadelphia and left the city. He spent the rest of his life in the North as an active leader in the antislavery movement. Although the exact date of his death is not known, most sources indicate that it was probably after 1865.[27] In his autobiography, Lane lists a number of prominent Raleigh citizens among his supporters, several of whom were connected with First Presbyterian Church. These include William McPheeters, Drury Lacy, John Primrose, and William Peace.[28]

---

[26]Ibid. Following the Turner Rebellion in 1831, North Carolina law forbid Chavis not only from preaching but also from educating free blacks and slaves thereby limiting his students to whites only.

[27]See Lunsford Lane, *Narrative of Lunsford Lane, Formerly of Raleigh, N.C.: Embracing an Account of His Early Life, the Redemption by Purchase of Himself and His Family From Slavery, and His Banishment From the Place of His Birth for the Crime of Wearing a Colored Skin*, 2nd ed. (Boston: J. G. Torrey, 1842), http://docsouth.unc.edu/neh/lanelunsford/lane.html. See also Murray, *Prehistory*, 274–75.

[28]Ibid., 30.

First Presbyterian Church of Raleigh

The resignation of William McPheeters in late 1829 began an unsettled period for First Presbyterian Church due largely to the fact that the church had no consistent pastoral leadership. The historical details of the first couple of years in this period are sketchy because no sessional records exist until 1831. From other sources it is known that one of the first names to be associated with the pastoral leadership of the church was Thomas P. Hunt. He is mentioned in connection with the church by the *Raleigh Register* on 21 September 1829, where it is written that he, along with McPheeters and Rev. Nehemiah H. Harding, met to establish a temperance society in Raleigh. The following spring (15 April 1830), he is again referenced in the newspaper as having delivered an address in the church's Session House related to the anniversary of the Sabbath School Union. Hunt is also mentioned as having delivered the sermon at the church on the fourth Sunday in July 1830, but by April 1831, he is described in the newspaper as being "late of this city."[29]

At this point, the sessional records reveal the church's attempt to establish pastoral leadership. The first entry in the oldest sessional record book speaks of a visit by Rev. John Witherspoon, agent from the Board of Missions of the General Assembly of the Presbyterian Church. Witherspoon remained for a few weeks and led the congregation to organize a mission society as an auxiliary to the General Assembly's Board of Missions. The reference then turns to the departure of Thomas Hunt and a plan put forth by Witherspoon to combine the "wisdom of age" with the "activity and zeal of youth" by providing to the church a "young man laboring under the direction and counsel of an experienced minister." The session developed a plan to invite William McPheeters "to become their stated supply, to have the oversight and government of the church, to

[29]William P. McPherson, ed., *The History of First Presbyterian Church, Raleigh, North Carolina: 1816–1991* (Raleigh: Commercial Printing, 1991) 26; Thomas Poage Hunt, *Life and Thoughts of Rev. Thomas P. Hunt: An Autobiography*, ed. S. C. Hunt (Wilkes-Barre, PA: Robt. Baur & Son, 1901), available through Google Books.

labor in preaching the word in communion with such a young missionary as the Board of Missions may from time to time station among them."[30]

Three days later, the session met and reported that the congregation approved the plan. Two elders were assigned the task of writing a letter to McPheeters requesting his help.[31] Mysteriously, there is no mention of a response from McPheeters, nor is there even any mention of McPheeters's name for a year until the following January. A letter from McPheeters dated 11 January 1832 is copied into the sessional records following the last entry for 1831. In the letter, McPheeters kindly rejects the congregation's request. What conversations transpired during the intervening year and why McPheeters did not respond earlier cannot be known from the records that exist. In his letter, he does mention that he wanted to "retire to some other field of labor," and that the size of his family caused him to "think of a location somewhere in the western country." He even mentions the "Valley of the Mississippi" as a place that might hold promise for him.[32] McPheeters, however, ultimately chose not to leave Raleigh, and the plan presented to the congregation by the elders was implemented beginning in June 1832, when the church extended an invitation to Rev. Nehemiah H. Harding of Oxford, North Carolina, "to come take charge of the Presbyterian Church in this city."[33] Harding's earlier work with Hunt and McPheeters in helping to establish a temperance society in the city in 1829 likely had provided the opportunity for the church to become acquainted with him. His first Sunday as the church's "pastor or stated supply" was 29 July 1832. He only stayed a few months, however, choosing to return to Oxford in September 1832. Rev. George H. Apthorpe, a missionary from the American Home Missionary Society, succeeded Harding in September 1832 but remained with the church for less than three months. McPheeters then agreed to supply the pulpit until another minister could be secured.[34]

[30]Minutes of the Session, 20 January 1831.

[31]Ibid., 23 January 1831.

[32]William McPheeters to the Elders of the Presbyterian Church, 11 January 1832, contained in Minutes of the Session.

[33]Ibid., 9 June 1832.

[34]Ibid., 29 July 1832; 19 September 1832.

There are no sessional records for the rest of 1832 and the first few months of 1833. On 13 May 1833, the record reports that the congregation unanimously selected Rev. Michael Osborn as the next pastor and that he would assume such duties in August of that year. Osborn was born in New Jersey on 21 March 1796. He attended Princeton Theological Seminary and was ordained by the Elizabethtown Presbytery on 23 February 1825. He came to North Carolina in 1829, first to the Presbyterian Church in New Bern, then to Raleigh. He spent two years in missionary work for the Orange Presbytery prior to his acceptance by the Raleigh congregation. Osborn eventually moved to Farmville, Virginia, where he served as pastor from 1848 until his death on 3 July 1862.[35]

Osborn seems to have remained with the church until spring 1836.[36] There is no specific mention of his leaving, but the sessional record for 6 March 1836 does not list him as present in that session meeting whereas he had been present in the previous meetings. Also, McPheeters performed an infant baptism at that meeting, and for the meeting on 11 July 1836 McPheeters was asked to moderate.[37] Returning briefly to the records for 1833, it should be noted that in the fall of that year one important development concerned the practice of pew rental. The session abolished the practice, and all the pews were declared to be free.[38]

Thus, by 1836, the First Presbyterian Church in Raleigh was in need of stability in pastoral leadership. For the previous seven years, the church had struggled with various "stated supply" pastors while McPheeters served sporadically in various interim capacities. The instability had a detrimental effect on the church. While the sessional records do not address the need for leadership stability overtly, there are three clues, in particular, that allow the careful observer to conclude that the elders were concerned. First, the session designated 31 March 1831 to be a special day of "humiliation and prayers." No specific reason is given for

---

[35]Biographical information taken from McPherson, *History of First Presbyterian Church*, 27–28.

[36]McPherson (*History of First Presbyterian Church*, 28) indicates that Osborn left the Raleigh church within a few months after he arrived. However, his name continues to be listed in the sessional records as moderator until 1836.

[37]Minutes of the Session, 13 May 1833, 6 March and 11 July 1836.

[38]Ibid., 24 October 1833.

this designation, but it is probable that the church's needs were on the minds of the members. The special day was to start with individual members praying at an early hour. Then at 9:00 a.m., they were asked to pray again. At 11:00 a.m., the men and women were asked to gather in separate locations for "social prayer." At 4:00 p.m., all members were to join together for "social prayer." Finally at "candle light," the church was to observe its weekly prayer meeting.[39] Several years later, the session declared that it is "expedient that the sacrament of the Lord's Supper be celebrated by this church as often as once in two months." That resolution may be a second clue as to the lack of pastoral stability, which may have led to neglect of that important practice. No further word, however, is given. In fact, the session meeting for that particular date mentions this as its only act of business.[40] One final clue that may reveal the elders' frustration with the lack of pastoral stability is seen in the sessional record for 18 October 1836: "Having no pastor and there being no minister of the Presbyterian Church to whom the elders could have access to act as Moderator, they conceived they were authorized to act under such circumstances."[41]

Although there is no official account of it in the sessional records, Drury Lacy became the pastor of the church on 7 January 1838, initiating a long tenure that lasted until 1855. Lacy brought pulpit eloquence, wisdom, leadership, and social grace to the pastoral role at the church, the likes of which had not been seen since the McPheeters pastorate. In retrospect, it is clear that Lacy was the perfect leader for the church at this crucial juncture in its early years.

Lacy was born in Ararat, a small town located in Prince Edward County, Virginia, on 5 August 1802. His father was a Presbyterian minister and ran a classical school in the town. After he completed the traditional classical education of the day at his father's school, Lacy enrolled at Washington College and then a year later enrolled at Hampden-Sydney College, where he received his bachelor's degree in 1822. Upon graduation, Lacy returned to his hometown and assumed the role of

---

[39] Ibid., 31 March 1831.
[40] Ibid., 3 December 1833.
[41] Ibid., 18 October 1836.

teacher that his father had occupied. He remained a teacher until 1828, when he decided to enter Union Theological Seminary in Virginia. Lacy's decision to enroll in seminary was the result of his conversion experience under the preaching of Asahel Nettleton.[42]

Nettleton's influence during the Second Great Awakening is often not recognized. He remained thoroughly Calvinistic and devoted to traditional Presbyterian doctrine in the face of other revivalists of the time such as Charles G. Finney. Controversy among Presbyterians over Finney's "new measures" led to the convening in 1827 of the New Lebanon Conference, where Nettleton and Lyman Beecher became leading voices in opposition to Finney's revival methods.[43] Nettleton's influence on the young Lacy provides a clue as to Lacy's later theological perspective, especially in matters related to revivalism among Presbyterians.

Upon completion of his seminary degree in 1831, Lacy was licensed by the West Hanover Presbytery. Two years later, the East Hanover Presbytery ordained him, and the following year, he became pastor of the Presbyterian church in New Bern, North Carolina, until 1837.[44] From there he came to Raleigh.[45] Lacy served the Raleigh church until 1855, when he accepted an invitation to become the president of Davidson College. Education was, no doubt, in his blood. Before he was born, his father, Drury Lacy Sr. served as vice president and, for a period, acting

---

[42]See "Rev Drury Lacy, II," findagrave.com; accessed 19 September 2013, http://www.findagrave.com/cgi-bin/fg.cgi?page=gr&GSln=Lacy&GSfn=Drury&GSby=1802&GSbyrel=in&GSdy=1884&GSdyrel=in&GScntry=4&GSob=n&GRid=42756954&df=all&.

[43]Sydney E. Ahlstrom, *A Religious History of the American People,* 2nd ed. (New Haven: Yale University Press, 2004) 455–61. Reportedly, Lyman Beecher said the following words to Finney in the conference: "I know your plan and you know I do. You mean to come into Connecticut, and carry a streak of fire to Boston. But if you attempt it, as the Lord liveth, I'll meet you at the State line, and call out all the artillery-men, and fight every inch of the way to Boston, and I'll fight you there" (461).

[44]"Rev Drury Lacy, II," findagrave.com.

[45]*Dictionary of North Carolina Biography,* s.v. "Lacy, Drury, Jr."

president of Hampden-Sydney College (1789–1797).[46] Early American Presbyterianism was known for its educated pastors who often served dual roles as educators. The most obvious example of that in Raleigh before Lacy was William McPheeters. The move to Davidson College was, therefore, a good move for Lacy and not a complete surprise.

Lacy's tenure as president at Davidson was successful although he inherited a difficult situation. The months prior to his assumption of the school's presidency witnessed a student uprising against the faculty that led to the exodus of many of the students. The episode, which occurred just before Christmas 1854, involved a conflict between the students and a faculty member Major Daniel Harvey Hill. Hill, who had joined the faculty as professor of mathematics earlier in the year, was a West Point graduate and a veteran of the Mexican War. He was also a strict disciplinarian and demanding instructor, two qualities that seem to have been the locus of the problem with the students. That problem escalated into an encounter between a number of the students and several professors, including Hill, in which rocks were thrown at the professors, one rock striking Hill on the shoulder. The faculty, after an investigation, expelled a student they believed was guilty of throwing the rock although the evidence against him was considered to be circumstantial. The students came to his defense, leading to an exodus of many students from the school. The following spring, only thirty-one of the seventy-five students who matriculated the previous fall were present. At graduation exercises in spring 1855, only three students received diplomas.[47] Lacy began his duties in spring 1855 just after the student uprising. Shortly thereafter, the school received a large gift from the estate of Salisbury businessman Maxwell Chambers. The gift of approximately $200,000 [$5,560,000] was so large that it made Davidson College the wealthiest private educa-

---

[46]See "Presidents of the College," accessed 17 September 2013, http://www.hsc.edu/Academics/Academic-Catalogues/Catalogue-2015-16/Presidents.html.

[47]Cornelia Rebekah Shaw, *Davidson College* (New York: Fleming H. Revell Press, 1923) 72–81.

tional institution in the South at the time.[48] The gift also led to the construction of the Chambers building on the campus.

Lacy's pastorate corresponded with one of the most volatile periods in American history. Whether it was his sense of the times or some other reason, Lacy resigned as the school's president in 1860 to serve as a domestic missionary with the Orange Presbytery. During the Civil War, Lacy served as a chaplain at the military hospitals in Raleigh and Wilson. Following the war, from 1866 to 1878, he served as a supply preacher at various churches in the Orange Presbytery and as a professor at Peace Institute (now William Peace University), where his wife was "lady principal."[49] Lacy was married twice. His first wife, Williana Wilkinson, died in 1846. He married Mary Ritchie Rice in 1849. Lacy died in 1884.

Several years before Lacy's arrival, a civic catastrophe forced the state of North Carolina to look to First Presbyterian Church for help. One challenge for Raleigh during the antebellum years was the containment of fires that broke out at various times in the city. In 1819, the city had purchased a small pumping engine. It was the responsibility of all citizens to respond and fight the fires whenever they broke out. The small engine and citizens' efforts with leather buckets, however, were hardly able to contain fires of the magnitude that the city saw in 1831, 1832, and 1833, which destroyed much of the heart of the city's business district. It was during the early morning hours of 23 June 1831 that Raleigh lost its most prized structure, the statehouse, to a fire. It was believed that the fire was accidently started by a worker who had been employed to install a new zinc roof on the building to replace the wood shingles (considered, ironically enough, to be a fire hazard). Fire had threatened the statehouse before, once in 1816 and again just five months before its final destruction in 1831. Joseph Gales, editor of the *Raleigh Register*, caught the terrible irony of the building's destruction saying, "It is a mortifying reflection that the very means adopted for the security of the building have been attended with a fatality that produced its destruction." Rebuilding the structure took seven years, and it was

---

[48]Ibid., 86–89.

[49]See "Biographical Information," accessed 19 September 2013, http://www2.lib.unc.edu/mss/inv/l/Lacy,Drury.html.

completed in 1840 at a cost of $530,684.15 [$14.8 million]—more than ten times the original projected cost. The first legislative session met in the new building in November 1840.[50]

Realizing the magnitude of the calamity and recognizing that they had one of the best structures in the young city, within twenty-four hours of the fire, the members of First Presbyterian Church offered use of its facilities for both the legislature and the state supreme court. The supreme court accepted the offer and met in the Session House until the new capitol was completed in 1840, making First Presbyterian the only church to "house" one of the three branches of the state government. The legislature displaced the governor and met at the "Government House" through the 1835 session, whereupon it relocated to several privately owned buildings until the completion of the new capitol.[51] It was in 1835, while the new capitol was still under construction, that the First Presbyterian Church hosted the North Carolina Constitutional Convention. The state's constitution, originally written in 1776, had not been amended or reformed, and by the 1830s, there was much discussion and debate generated about the need for revision. William McPheeters along with Rev. James Jamieson of the Methodist Episcopal Church served as chaplains to the convention.[52] The convention made several significant

---

[50]Murray, *Prehistory*, 252–55. Eleven years later, the most destructive fire that the city had experienced came on 15 December 1851. That night a fire erupted in H. A. Depkin's boot and shoe store located at the corner of Fayetteville and Hargett streets. The fire ultimately spread to and destroyed more than seventeen buildings on Fayetteville, Hargett, and Wilmington streets. Two months later, the city employed Seymour W. Whiting as the first salaried fire chief (Murray, *Prehistory*, 409–11).

[51]Murray, *Prehistory*, 206–207, 230. The executive residence, originally built in 1816, was called both the "Government House" and the "Governor's Palace" in its day. It served as the residence for all of North Carolina's governors from William Miller through Zebulon Vance. It was constructed at the end of Fayetteville Street on a location occupied later by the Centennial School and still later by Memorial Auditorium.

[52]See *Journal of the Convention, Called by the Freemen of North-Carolina, to Amend the Constitution of the State, Which Assembled in the City of Raleigh, on the 4th of June, 1835, and Continued in Session Until the 11th Day of July Thereafter*

changes to the state constitution, such as denying the right to vote to free blacks and amending an article in the original document that held that only Protestant Christians could hold public office. The wording was changed from "Protestant" to "Christian."[53] The new constitution also excluded an article from the old that denied ministers who were currently serving churches from holding public office. The membership totals of the Senate and House were fixed at fifty and 120, respectively. The office of governor was also made a popularly elected office with a two-year term.[54]

Church discipline was an important concern for Protestant churches in the antebellum years, particularly in the South. A few blocks away from First Presbyterian Church in Raleigh, the Baptists were also deeply interested in moral lapses among their membership.[55] The sessional records at First Presbyterian also contain numerous church discipline matters during the pastoral tenure of Drury Lacy. It is noteworthy that before Lacy became the church's pastor there are no instances of church discipline mentioned in the records even though the surviving records only extend back to 1831. Nevertheless, during the period of pastoral vacancy in the 1830s, there are no instances of discipline mentioned. Apparently, Lacy brought a greater focus on matters of morality than the church experienced in the years immediately preceding his arrival.

Concern for personal morality was imparted into the American religious consciousness by the Puritans, and as Sydney Ahlstrom notes, "Re-

---

North Carolina. Constitutional Convention (1835) (Raleigh, NC: Joseph Gales & Son, 1835) 103, http://docsouth.unc.edu/nc/conv1835/conv1835.html.

[53]See *Raleigh Register*, 20, 27 July and 3 August 1821, as cited by Murray, *Prehistory*, 180. Openness to Catholicism within the city of Raleigh was aided in 1821 when the Right Reverend John England, bishop of Charleston, visited the city and delivered a series of lectures on Catholicism in the sanctuary of First Presbyterian Church. The lectures spanned a ten-day period, and newspaper publisher Joseph Gales said that they were delivered in an "uncommonly impressive manner" and succeeded in removing "much previous misconception and many unwarranted opinions" about the Roman Catholic Church.

[54]See *Encyclopedia of North Carolina*, ed. William S. Powell et al. (Chapel Hill: University of North Carolina Press, 2006) s.v. "Convention of 1835.

[55]W. Glenn Jonas Jr., *Nurturing the Vision: First Baptist Church Raleigh, 1812–2012* (Macon: Mercer University Press, 2012) 33.

formed preaching never neglected to stress radical amendment of behavior as a necessary concomitant and sign of true conversion."[56] Temperance became one of the first great moral crusades as American religion emerged from the Second Great Awakening. The Puritans and most of the other religious groups in colonial America generally were not teetotalers. But abuse of alcohol, along with drunken behavior, was a social ill that captured the attention of many American Christians by the early nineteenth century.

The great Presbyterian preacher Lyman Beecher became one of the first voices to call for temperance and moral reform. He was instrumental in the formation of the Connecticut Society for the Reformation of Morals in 1813, while in Massachusetts, lawyer Jeremiah Evarts launched a similar effort with the Massachusetts Society for the Suppression of Intemperance. A little more than a decade later (1826), the American Society for the Promotion of Temperance was formed in Boston, and by 1836, the American Temperance Union was formed, advocating total abstinence from alcohol. Although national Prohibition was decades in the future, according to Ahlstrom, the "extraordinary success of the temperance movement during the next two decades forms a familiar chapter in American social history," so much so that the state of Maine in 1846 passed the first prohibition law in the nation.[57]

The temperance movement made its way into North Carolina as early as 1828 and spawned numerous county-wide organizations. The North Carolina Temperance Society was formed in 1839 in an effort to bring unification to the various disparate local groups.[58] It comes as no surprise, therefore, that the first instance of church discipline mentioned in the First Presbyterian sessional records during Lacy's pastorate concerned the abuse of alcohol. On 13 August 1842, the elders discussed the case of Nelson B. Hughes, a member of the church and prominent Raleigh businessman, "who has been reported as guilty of the sin of intemperance." Attempts were made to bring him to repentance, but those at-

---

[56]Ahlstrom, *Religious History*, 425.

[57]Ibid., 426.

[58]See *NCpedia*, s.v. "Temperance Movement," accessed 3 October 2013, http://ncpedia.org/temperance-movement.

tempts failed. Consequently, the session instructed the pastor and one other elder to visit with Hughes "and in the name of the Session represent to him the great sin of which he is reported as guilty," and that "the reproach of the church suffers by his conduct." The resolution also instructed that Hughes should be informed as to "the ruin he is bringing on himself."[59] Within six days, the pastor reported back to the session the contents of a letter written to him by Hughes "which makes a full and candid acknowledgement of his offence [*sic*], confesses his unfeigned sorrow and deep penitence for having sinned against God, and brought reproach on the church, and asks the forgiveness of his brethren." Lacy also indicated that Hughes included a note to the session "proposing that they should suspend him from church membership until he should prove himself clean of this sin."[60] The session decided that he had shown the proper remorse and that the church should not go to the extent of suspending his membership.

The modern reader of the sessional records would perhaps identify the sickness of alcoholism in the situation with Nelson Hughes, and unfortunately, it was not over. On 4 October 1845, the session was forced to deal with Hughes and his alcohol abuse once again. It is interesting to read the way that the clerk of the session described the case: "Resolved, that the charge of intemperance is hereby proffered against Nelson B. Hughes by general rumor." The session then ordered that the clerk should notify him to appear in person before them and that he was also to be informed that he was to refrain from observance of the Lord's Supper until his situation was resolved.[61] Nine days later, the clerk reported that Hughes sent a letter in reply to the session's request. The letter was read before the session although it was not included with the official record of the meeting. Upon hearing the letter, the session made two resolutions: (1) although Hughes did not appear in person before the session, "he does not deserve the censure of the Session for contumacy—as the whole tenor of his letter just read clearly shows that none was intended" and (2) although he made a full acknowledgement of his wrong-doing,

---

[59]Minutes of the Session, 13 August 1842.

[60]Ibid., 19 August 1842.

[61]Ibid., 4 October 1845.

the session determined that "for the warning of all others, for the purity of the church, for the promotion of God's glory" he should be "suspended from the privileges of the church until he shall give sufficient evidence of repentance."[62] The last mention of Nelson B. Hughes in the sessional records occurred three years later, a sign that he still struggled with alcoholism. The clerk referred back to the session's action in 1845 and stated that Hughes, "far from manifesting any signs of repentance and reformation, continues to grow more confirmed in the habit of intemperance and that this habit has become so fixed and habitual as to give no hope whatever of amendment." The session then ordered that "as the last means that can be used, under God, of reclaiming him, but especially to deliver the church from the scandal of his offence and to inspire all others with fear by the example of his punishment," he was to be "cut off from all communion with the church." Secondly, the session determined that the pastor was to publicly announce this action from the pulpit on the following Sunday morning.[63]

Another situation of personal morality that came to the attention of the session concerned a woman named Rebecca Wedding. Little is known of her other than the fact that she was a member of the church. On 24 March 1849, the sessional record contains this statement:

> It being notorious that Rebecca Wedding, a non-married female member of this church has given birth to a child a few months since. On motion, ordered that the Clerk cite this said Rebecca to appear before the Session in the Session House on Tuesday 24th day of April next at 4 o'clock in the afternoon to show cause why she should not be dealt with according to her offense, so ____________ a member of the church of Jesus Christ.[64]

The matter was "unavoidably delayed" until a year later though no reason is given for the delay. The minutes for the 31 May 1850 meeting disclose that she wrote a personal letter of confession to the session "expressing her deep sorrow." After consideration of the situation and her confession, the session determined to "suspend her from the privileges

[62]Ibid., 13 October 1845.

[63]Ibid., 12 July 1848.

[64]Ibid., 24 March 1849. The blank indicates one word that is unintelligible.

and ordinances of the church until she gives further evidence to this session that she has repented of her sin and offense against God and His Church."[65] There is no further mention of Rebecca Wedding in the sessional records. It is noteworthy that there is no mention of the child's father. Who was he? Was he a member of the church as well? What became of that situation and what happened to Wedding and her child? Unfortunately, there are no answers to these questions. The episode simply stands as another example of antebellum piety and concern for personal morality in a bygone era.

One more example of church discipline that the modern reader may find interesting concerns a church member named Karl Petersilia, an immigrant from Germany. He and his wife, Lucy, joined the church on 24 March 1849, transferring their membership from First Presbyterian Church in Greensboro.[66] The Petersilias were professors at the Female Classical Institute, which opened on Hillsborough Street in 1849. Karl was professor of music while his wife taught drawing and painting. He also opened on Fayetteville Street a music store, which sold a variety of musical instruments including pianos.[67] There is no further mention of Karl in the sessional records for the next three years. Presumably, he and Lucy were upstanding citizens of the city and loyal members of the Presbyterian Church. On 7 April 1852, the sessional record contains the following notation: "Reports being current of the intemperate habits and also the frequenting of the Billiard Room of Mr. Karl W. Petersilia, a member of this church."[68] The session followed its standard procedure for those cases by appointing a committee of two elders to visit with him to determine if he felt remorse and showed evidence of repentance. Several months later, the sessional records report that the committee went to see Petersilia but did not find him at home. The session then composed a letter to him requesting that he "not come to the Lord's Table on the next communion" until the reports about him could be investigated.[69]

---

[65]Ibid., 31 May 1850.

[66]Ibid., 24 March 1849.

[67]Murray, *Prehistory*, 314, 342.

[68]Minutes of the Session, 7 April 1852.

[69]Ibid., 29 September 1852.

Perhaps showing evidence that Petersilia was not too concerned about what his church thought of his behavior, he never appeared before the session in person to speak to their concerns. The sessional records mention the situation several times, and on 4 March 1854, the session "spent a considerable length of time in solemn deliberation" trying to determine the proper way to proceed with the situation. At that meeting, they passed a resolution indicating that Petersilia had "given no satisfactory evidence of repentance for the sin of intemperance of which he is known by the members of the session to have been for a long time guilty.... Resolved, that [he] is duly excluded from the communion of the church, not only for his intemperance, but for his contumacy until he repents."[70]

The modern reader may be inclined to consider the church's attention with such personal moral matters to be a serious invasion of privacy. After all, what right did the church have in making judgments on an individual's moral choices? Most congregations do not involve themselves in the personal moral decisions made by their members anymore. The antebellum years, particularly just after the Second Great Awakening, were different. These cases provide a glimpse into the culture of Raleigh religion in the middle of the nineteenth century and also provide insight into how seriously the Raleigh Presbyterians took personal morality. A lapse in personal morality was a direct and negative reflection upon the witness of the First Presbyterian Church itself. For the sake of the congregation's witness, those matters needed to be dealt with in a serious, yet fair way. We should also be reminded that the Christians in the nineteenth century did not understand the disease of alcoholism as it is understood today. Neither did they have the same sense of compassion toward a young, unmarried woman who became pregnant that a modern congregation might have today. Most churches today would seek to find ways to minister to these people rather than exclude them from the fel-

[70]Ibid., 4 March 1854. There are several other church discipline cases mentioned in the sessional records dealing with matters such as intemperance, lack of church attendance, "riotous behavior," and "keeping wicked company visiting a house...of ill fame" (see Minutes of the Session, 12 July 1850, 8 November 1850, and 14 November 1854).

lowship. While that was not necessarily a lesser concern back then, the means of dealing with such situations was very different.

During the period from 1831 to 1855 (as previously noted, the extant sessional records only go back to 1831), the church showed remarkable numeric growth. Membership totals were occasionally reported in the sessional records as the church year came to a close because such statistics were also sent to the presbytery. Although these reports (always in April) are not consistently present, the reader of the sessional records can see how the church grew over the two and a half decades. The chart below shows the membership totals that are reported in the sessional records:

Year	Membership[71]
1832	39
1833	49
1834	54
1835	55
1842	71
1843	79
1852	108
1853	131
1854	114
1855	108

The chart shows a trend of consistent growth until the final years of Drury Lacy's pastoral tenure. The sessional records provide no explanation about the decline in membership from 1853 to 1855.

In 1847, a controversy erupted in the church related to the North Carolina Institution for the Deaf and Dumb. Wake County led the state in seeking to provide a means of education to both deaf and blind citizens. As mentioned in chapter 2, William McPheeters, along with Joseph Gales and other Wake County citizens, advocated as early as 1827

[71]Minutes of the Session, 20 April 1832; 20 April 1833; 21 April 1834; 13 April 1835; 6 April 1842; 17 April 1843; 11 April 1852; 1 April 1853; 1 April 1854; 1 April 1855.

on behalf of that cause. For the next seventeen years he and others continued to promote the erection of a school to educate those unable to hear or speak.[72] On 28 December 1844, in a "dramatic presentation" before the General Assembly, the legislators and the public saw a demonstration of techniques used to instruct deaf children so that they could communicate and learn. William Dewey Cooke, from Staunton, Virginia, was in charge of the demonstration. Cooke had studied under Harvey Prindle Peet, considered at the time to be a pioneer in the field, at the New York Institution for the Instruction of the Deaf and Dumb. The legislators were so impressed that they appropriated $5,000 [$159,000] for the establishment of a school in Raleigh. Cooke moved to Raleigh in early 1845, and the school was formally established on 1 May 1845, with the state committing to finance half of each student's expense.[73]

In April 1846, Cooke and his wife, Lucy Ann, were admitted to the membership of First Presbyterian Church in Raleigh by certificate from the First Presbyterian Church in Staunton, Virginia.[74] In January 1847, Cooke sent a letter to the elders and trustees of his church requesting that a "vocal and instrumental concert for the purpose of raising funds to pay for a printing press" for the school's use be allowed. The session declined to grant permission over concerns that such an event might violate the proper decorum of the building constructed as a sacred space and devoted to worship.[75] Although just a few years earlier the North Carolina Supreme Court used the Session House until the new capitol was built and the church structure was used for the North Carolina Constitutional Convention, several ruling elders considered the fundraiser "in the sight of God an improper and unholy use of said Church."[76]

The following month, three elders, James M. Towles, Jesse Brown, and Charles Dewey, sent a letter to the session informing of their resignation from their offices as ruling elders. They believed that their opposition to the fundraiser had caused dissension in the congregation and that

---

[72]Murray, *Prehistory*, 326.
[73]Ibid.
[74]Minutes of the Session, 1 April 1846.
[75]Ibid., 20 February 1847.
[76]Ibid.

their "actions as officers of the Presbyterian Church...are not amicably entertained by the church, or a considerable number thereof." They continued by suggesting that some members of the church had considered their acts "accounted unworthy of our station and unchristian." Finally, they were given the impression from some in the congregation that "unless we make confession for and reconsider the stand we have taken...division and separation will take in the membership."[77] In the same entry in the sessional records that described this event, the elders reluctantly accepted their three brothers' resignations and penned a two-page resolution of support and appreciation for their good service as elders in the past. Finally, they determined that at the call of the pastor an election for three replacement elders would be held on 22 February, just ten days later.[78]

The story has a happy ending. In what must have been a show of unity in the congregation, the three elders who resigned were re-elected "by a large majority" of the congregation and agreed to resume their duties.[79] The only other reference to the matter came one year later. On 21 February 1848, the session met at Cooke's request. He sought a meeting of the session to clear up any misunderstanding that may have arisen during the previous year regarding his request for the use of the building for the fundraiser. A reading of the minutes of the meeting suggests that there may have been some residual effect from the conflict the previous year and Cooke wanted reassurance of his good standing in the church. In response to his concerns, the session reported that he was "a member of the Presbyterian Church in Raleigh in full and regular standing, that no charges whatever have been brought against him by this Session and that as far as their influence can reach...they are cheerfully given by this their action for the correction...of any report that may have circulated...to him."[80] It would appear then that although the church had different notions about whether or not such a fundraiser would violate the de-

---

[77]Ibid.

[78]Ibid.

[79]Ibid.

[80]Minutes of the Session, 21 February 1848.

corum of the church, nevertheless, the issue did not have any long-term negative consequences.

During the pastorate of Drury Lacy, an important milestone occurred for the First Presbyterian Church due to the generosity of one of the most prominent women in Raleigh before the Civil War. Frances Pollock Devereux (1771–1849) came to Raleigh with her husband, John, in the 1820s from New Bern. The Pollock and Devereux families were among the wealthiest families in North Carolina in their day, owning thousands of acres of land and hundreds of slaves. John Devereux (1761–1844) was born in Ireland and had a fascinating life before he met Frances Pollock. According to one family source, as a child, he was sent by his family from Ireland to France to prepare for the priesthood in the Roman Catholic Church. Although he later changed his plans, he remained a faithful Roman Catholic throughout his life. He joined the British Royal Navy before the American Revolution and served at the rank of lieutenant during the war. He resigned his commission, settled in Charleston, South Carolina, following the war, and joined a shipping business as a partner.[81]

On a business trip during the 1780s, Devereux became shipwrecked near Cape Hatteras, off the coast of North Carolina. He remained in North Carolina for some time in order to help determine the company's losses and at some point made a trip to New Bern. There he met Frances Pollock, the daughter of Thomas and Eunice Edwards Pollock. The Pollock Family had deep roots in North Carolina. Frances's great-grandfather was Governor Thomas Pollock, who governed the colony from 1712 to 1714 and again in 1722. Frances was also the granddaughter of Jonathan Edwards, one of the greatest preachers in colonial America and, by some accounts, one of America's greatest theologians. The couple married in 1790. Through her father, Frances inherited eight plantations as well as 7,500 "milled Spanish pieces of eight."[82] John made his own fortune following the couple's marriage. He continued in the business, establishing trade between New York, Charleston, and the West Indies. He probably studied law at some point because he amassed

[81]*Dictionary of North Carolina Biography*, s.v. "Devereux, John."
[82]Ibid.

a law library, which he bequeathed to Thomas Pollock Devereux, the only son to outlive him. John and Frances had one daughter, Frances Ann Devereux, who married Leonidas Polk, the famous Episcopal bishop and Confederate chaplain.[83]

Devereux was a generous supporter of the University of North Carolina and the Griffin Free School in New Bern. He also wanted the best education possible for his sons, sending them both to Yale for training in law. Frances Devereux also supported a number of charitable organizations and was a charter member of the First Presbyterian Church in New Bern. When the couple moved from New Bern to Raleigh, Frances brought her generosity to the First Presbyterian Church in the capital city also. Most significantly, she provided the means by which the church built its first manse.

The process that led to the building of the manse and the donation of the property to the church is an interesting, and to some extent unique, tale. On 23 January 1840, William F. Clark conveyed an acre of land located at the southwest corner of West Hargett and South Dawson Streets to the church. Written into the deed to the land are the following provisions:

> That the said lot of land shall be used for erecting thereon buildings suitable for the comfortable accommodation of the Pastor of the Presbyterian Church, in the city of Raleigh, so long as the leading doctrines declared in the confession of Faith and Catechizing of the Presbyterian Church, such as the doctrine of universal and total depravity, the doctrine of election, the doctrine of the atonement, the doctrine of the imputation of Adam's sin to all his posterity and the imputation of Christ's righteousness to all his people, for their justification, the doctrine of human inability, the doctrine of the necessity of the influences of the Holy Spirit in the regeneration, conversion and sanctification of sinners, as these doctrines are now understood and explained by the General Assembly of the Presbyterian Church at present known as the

---

[83]Ibid. The couple had another son named George Pollock Devereux who died in 1837 after a brief illness.

> Old School General Assembly, shall be faithfully taught by the Pastor of the said Presbyterian Church in the City of Raleigh.[84]

Frances Devereux paid for the property and built a house upon it. On 20 June 1843, the trustees of the church conveyed the property by deed to Mrs. Devereux for the payment of $1 [$32.50], who in turn deeded it back to the church. Language similar to the 1840 deed was present in the 1843 deed as well, requiring that the church

> shall at all times continue (as now) in communion with the Presbyterian Church in the United States of America, subject to its proper Presbytery and Synod and other ecclesiastical officers and authorities under the ultimate and general control of the General Assembly...and shall in all things conform to the doctrine, discipline and form of government of the said Presbyterian Church in the United States under the jurisdiction of the said (old school) General Assembly.[85]

The language in the 1840 and 1843 deeds and the requirements that were placed upon the church are relatively unique for typical land transactions. Clearly, Frances Devereux was concerned that her church should maintain its ties to traditional "old school" Presbyterianism into the future beyond her era. As the grandchild of Jonathan Edwards, it is not surprising that doctrinal matters would have been a topic of concern and likely were discussed around the dinner table as she was growing up. She had been a charter member of the First Presbyterian Church in New Bern and was one of the earliest members of the First Presbyterian Church in Raleigh. Furthermore, as seen earlier, both the First and Second Great Awakenings presented challenges to Presbyterianism in America. These differences between the Old Side and New Side groups became particularly acute during the Second Great Awakening with the success of Charles G. Finney's evangelistic efforts. Finney left a career in law to become an evangelist and openly declared his disdain for the doc-

[84]A copy of the deed is recorded on page 275 of Book 15 of the Wake County Registry, and through a search of Wake County's online Consolidated Real Property Index, it can be accessed at http://services.wakegov.com/books web/PDFView.aspx?DocID=108474488&RecordDate=01/24/1843.

[85]*Church v. Refining Co.* 200 N.C.469 (1931).

trinal parameters of the *Westminster Confession of Faith*.[86] Asahel Nettleton's influence seen earlier upon Drury Lacy would suggest that Mrs. Devereux had a sympathetic audience with her pastor in her concerns for her church's future doctrinal positions as well.

It is also worth noting that a few blocks away from Raleigh's First Presbyterian Church, the Baptist Church was experiencing dire financial problems at the same time that Mrs. Devereux donated the land for the manse. Amos J. Battle, the Baptist pastor, paid $2,100 [$68,200] of his own money for a parcel of land located at the southeast corner of Wilmington and Morgan streets. He proceeded to contract for a new church building to be constructed on the site with the understanding that the congregation would eventually pay him back. Unfortunately, just as the construction on the building was completed, Battle, whose family was one of the wealthiest in North Carolina before the Civil War, lost his entire fortune due to some risky investments. The building's contractors could not be paid, and the congregation was forced to either raise the money or sell the property. Great concern issued forth in the newspapers about that difficult moment in the life of the Baptist congregation. One concern was that the sacred property might eventually be purchased by a saloon! In the end, the debt was satisfied and the church was saved.[87] Nevertheless, one could speculate that this episode in the life of a sister

---

[86](Charles G. Finney, *Lectures on Systematic Theology: Embracing Ability [Natural, Moral, and Gracious], Repentance, Impenitence, Faith and Unbelief, Justification, Sanctification, Election, Reprobation, Divine Purposes, Divine Sovereignty, and Perseverance* [Oberlin, OH: James M. Fitch, 1847] 3–4, http://babel.hathitrust.org/cgi/pt?id=yale.39002088676441;view=1up;seq=12). Finney said,

> Every uninspired attempt to frame for the church an authoritative standard of opinion which shall be regarded as an unquestionable exposition of the word of God, is not only impious itself, but it is also a tacit assumption of the fundamental dogma of the Papacy. The assembly of divines did more than to assume the necessity of a pope to give law to the opinions of men; they assumed to create an immortal one or rather to embalm their own creed and preserve it as the pope of all generations. That the instrument framed by that assembly should in the nineteenth century be recognized as the *standard* [emphasis Finney's] of the church...is not only amazing but I must say it is highly ridiculous.

[87]Jonas, *Nurturing the Vision*, 62–71.

congregation may have influenced Mrs. Devereux to make assurances that in the future the property she gave to her church would be protected and preserved for the use that she desired.

As Drury Lacy's pastoral tenure came to a close in 1855, he could look back over eighteen years of a successful ministry. Lacy's experience and leadership were exactly what the First Presbyterian Church needed when he arrived on the scene in 1837. The church had endured almost eight years without a consistent pastoral presence. Lacy brought stability and the kind of visionary direction that McPheeters had shown. The church grew, endured some difficult times, and established itself as an important presence in the city of Raleigh. One nineteenth-century interpreter described Lacy's arrival and commencement of his pastoral duty with these words:

> The new pastor, clothed with authority and full of zeal for the glory of God, went to work in earnest not only in preaching, but in urging on important church enterprises. The church was repaired and refitted, the Sabbath School resuscitated, prayer meetings conducted in private families, quarterly meetings held by the Session, and cases of discipline adjudicated.[88]

As Lacy left to become the president of Davidson College, most of the members who read the newspapers could probably sense that the next ten years were going to be very difficult, as the nation was about to be plunged into the midst of its most disastrous war ever. How the church endured during those years and the years of Reconstruction is told in the next chapter.

[88]McPherson (*History of First Presbyterian Church*, 29) cites an untitled article from the *North Carolina Presbyterian*, 19 March 1879, written by Jethro Rumple. No further biographical information is given.

4

Leading the Way

The Context

By 1850, slavery was the dominant political issue in the United States. While the nation could not have foreseen what was ahead for the next decade, looking back, it is easy to see how the events of the 1850s laid the groundwork for the tragedy that was to be the Civil War. The decade began with the Compromise of 1850, a series of five laws designed to ease the tension between the slave-holding South and the free states in the North. Unfortunately, the compromise did not work. Expansion brought settlement to new territories in the West, and the conflict between slave and free states continued. Then in 1852, the publication of *Uncle Tom's Cabin* by Harriet Beecher Stowe brought the horrors of slavery into the consciousness of the average American in the North. Five years later, in 1857, the Supreme Court ruling in *Dred Scott v. Sanford* declared that blacks (slave and free) were not to be regarded as citizens of the United States. Two years later, in 1859, abolitionist John Brown led a raid on the federal arsenal at Harpers Ferry, Virginia, which further heightened the tensions between North and South.

The tension between North and South over slavery finally erupted into full-scale war in 1861. The Civil War, which lasted until 1865, was the most destructive and costly war in American history, with more than one million Americans either killed or wounded. While the war itself lasted for four years, the tensions between North and South lasted for decades, and one could argue that they still exist in some quarters. In many ways, the war had devastating effects for the South in both rural and urban areas, from which it would take decades to recover.

The sectional crisis also had a direct impact on American Presbyterianism. The division between Old School and New School Presbyterians in 1837 could be regarded as the first major North-South split in a denomination. The Old School stronghold was in the South while the New

School Presbyterians tended to be centered in the North. There were, of course, Old School Presbyterians in the North as well as New School Presbyterians in the South. When the Old School General Assembly convened in 1861 and expressed loyalty to the Union, the Southerners met in Augusta, Georgia, in December, where they quickly produced a declaration that slavery was the cause of their disunion and published a defense of the institution. Meanwhile, the New Schoolers had already split over the issue in 1857. The Southern New School Presbyterians merged with the Old School Church in the South. Following the war, this united group continued as the Presbyterian Church of the United States.[1]

In 1869, the first transcontinental railroad was completed, joining both coasts. While that accomplishment brought rapid expansion to the West, it also brought conflict between white settlers and Native Americans over territory. Ultimately, the saga would end tragically for the Native Americans of the Western Plains, who all but lost their way of life to white settlement and development.

As the political landscape in the United States experienced upheaval with disputes between North and South over slavery, the publication of Charles Darwin's *Origin of the Species* in 1859 changed the intellectual landscape. While its full impact would not be felt until decades later, *Origin of the Species* brought science and theology into direct conflict as it challenged the traditional literal interpretation of the creation stories in Genesis.

Biblical scholars and theologians, beginning first in Germany, also began to raise questions about traditional Christian assumptions about the Bible and theology. Julius Wellhausen, a German biblical scholar, was one of the first to lead the way in nineteenth-century biblical criticism as his Documentary Hypothesis raised questions about the traditionally accepted single-author theory of the Pentateuch. Wellhausen concluded that Moses did not write the first five books of the Old Testament. Instead, those books evolved gradually over a number of centuries as differing Jewish traditions were written down and edited together,

---

[1]Sydney E. Ahlstrom, *A Religious History of the American People,* 2nd ed. (New Haven: Yale University Press, 2004) 659–61.

finally reaching completion in the late sixth century BCE. Though largely accepted today by biblical scholars, Wellhausen's conclusions were highly controversial in the nineteenth century.

Biblical criticism also led to new questioning of traditionally accepted notions about Jesus. His miracles, virgin birth, bodily resurrection, and literal return all became topics of discussion as the Gospels were studied from an objective perspective as ancient literature rather than from the eyes of faith as the revealed message of God. The search for the historical Jesus began with the dawn of the nineteenth century and for most of the century, New Testament scholars were occupied with these questions.[2]

During the last half of the nineteenth century, many American intellectuals traveled to Europe, especially Germany, for education. Their return to the United States and employment by the nation's leading academic institutions disseminated the new theological ideas among new generations of students. As might be expected, the new ideas brought controversy. Many American Christians were not as eager to jettison the traditional way of viewing the Bible. It did not take long before some of the leading theological institutions in the United States came under fire by conservative critics.[3]

---

[2]See Stephen Neill, *The Interpretation of the New Testament 1861–1961* (Oxford: Oxford University Press, 1964) for a good discussion of these issues.

[3]See *Dictionary of Christianity in America*, ed. Daniel G. Reid et al. (Downers Grove, IL: InterVarsity Press, 1990) s.v. "Heresy Trials (1878–1906)." Most of these battles took place in the North. Among the Baptists, Ezra P. Gould was dismissed from Newton Theological Seminary in 1882 and Nathaniel Schmidt from Colgate Rochester Theological Seminary in 1896. The Methodists, although not as concerned with doctrinal matters as some of the other Protestant denominations at the time, nevertheless, leveled charges of liberalism against Hinkley G. Mitchell and Bordon P. Bowne, both members of the Boston University faculty. The most publicized cases occurred in the Presbyterian denomination with Charles A. Briggs from Union Theological Seminary and Henry Preserved Smith of the Lane Theological Seminary. See also William R. Hutchison, *The Modernist Impulse in American Protestantism* (Oxford: Oxford University Press, 1976).

The City of Raleigh in the Aftermath of John Brown's Raid

By the 1850s, the residents of Raleigh were aware that the nation's unity was at risk as tensions between North and South continued to grow, and they were naturally apprehensive about the current events of that day. The publication of Hinton Rowan Helper's *The Impending Crisis of the South: How to Meet It* (1857), which blamed the Southern support of slavery for the region's lack of financial progress, brought a swift reaction from Southerners. The fact that Helper was a native North Carolinian added to the local fury unleashed against the book.[4]

John Brown's raid at Harper's Ferry in 1859 also created tension among Raleigh residents, exacerbated by the fact that one of Brown's co-conspirators was a Raleigh native named John A. Copeland Jr. Copeland, a freeborn African American who had moved with his parents to Oberlin, Ohio, was eventually executed, along with the other conspirators, for his part in the affair. Then when two fires broke out within a week—one at the store of prominent Raleigh citizen Jordan Womble and the other at the home of his son—many in Raleigh feared that Brown's raid was part of a larger conspiracy to encourage slave uprisings all over the South.[5] Given the turmoil of the time period, it was important to the members of First Presbyterian Church that they have solid, consistent leadership, especially in the role of pastor.

First Presbyterian Church of Raleigh

Joseph M. Atkinson. As Drury Lacy ended a successful eighteen-year pastorate at First Presbyterian Church, the congregation focused its energy on finding a new pastor. Lacy tendered his resignation on 14 March 1855, indicating that it would take effect on 1 July of that same year.[6] By September, the sessional records refer to Rev. Joseph M. Atkinson as "pastor-elect."[7] The installation for the new pastor occurred on 25 No-

---

[4]Elizabeth Reid Murray, *Prehistory Through Centennial*, vol. 1 of *Wake: Capital County of North Carolina* (Raleigh: Capital County Publishing Co.,1983) 452–53.

[5]Ibid., 453.

[6]Minutes of the Session, 14 March 1855.

[7]Ibid., 17 September 1855.

vember. Representatives from the Orange Presbytery were present. Rev. J. Jones Smyth of Greensboro preached the installation sermon from Ephesians 1:22, "And he has put all things under his feet and has made him the head over all things for the church." Dr. Alexander Wilson of Alamance proposed the constitutional questions to the new pastor and the congregation and also gave the charge. According to the sessional record, the event was "solemn and impressive." The clerk closed the account with this benediction: "May the great head of the church bless this union of pastor and congregation."[8]

Joseph Mayo Atkinson was born on 7 January 1820 in Mansfield, Virginia. He was one of eleven children born to Robert and Mary Tabb Mayo Atkinson. Like several of his brothers, Joseph chose a career in vocational ministry. His elder brother Thomas served as the third Episcopal bishop of North Carolina from 1853 to 1881. Another brother, John, was ordained into the Presbyterian ministry and served as president of Hampden-Sydney College in Virginia from 1857 to 1883. Joseph heard a variation of the calling to ministry, choosing instead to serve a local parish as a pastor. After a brief educational foray following his brothers at Hampden-Sydney College, he transferred to the College of New Jersey (now Princeton University) and graduated in 1841.[9]

Two years later, he completed his theological education at Princeton Theological Seminary. Atkinson received his license to preach from the Winchester Presbytery in 1843, and in 1845 the same presbytery ordained him. For the next six years, he served a variety of small Presbyterian parishes in Virginia. In 1849, he moved to Frederick, Maryland, where he became the pastor of the church there and remained until relocating to Raleigh in 1855. During his time in Frederick, his pastorate was characterized by steadiness and consistency rather than large numerical growth. One contemporary account, quoted by the *North Carolina Presbyterian* in 1858, indicated that his time in Frederick "was not marked by any great accessions to his church or congregation," concluding that the

---

[8]Ibid., 25 November 1855.

[9]*Dictionary of North Carolina Biography*, ed. William S. Powell (Chapel Hill: University of North Carolina Press, 1979–1996) s.v. "Atkinson, Joseph Mayo."

large German immigrant population in the area was more disposed to the Lutheran and German Reformed churches than to the Presbyterian church.[10]

In the pulpit, Atkinson might best be characterized as a reserved teacher-preacher. One contemporary declared that the "pulpit ministrations of Mr. Atkinson were not calculated to produce great excitement, and sudden reformation, but rather to lay those deep foundations of doctrinal truth, so absolutely essential to all true godliness and Christian usefulness."[11] Several of Atkinson's sermons were published. One of his sermons preached during the Civil War was titled "God the Giver of Victory and Peace." It was reproduced and distributed as a tract for the soldiers of the Confederate army to build morale among the troops. Atkinson published another tract for the Confederate army titled *Casting Our Burden on the Lord*, which more than likely originated as a sermon as well.[12]

In 1860, Atkinson published a book titled *The True Path: or the Young Man Invited to the Saviour.* The book was the result of a series of lectures given by Atkinson although there is no mention in the introduction of the book about the location of the lectures. Were they sermons delivered from the pulpit? Were they delivered on the campus of Hamp-

---

[10]*North Carolina Presbyterian* (Fayetteville, NC), 20 April 1858, 2. The writer is not identified. The writer seemed to be impressed with the effective catechesis of the Lutheran and German Reformed churches in the area to the extent that it should be emulated by the Presbyterians: "The congregations of both these denominations are large and flourishing, and as their children are instructed in the catechisms and confessions of their own faith, with a particularity which Presbyterians might well imitate, it is rarely that they are found uniting with other churches."

[11]Ibid.

[12]Joseph M. Atkinson, *God, the Giver of Victory and Peace: A Thanksgiving Sermon, Delivered in the Presbyterian Church, September 18, 1862, Raleigh, N.C.* (Raleigh, NC: n.p., 1862), http://babel.hathitrust.org/cgi/pt?id=dul1.ark:/13960/t2t44hr74;view=1up;seq=3. The correspondence and sermon text of this tract is reproduced in this book as Appendix 1. Atkinson, *Casting Our Burden on the Lord* (Raleigh, NC: n.p., n.d.), http://babel.hathitrust.org/cgi/pt?id=dul1.ark:/13960/t5m911z1p;view=1up;seq=2. The text of this tract is reproduced in this book as Appendix 2.

den-Sydney College in Virginia, where his older brother John M. P. Atkinson served as president and to whom the book is dedicated? Atkinson was, however, clear that the purpose of the book was directed to "young men of whom the number is very great and perpetually increasing, who are pursuing a course of liberal study in high schools, academies, and colleges."[13]

Prior to the Civil War in America, there was great concern among many Protestant ministers for the state of morality among the young men of the day. Atkinson acknowledged this in the preface, recognizing the growth of the Young Men's Christian Associations as a "partial remedy" to the "disease" found in many cities and towns whereby too many young men were succumbing to temptations to vice.[14] Atkinson wrote the book with himself in mind, imagining that it "would have been useful to me…[as] a young man in college." He thought the book would also be useful to Christian parents who might want to give the book to their sons "with the confidence that its teachings were scriptural…[and] with the hope that…they might be saving."[15]

Regardless of how useful the book might have been in aiding the moral development of young men in the South less than one year before the Civil War began, it does provide helpful insight into the theology of Joseph M. Atkinson. To understand the context for his theology, it should be noted that Atkinson's years at Princeton Theological Seminary (1841–1843) corresponded to a period of theological conflict between the so-called "Princeton Theology" and the "New Haven Theology." The theological conflict played out in the years succeeding the Second Great Awakening largely within the Reformed tradition in Presbyterian and Congregationalist circles.[16]

Nathaniel William Taylor (1786–1858), professor of theology at Yale Divinity School, is generally regarded as the originator of the New

---

[13]Joseph M. Atkinson, *The True Path or the Young Man Invited to the Saviour in a Series of Lectures* (Philadelphia: Presbyterian Board of Publication, 1860) 9.

[14]Ibid.

[15]Ibid., 10.

[16]See Ahlstrom, *Religious History*, 415–20, 462–71, for a summary of these issues.

Haven Theology. Taylor sought to modify the strict Calvinism of the Reformed tradition. He believed that humans sin because sin is universal, not because sin is inherited from Adam. This denial of "original sin" logically leads to a view that humans, theoretically, have the capacity not to sin. Furthermore, Taylor rejected the doctrine of predestination as espoused by Old Side Presbyterianism. Although he steadfastly maintained his commitment to the *Westminster Confession of Faith* throughout his life, his theology nevertheless created a "reasonable revival theology that could prosper in the democratic ethos of Jacksonian America."[17]

The strongest opposition to Taylor came from the faculty of Princeton Theological Seminary, led especially by Archibald Alexander (1772–1851) and later by Charles Hodge (1797–1878). Under Alexander's influence, Princeton Theological Seminary became the most important and influential defender of Old School Presbyterianism and strict adherence to the *Westminster Confession of Faith*. This steadfast devotion to strict Calvinism is best portrayed by Hodge in a remark he made in 1872 upon the fiftieth anniversary of his association with Princeton: "A new idea never originated in this Seminary."[18] For most of the nineteenth century, Princeton Theological Seminary served as the vanguard for resistance to Modernism as it related to biblical criticism and theology.

The True Path reveals the heart of a pastor with a theological mind hewn from the stone of Presbyterian orthodoxy. A careful reading of Atkinson reveals his concern for the changes beginning to occur in the American intellectual landscape at the time. Published just one year after Charles Darwin's *Origin of the Species*, Atkinson articulates the book's theological tenor in the preface: "the staple of the book is the doctrines of Evangelical Protestant Theology, as opposed to the perversions of Popery on the one side, and the negations and errors of Rationalistic infidelity on the other."[19] Atkinson was aware of three things: (1) the intellectual challenges to Christianity and the Bible brought about by scientific inquiry along with new trends in theological studies such as biblical criti-

---

[17]Ibid., 420.

[18]Thomas E. Jenkins, *The Character of God: Recovering the Lost Literary Power of American Protestantism* (New York: Oxford University Press, 1997) 49.

[19]Atkinson, *True Path*, 10.

cism; (2) the growing presence of Roman Catholicism as a result of European immigration to America and its challenge to Protestant hegemony; and (3) the debate (mentioned above) within the Reformed theological tradition in America.

In the book, Atkinson wastes no time attacking the trends in theology that were developing by the middle of the nineteenth century. Intellectuals had drunk deeply from the well of the Enlightenment and were charting new paths in theology based on rationalism and scientific inquiry. Atkinson rejected such an approach to the study of the Bible and accepted the literal truth of the Bible. In fact, for him only two choices existed: "The only schemes of theology self-consistent throughout are evangelical Christianity at the one pole, and absolute atheism at the other. Every intermediate system is a compromise and a contradiction."[20] He believed that the "doctrines and declarations of the whole Bible [were] clear and harmonious." Those who deny the divine claims of Christ in the Bible "are inevitably forced to deny other truths, and often lapse by degrees into the fathomless abyss of Atheism."[21] Atkinson believed that the Bible was divine in origin though produced through the agency of humans. The "rationalist" chooses to read it only as a human book whereas the "enlightened believer" should "contemplate it as essentially a revelation *from* God and *of* God; inspired by his Spirit, and instinct with his presence."[22] When studied from this perspective "its glorious divinity shines out…its ineffable sweetness streams out…its sovereign majesty is felt…its matchless and mysterious power to subdue, to sanctify and to cheer the soul, is infallibly evinced."[23]

Atkinson was no friend to Enlightenment rationalism as applied to theological understandings of truth. As an example, he identified the French philosopher Auguste Comte and his philosophy of positivism. Comte taught that human societies evolve through three successive stages: (1) the theological, whereby humans explain universal inconsistencies as divine in origin; (2) the metaphysical, a stage similar to the first but

---

[20]Ibid., 15.

[21]Ibid.

[22]Ibid., 20. The emphasis is Atkinson's.

[23]Ibid., 21.

more nuanced in its attempts to understand the supernatural; and (3) the scientific, where humans cease looking for divine causes and focus instead on the laws that govern universal phenomena. He concluded that once a human society reaches the scientific stage it will naturally reject Christianity.[24] Atkinson's response is that the Bible is not a scientific book but instead a book of revelation. As such, there cannot be any "scientific" errors in the Bible. Furthermore, the Bible continues to be revered by Christians despite all attacks from rationalists. In terms of human experience the Bible's revelation continues to bring positive change to both individuals and communities. Finally, both the "peasant" and the "philosopher" can find meaning in the Bible. Consequently, in Atkinson's mind, "there is no real conflict between Scripture and Science—the word and the works of God—and…any apparent discrepancy arises from our misconception of the true teachings of one or of both."[25]

Atkinson was open, however, to the possibility of a non-literal interpretation of Genesis 1–2 such as may be embraced today in the "Day/Age Theory" or the so-called "Gap Theory."[26] In fact, one statement reveals that Atkinson might even be open to some kind of Darwinian interpretation: "There are many things in regard *to the mode* of the creation, in respect to which intelligent believers may innocently differ; but in regard to *the fact*, there can be no differences of sentiments, because he who denies it, not only ceases to be…a Christian, but proclaims himself an Atheist."[27] For Atkinson, the questions of *how* the world was

[24]Ibid., 30. For a good explanation of the thought of Comte, see *Stanford Encyclopedia of Philosophy*, s.v. "Comte, Auguste," accessed 9 June 2014, http://plato.stanford.edu/entries/comte/.

[25] Atkinson, *True Path*, 35.

[26]Ibid., 112. The "Day/Age Theory" is proposed on the basis of the various interpretations in the Old Testament that the Hebrew word *yom* might have. In some places the word is translated as a 24-hour period of time, from sundown to sundown. In other places the word is translated into English to refer to an era or an epoch, revealing an indistinguishable period of time. The "Gap Theory" is the idea that suggests that between Genesis 1:1–1:2 there might exist a "gap" whereby as many as millions of years of creation might have taken place, none of which is described in the creation stories.

[27]Ibid., 113. The emphasis is Atkinson's.

created are fair game for Christians to debate and may best be left to science. On the matter of *who* did the creating, he leaves no room for discussion, believing that true Christians will naturally affirm that the world came into being through the creating power of God.

The True Path also reveals Atkinson's anti-Catholicism, although this is only apparent in a few places. Such would be expected from a Protestant minister in the middle of the nineteenth century. Large waves of Catholic immigrants came from Europe to America in the nineteenth century, which brought a challenge to the Protestant hegemony that had existed since the nation's founding. For the most part, Atkinson avoids direct references to Roman Catholicism. There are, however, a few places in the book where he seems not to have been able to resist. In addition to the "perversions of Popery" comment cited above, he takes a couple of additional jabs at Catholicism. For example, toward the end of the book, in a chapter devoted to the providential activity of God in the world, he makes this startling claim:

> In the dispersion of the fleets of the Spanish Armada…who can deny that the hand of God was as plainly revealed for the preservation of the true gospel in England, as it ever had been for the confusion of the idolatry of Baal or of Ashtaroth? Who but the Lord of all the earth raised that tempest, which scattered the ships of Spain, confounded the counsels of the Pope, and dashed the hopes of Philip? Who but God alone?[28]

In a chapter devoted to the doctrine of salvation he mentioned the sixteenth-century Reformers Luther, Calvin, Zwingli, Knox, and Cranmer, calling them "true penitents," who turned away from "the cruel and debasing superstitions of Rome."[29]

Atkinson devotes a considerable amount of space throughout the book to the Calvinist understanding of God's activity in the world. His views are in the camp of the Presbyterian orthodoxy of his day although it is apparent that he espouses a gentler orthodoxy, recognizing that while salvation rests entirely upon the initiative of God, nevertheless,

---

[28]Ibid., 255.
[29]Ibid., 275.

humans have the capacity to respond. He affirms God's decrees of election, although not the exclusion of human freedom.

> We are not bound to evince the logical consistency...between divine sovereignty and human responsibility, the election of God and the free agency of man. The one is assumed, the other affirmed throughout the Scriptures. The one is necessary to the constitution of man, the other to the authority of God. The one is an intimate and universal fact of consciousness; the other is an essential and inalienable prerogative of God. Without the one we cease to be men; without the other, he ceases to be God. Without the one, we should not be capable of salvation; without the other, there could be no salvation for us.[30]

Most of Atkinson's theological attention is devoted to the providence of God, which he regards as a "sort of test doctrine, the reception or rejection of which determines a man's religious character; for no doctrine is more explicitly affirmed by Christ, and none is more truly grateful to one who has imbibed the spirit of Christ."[31] He still affirms that God chose salvation for some, but not all.[32]

He believes that God presided over the entire universe and that everything that happens is always under his guiding eye. In the natural order, God's presence is seen "not only in the sunny and smiling landscape, but in the tornado and tempest."[33] God is the author of all good things in the world but also directs bad events like famine, disease and death, "the awful terrors of injured justice, of outraged and indignant majesty."[34] Human suffering is not the folly of a capricious God. Instead, Atkinson considers it to be "the frown of God on sin."[35] In short, Atkinson believes that God created the world and therefore is the rightful owner of it. "He declares his presence in every place, his agency in every event, his power

---

[30]Ibid. 98. In another place (p. 268), he affirms that "the moving cause of our salvation is in God and not in man."

[31]Ibid,. 265.

[32]Ibid., 260. "God's providence appears, in so ordering all things—the most trivial and minute, the most unwelcome and painful, things seemingly most adverse and injurious—as to secure the salvation of his chosen."

[33]Ibid., 73.

[34]Ibid., 74.

[35]Ibid., 103–104.

over every person, his sovereign sway over every department and every manifestation of nature."[36]

The True Path is a helpful book, providing the modern reader with an important window into understanding the theological reflections of one of Raleigh's most prominent pastors in the middle of the nineteenth century. Atkinson was a product of his era. He was not a trendsetter nor was he particularly creative in his theology. As a parish minister, such characteristics would not be expected. His theology comports with the Presbyterian orthodoxy of his day and shows a growing concern with the changing intellectual environment around him. He was not afraid to engage the new ideas, but neither was he willing to embrace them.

William Peace and the Establishment of the Peace Institute. One of the most important members of First Presbyterian Church during the antebellum years was William Peace. He was a charter member and was selected as one of the first four ruling elders in the church. He was also an important citizen in the nascent years of the city of Raleigh.

Peace was a native of Granville County, born to John and Margaret Scott Peace on 7 March 1773. His father was a wealthy planter, and his family was among the first settlers in the county. William had three brothers: Joseph, Pleasant, and John. His only sister was named Lucy, who married Thomas J. Lemay, one of the earliest newspaper editors in Raleigh.[37] William is said to have been enrolled in the first class of the University of North Carolina, where he studied until 1796, but did not graduate. Instead, he and his older brother Joseph opened a general merchandise business in Raleigh, which was in operation by 1798. The small building that the business occupied was located in the first block on the

---

[36]Ibid., 251.

[37]Samuel A. Ashe, ed. *Biographical History of North Carolina: From Colonial Times to the Present*, 8 vols. (Greensboro: Charles L. Van Noppen, 1905–1917) 6:391–95. See also "16. Thomas J. Lemay," under "NC Newspaper History," accessed 15 June 15, 2014, http://ncpressfoundation.org/wp-content/uploads/2013/03/Website-16Lemay-Parker.pdf. Thomas J. Lemay (1802–1863) was the editor and owner of the *Raleigh Star* and the *North Carolina Gazette* from 1826 to 1853.

west side of Fayetteville Street.[38] When war broke out against England in 1812, he took a break from his business pursuits to serve in the army as a lieutenant and later as a captain of a militia.[39] Following the war, he became the commissioner of city government in Raleigh and oversaw the construction of the first governor's mansion in 1816. The building remained the governor's residence until it was converted into a school in 1876.[40]

Following Joseph's death in 1842, William became the sole owner of the business, which became even more successful during the next several decades. His interests also branched out into banking, as he served as the director of the Bank of the State and the Bank of North Carolina for forty-five years.[41] He also served as the chief trustee of the Rex Hospital Fund, which was given by John Rex and eventually used to build Rex Hospital. Additionally, Peace was an early supporter of the Raleigh Academy. In 1830, he purchased the original building and contents and served as the treasurer of the school, providing private donations to keep the school operational until 1855.[42]

In 1857, Peace led efforts "to establish a superior school for young ladies—an institution which will furnish thorough instruction and prepare young women for the discharge of the duties and responsibilities of life."[43] The idea of such a school had been discussed a decade before by at least one church within the Orange Presbytery. The sessional records for the Spring Branch Church in 1847 contain a resolution "that the Reverend William N. Mebane and Elder Alfred M. Scales respectfully bring to

---

[38]Murray, *Prehistory*, 116. A list of the types of goods sold at the business can be seen here: "Joseph & William Peace," *Raleigh* (NC) *Register, and North-Carolina Weekly Advertiser* [Raleigh, North Carolina] 22 November 1804, n.p.

[39]*Dictionary of North Carolina Biography*, ed. William S. Powell (Chapel Hill: University of North Carolina Press, 1979–1996) s.v. "Peace, William."

[40]Ibid.

[41]Ibid.; see also *From Colonial Times to the Present*, ed. Samuel A. Ashe, vol. 6 of *Biographical History of North Carolina* (Greensboro: Charles L. Van Noppen, 1907), s.v. "William Peace."

[42]*Dictionary of North Carolina Biography*, s.v. "Peace, William."

[43]"Multiple News Items." *Fayetteville* [North Carolina] *Observer*, 19 May 1859, n.p.

the notice of the Orange Presbytery meeting in Raleigh the importance of establishing a female institution of learning to be under the direction of Orange Presbytery."[44]

Peace donated eight acres of land and $10,000 [$292,000] for the construction of a building to house the school, which was incorporated on 1 October 1858 under the name Peace Institute of Raleigh.[45] The school was organized as a private stock company with the membership of the First Presbyterian Church as its shareholders, and it was operated by a board of trustees.[46] Construction on the first building, located at the northern end of Wilmington Street, began within a year after the school's incorporation. By autumn 1860, the foundation was being constructed. One contemporary account of the building's construction in process said that it measured about 118 feet in length and would "contain ample accommodations for more than 100 pupils, besides the necessary lecture rooms, chapel, etc." Plans were for the building to be complete by 1 July 1861, and the cost was reported to be more than $20,000 [$578,000].[47]

Unfortunately, however, the Civil War interrupted the plans to open the school, and the building was not completed as anticipated. Instead, despite its incomplete state, the Confederate Army used it as a hospital. Dr. Thomas Hill was sent to Raleigh with orders to open a

---

[44]Sidney Ann Wilson, *Personae: The History of Peace College* (Raleigh: Peace College, 1972) 5. The Spring Branch Presbyterian Church was dissolved in 1859, and the remaining members united with the Madison Church. See Robert Hamlin Stone, *A History of Orange Presbytery: 1770–1970* (Greensboro, NC: Heritage Printers, 1970) 360.

[45] Wilson, *Personae: The History of Peace College*, 5.

[46]The original board members were Daniel Gould Fowle (who served as governor of North Carolina from 1889 to 1891), William H. Crow, Thaddeus McGee, Richard Stanhope Pullen, and Joseph M. Atkinson. Atkinson served as the president of the board.

[47]"Peace Institute," *North Carolina Presbyterian*, 8 September 1860, 2. Joseph M. Atkinson seems to have been deeply involved in raising further funds for the institution. There are two references in the *North Carolina Presbyterian* in 1859 indicating his efforts to raise the $20,000, which, along with Peace's initial $10,000, comprised the cost of the building. See *North Carolina Presbyterian*, 1 January 1859, 2, and *North Carolina Presbyterian*, 7 May 1859, 2.

hospital in May 1862. Years later, he wrote that the original plan was to utilize St. Mary's School on Hillsborough Street, but soon the idea shifted to the Peace Institute since using it would not displace any students. Describing the incomplete state of the building, he said, "I visited the place and found a large brick framework,—the roof on,—but no floors and windows.... General Holmes' orders were to hurry up matters and...to impress every able-bodied man in Raleigh and put him to work—to get the building ready." The first patients entered the hospital on 6 June 1862.[48] In the years immediately following the end of the war the building was used as the headquarters for the Freedman's Bureau. In the meantime, William Peace died at the age of ninety-two on 11 July 1865. He never saw the institution that bore his name in session.[49]

When the building was finally returned to the trustees for its original purpose, they realized that they needed to raise money for much-needed renovations before the school could open. They borrowed $5,000 [$75,700] in 1866 and then mortgaged the building and land to Richard Stanhope Pullen, a Methodist layman and member of the board. Pullen realized that the original charter of the school called for it to be "Presbyterian in its influence and course of education," so he offered the largest portion of the stock to the members of First Presbyterian Church.[50]

In fall 1872, the school was finally ready to open. The renovation of the main building was complete, providing fifty-seven bedrooms, classrooms, a library, music rooms, a combination gymnasium and art studio, chapel, dining hall, office space and space for other uses.[51] The board leased the school property to Reverend Robert Burwell and his son John Bott Burwell, who served as the first principal and associate principal. Mary Rice Lacy (wife of Drury Lacy), who had operated a private school in Raleigh for girls, became the first "lady principal" of the school incor-

---

[48]Wilson, *Personae*, 6.

[49]William Peace never married. He died at the home of Governor William W. Holden, where he had lived for a number of years. He was buried in Raleigh's City Cemetery beside his brother Joseph.

[50]Wilson, *Personae*, 6; Murray, *Prehistory*, 614. The quote is from the school's original charter.

[51]Murray, *Prehistory*, 614.

porating her students into the student body. The operation of the school began on 23 September 1872 with 104 students.[52]

Burwell and his family operated the school until 1890. James Dinwiddie became the school's second principal that year and remained in the position until 1907, when First Presbyterian Church purchased the school and invited the Presbyteries of Albemarle, Granville, Kings Mountain, Orange, and Wilmington to take joint ownership and operational responsibilities.

First Presbyterian Church of Raleigh maintained a long and close contact with the school from its inception into the later decades of the twentieth century. In the early decades of the school's history, the students from Peace walked together to worship services at the church, where they sat in the gallery. Faculty were also involved in the life of the church, none more so than the school's music professor Albrecht Baumann and his wife, Mary Penick, who were two early faculty members and music faculty for twenty years. Albrecht Baumann also served as the first organist of the church. In the early years of the church's history, the ruling elders had opposed instrumental music. Baumann's expertise and musical giftedness helped to transform the congregation's views on the matter.[53] More will be said in later chapters about the relationship between Peace Institute and the church.

The Civil War. The Civil War and Reconstruction years were difficult for Raleigh residents. Although slow to accept the secessionist sentiment, when the war began at Fort Sumter, South Carolina, Raleigh citizens (like most North Carolinians) became ardent supporters of the Confederacy.[54] The city joined the war effort in full force. John Lewis Peyton observed in the opening days of the war that the city seemed to possess "a good deal of the 'pomp and circumstance of glorious war.'"[55] Wake County historian Elizabeth Reid Murray reports that so much

---

[52]Ibid., *Prehistory*, 614–15.

[53]Ibid., 615.

[54]See Ibid., 457–542 for a complete summary of the impact that the Civil War had on Wake County in general and the city of Raleigh in particular.

[55]John Lewis Peyton, *The American Crisis: Or, Pages from the Note-book of a State Agent During the Civil War*, 2 vols. (London: Saunders, Otter and Co., 1867) 1:16, cited in Murray, *Prehistory*, 470.

eagerness for the war effort existed in the county, such that even before North Carolina declared secession, four companies of volunteers were already prepared to deploy.[56] By November 1861, the North Carolina Presbyterian Synod, meeting in Raleigh that year, voted to secede from the Presbyterian Church of the United States and urged all of the state's Presbyterians to support the Confederacy.[57]

The city's eagerness for the glories of war soon subsided as Raleigh residents came to realize the difficulties that war brings. Of the nearly 125,000 soldiers that North Carolina provided for the Confederate war effort, between 33,000 and 35,000 were killed, and when the war ended in 1865, thousands of soldiers returned home injured, maimed, sick, or mentally debilitated.[58] On the home front, Raleigh citizens encountered shortages of almost all the necessities of everyday life. As the supply of goods dwindled, prices rose and along with them the tempers of many people. One citizen described the crisis in a letter to the *Observer* of Fayetteville: "People who cannot get enough to eat…grumble at everything [and] vent their spleen upon the war, which is the immediate cause of their suffering.… I do not wonder that the patriotism of some waxes cold and their wrath hot."[59]

Joseph Atkinson was a vocal, early supporter of the war effort and considered the war to be "the spontaneous uprising of a whole people to repel a lawless and atheistic aggression."[60] Like hundreds of other Southern clergy, Atkinson was deeply concerned for the spiritual welfare of the

---

[56]Murray, *Prehistory*, 470.

[57]W. Buck Yearns and John G. Barrett, *North Carolina Civil War Documentary* (Chapel Hill: University of North Carolina Press, 1980) 226.

[58]*NCpedia*, s.v. "North Carolina in the Civil War," accessed 17 November 2013, http://ncpedia.org/history/cw-1900/civil-war. Additionally, there were approximately from North Carolina 5,000 African American men and 10,000 white men who joined the Union Army.

[59]Mary Shannon Smith, "Union Sentiment in North Carolina During the Civil War," *Meredith College Quarterly Bulletin* 9 (November 1915): 14–15, cited by Murray, *Prehistory*, 485.

[60]Joseph M. Atkinson, "Address to the Public," *North Carolina Presbyterian*, 15 November 1862, 2.

Confederate soldiers.[61] Great effort was made in the South to provide Bibles to soldiers. Southern clergy volunteered time among the troops as chaplains and evangelists in the camps. Clergy also allowed their sermons to be published and distributed among the troops. One historian determined that notwithstanding paper and labor shortages, the Confederacy was able to publish and distribute 200 million pages of tracts to the soldiers.[62] The effort to win the soldiers' souls was as intense as the effort to equip the soldiers to destroy the enemy. In a very real sense, "the mobilization of the southern clergy to confront the wartime challenge paralleled the mobilization of Confederate military resources."[63] In Raleigh, the General Tract Agency published thousands of pages of devotional tracts for distribution to the soldiers. The tracts were chosen for publication and edited by the cooperative efforts of the pastors of the Episcopal, Methodist, Baptist, and Presbyterian churches in Raleigh.[64]

The two tracts, mentioned above—*Casting Our Burden on the Lord* and *God, the Giver of Victory and Peace*—that Atkinson published were both designed to minister to the troops although in different ways. *Casting our Burden on the Lord* is shorter and only makes reference to the war in the first sentence: "There is no class of men who excite a deeper interest in every loyal son of the South than our gallant soldiers, who have

---

[61]There are scores of articles and books written about the Southern churches and their concern for the spiritual well-being of the soldiers in the Confederate Army. For a sampling, see W. Harrison Daniel, "An Aspect of Church and State Relations in the Confederacy: Southern Protestantism and the Office of Army Chaplain," *North Carolina Historical Review* 36 (January 1959): 47–71; W. Harrison Daniel, "Bible Publication and Procurement in the Confederacy," *Journal of Southern History* 24 (May 1958): 191–202; Herman Norton, *Rebel Religion: The Story of the Confederate Chaplains* (St. Louis: Bethany Press, 1961); Herman Norton, "Revivalism in the Confederate Armies," *Civil War History* 6 (December 1960): 410–24; Charles F. Pitts, *Chaplains in Gray: The Confederate Chaplains' Story* (Nashville: Broadman Press, 1957); Sidney J. Romero, "The Confederate Chaplain," *Civil War History* 1 (June 1955): 127–40.

[62]Drew Gilpin Faust, "Christian Soldiers: The Meaning of Revivalism in the Confederate Army," *The Journal of Southern History* 53/1 (February 1987): 66, http://www.jstor.org/stable/2208627?origin=JSTOR-pdf&.

[63]Ibid., 70.

[64]Yearns and Barrett, *North Carolina Civil War Documentary*, 229.

exposed themselves to the manifold hazards of the battlefield and of the camp, in defence [*sic*] of our honor, our liberties and our lives."[65] It may have originated as a sermon before being published for distribution although its brevity suggests that it was written for direct publication. Atkinson's purpose was to provide hope and comfort to soldiers who may be suffering homesickness, illness, battle wounds, or grief with the ultimate goal to "lead such directly to the Savior."[66] This tract attempted to encourage the suffering soldier by suggesting that all of God's faithful suffer afflictions at times and that "[t]rue godliness does not require us to deny that we are afflicted when God has laid His heavy hand upon us."[67] Atkinson suggested that when afflictions come, "it is not enough that we bear a burden; we must cast our burden upon the Lord."[68] Those who trust in the Lord during times of suffering "shall be sustained."[69] As one might expect, Atkinson also included an evangelistic appeal in this tract for the suffering soldier who might not be a believer. He suggested that "in the Gospel," there is "encouragement for those most deeply dejected and a hope full of immortality for the most despondent."[70] Atkinson concluded with the story of the Apostle Paul's thorn in the flesh. Paul learned that even though God did not remove the "thorn," God's grace was nevertheless "sufficient" because God's strength is "made perfect in weakness." Consequently, as ironic as it may sound to the non-believer, "We may therefore gather from his experience…that it is possible to glorify God in suffering."[71]

The other tract that Atkinson published in 1862 was titled *God, the Giver of Victory and Peace*. This tract is identified as a sermon that he originally preached in the pulpit of the First Presbyterian Church of Raleigh on 18 September 1862. Atkinson did not volunteer the sermon for publication; rather it was requested of him. A short letter, following the title page and signed by eleven men, explains the request: "We think that

---

[65]Atkinson, *Casting Our Burden on the Lord*, 1.
[66]Ibid.
[67]Ibid.
[68]Ibid., 2.
[69]Ibid., 3.
[70]Ibid., 5.
[71]Ibid., 6.

the very original and forcible manner in which you presented the issue involved in our present struggle, would not only prove instructive to the reading public generally, but that, if sent to our soldiers in camp, *as a tract*, it would prove very acceptable to them, and would tend to keep constantly before their minds the great truth—*that to God alone belongs the glory!* 'Tis He, who in fact fights our battles; and to Him should our thanks and praises be ascribed."[72] Like many North Carolinians, Atkinson was opposed to slavery before the outbreak of the war and was weary of secession. Once the war began, however, he became a vocal supporter of the Confederacy. This tract has been described as "one of the most ringing sermons heard in Civil War North Carolina."[73] The date that Atkinson originally preached the sermon is significant, just one day after the Battle of Antietam. Antietam produced the bloodiest single day in American military history with more than 22,000 Americans (North and South) dead, wounded, or missing. At Antietam, the Confederate advance into the North was halted and knowing that the battle occurred only the day before this sermon was preached makes it even more chilling to the modern reader because of the optimistic tone that Atkinson portrayed.

Atkinson used a phrase from Psalm 30:5 as a refrain throughout the sermon: "Weeping may endure for a night; but joy cometh in the morning." He began by recognizing that in the early months of 1862 there had been some sobering Confederate setbacks, causing the "head of every patriot [to be] bowed in profoundest grief."[74] But, a reversal of fortune came, according to Atkinson, with the defense of Richmond in late May 1862. This was the result "not only of human heroism but of Divine might," evidence of God's favor toward the Confederacy. Atkinson assumed that "never in the history of mankind has the wonder-working providence of God been more strikingly manifest than in the successive phases of this contest."[75]

---

[72]Atkinson, *God, the Giver of Victory*, 3.
[73]*Dictionary of North Carolina Biography*, s.v. "Atkinson, Joseph Mayo."
[74]Atkinson, *God, the Giver of Victory*, 6.
[75]Ibid., 7.

God sided with the Confederacy, according to Atkinson, because of the South's moral superiority. It was inconceivable that God would not be supportive of the Confederacy because the Southern cause was identical to that of the Founding Fathers in the American Revolution. Just as they broke from the tyranny of England, so the South was breaking from the tyranny of the federal government. Just as there were once heroes with names like Washington, Jefferson, Madison, and Marshall, the South's cause produced the same kind of "godly leaders" named Lee, Jackson, and Hill.[76] Atkinson reasoned that as "long as we shall deeply feel our dependence on God alone, and put our trust in Him, He will favor us, and our progress will be irresistible as the march of time."[77] Owing to God's favor, Atkinson believed that although the South was currently "involved in the heat and dust and blood of the battle: Hereafter she shall repose in victory and triumph and peace."[78]

Beyond a Southern victory and vindication, Atkinson thought that the South's moral superiority culminating in victory could be a valuable lesson to "the proud and heartless Tyrants, who in other lands and in future days, may seek to degrade the noble and enslave the free."[79] The modern reader might find a measure of irony in that statement, as Atkinson condemned those who "enslave the free" while in the midst of arguing the case that the Almighty favored the South, which desperately

---

[76]Ibid., 8–9. The belief among Southerners that they were morally superior to their Northern counterparts has been explored by numerous scholars. One of the most famous expositions of the notion is found in Charles Reagan Wilson, *Baptized in Blood: The Religion of the Lost Cause, 1865–1920* (Athens: University of Georgia Press, 1980). Wilson argues that following the war, the devastation of the South and its humiliation were so heavy that within the Southern psyche the notion developed that although they had suffered defeat on the battlefield, they nevertheless were morally superior: "The Southern civil religion emerged because the experience of defeat in the Civil War had created a spiritual and psychological need for Southerners to reaffirm their identity, an identity which came to have outright religious dimensions. Each Lost Cause ritual and organization was tangible evidence that Southerners had made a religion out of their history" (36).

[77]Atkinson, *God, the Giver of Victory*, 10.

[78]Ibid., 11.

[79]Ibid.

sought to defend slavery. That Atkinson saw no contradiction between what he wrote and the culture around him shows the degree to which the South was unable to discern its own moral deficiency.

There are only several brief allusions to the war in the First Presbyterian Church's sessional records. On 7 July 1864, there is a notation about a woman named Jane Cunningham who was approved for membership by the session. It is noted that the certificate of membership from her previous church in Virginia could not be obtained because the church was "now within the enemy's lines."[80] Several months later, the records mention a slave named "Joseph, servant boy of Mr. Wright Hunt from Camp Holmes." After examination, "Joseph" was admitted as a member upon his profession of faith in Christ, and he was to be baptized the following Sunday. The record also mentions that he presented a letter of permission to join the church from his owner.[81]

Following the fall of Richmond and Lee's surrender at Appomattox in 1865, General Sherman ordered his army to move into North Carolina. General Judson Kilpatrick's 3rd Calvary Division was ordered to move into and occupy the city of Raleigh. Fortunately for Raleigh residents, the city was spared the fate of complete destruction that befell the capital city of South Carolina. Sherman promised that the state capitol, as well as other buildings and benevolent societies, would be spared, along with the mayor and other local government leaders, as long as the Union troops met no resistance when they occupied the city.[82] The city was surrendered on 13 April 1865. The federal occupation lasted until the end of 1865, but with the Congressional Reconstruction Acts, military rule was implemented again from March 1867 through July 1868. Troops remained stationed in North Carolina until 1870.[83]

The most direct reference to the war presented in the sessional records is found a few days following the end of the war. On 17 April 1865,

---

[80]Minutes of the Session, 7 July 1864. The complete citation reads "Miss Cunningham has been a member of a Presbyterian Church in North Watson, Virginia for about one year (now within the enemy's lines). She could not obtain a Certificate of Membership hence she again appeared before the Session."

[81]Ibid., 6 November 1864.

[82]Murray, *Prehistory*, 503–506.

[83]Ibid., 543.

the session met and determined that the church might be used for purposes of worship by the chaplains of the occupying federal army. The entire entry in the minutes is interesting and merits quoting here:

> It being feared that the Presbyterian Church in this city might be pressed by the military authorities, and in view of the assassination of President Lincoln, and in order to maintain quiet in our city and prevent any exercise of military rule in the matter, the Session unanimously deems it wisdom to offer the use of the Presbyterian Church to the chaplains (Presbyterian) of the Federal Army, through General Stiles, Commander of the military post at Raleigh, on the afternoon of every Sabbath for the purpose of divine worship only so long as they may desire to occupy it for the purpose of preaching to their respective brigades, regiments, or companies.[84]

The statement provides a few interesting insights into the tension that existed in the city following the surrender of Raleigh. The elders seemed concerned about two things: (1) the possible confiscation of the church by the federal army for use and (2) the violence and unrest related to the assassination of Abraham Lincoln that could occur in the city.

The incident involving "Lt. Walsh" upon the surrender of the city might have justified the elders' concern and fear of potential violence. On 12 April 1865, a delegation presented a letter offering Raleigh's surrender to General William T. Sherman, who was headquartered outside of the city. They secured the general's promise that the city would be spared destruction if no hostility was shown to the Union troops as they moved into the city. The next morning, as General Hugh Judson Kilpatrick rode at the head of a column of Union troops coming up Fayetteville Street, Walsh, hiding in an alleyway drew his revolver and fired six shots at the advancing troops. According to one eyewitness, Kilpatrick's troops gave chase, and within just a matter of a few minutes, Walsh was captured. Kilpatrick ordered his immediate execution by hanging, refusing even to allow the young soldier to write a letter of farewell to his wife.[85] Fortu-

---

[84]Minutes of the Session, 17 April 1865.

[85]The story is recounted in Murray, *Prehistory*, 507. Walsh's first name is not known. Murray suggests that it may be "Robert." There is a grave in the Confederate section of Oakwood Cemetery with an inscription: "Lt. Walsh, 11th Texas Calvary, April 13, 1865."

nately, Kilpatrick did not retaliate against the entire city. Had Walsh's shots hit the general, it is very likely that the capital city would have been utterly destroyed and burned as were other Southern capital cities.

With the end of the Civil War came Reconstruction, a challenging period for the South, Raleigh notwithstanding. Federal law established the Freedmen's Bureau on 3 March 1865, just before the conclusion of the war. In Raleigh, the Freedmen's Bureau was first housed in the building originally built for the Peace Institute. The Bureau was created to provide food, clothing, and shelter to former slaves as well as to needy white citizens following the end of the war. In 1867, the Freedmen's Bureau's headquarters moved from the Peace Institute building to the A. M. Lewis house and the following year to Dawson Street and the home of Ruffin Tucker.[86]

With the ratification of the Thirteenth Amendment in 1865, whites and blacks were forced to relate to one another in new ways. Rather than assimilation, segregation eventually developed in the South. Churches were no different. In Raleigh, as early as 1868, the black members of

---

[86]Ibid., 552–53. According to Annie Ramsey, after the directors of Peace Institute reacquired the property from the Freedman's Bureau, they were faced with a dire situation due to the condition of the buildings and "all the funds belonging to the corporation having either been expended or lost." Moreover, "so hopeless seemed the enterprise that the directors thought it best to sell the property and negotiations were entered into with the Reverend Mr. Tupper, Principal of Shaw Institute, with a view to purchase for the use of a large male and female school for colored youth." Yet, "at the last moment Mr. Atkinson and other friends of the institution came to the rescue" by securing the needed funds (see Annie Sabra Ramsey, *Early History of Peace Institute* [Chapel Hill: n.p., 1964] 2, North Carolina Collection, Wilson Library, UNC Chapel Hill). Henry Martin Tupper of Massachusetts was honorably discharged from the Union Army on 14 July 1865. He and his wife arrived in Raleigh in October of that year after Tupper was commissioned by the American Baptist Home Mission Society to serve as a missionary to the freedmen (see Wilmoth A. Carter, *Shaw's Universe: A Monument to Educational Innovation* [Raleigh, NC: Shaw University, 1973] 2). Interestingly, a version of these events has been preserved in a tradition handed down in the church to Virginia Doughton, a recently-deceased member of First Presbyterian (David H. Permar, e-mail message to author, 27 August 2014).

First Baptist Church formed their own congregation and eventually built a structure at the corner of Wilmington and Morgan Streets.[87] African-American Presbyterians in Raleigh soon followed suit.

The sessional records for First Presbyterian Church occasionally refer to "Colored" members. As early as 1857, there is a reference to "Mawkins Lam, a man of color." Lam served as the church's sexton for several decades and was received into membership with baptism and communion in 1857.[88] There is a reference (mentioned above) to a slave named "Joseph," owned by a soldier stationed at Camp Holmes during the Civil War, who was admitted as a member to the church in 1864.[89] In 1866, "William John Williams" and his wife "Jane," also designated as "persons of color," presented themselves for membership before the elders and were received.[90] In 1874, a "colored woman" named "Sugar Hall" was received into the church's membership.[91]

Although there is evidence that both slave and free blacks were members at First Presbyterian Church before the Civil War and after, there is also evidence after the war that black Presbyterians in Raleigh began to meet on their own. Thoughts of organizing an African-American Presbyterian church surfaced as early as 1868. Under the leadership of Godfrey Rainey, a representative from the Board of Missions for Freedmen of the Presbyterian Church in the U.S., the seed of a congregation began to grow, first in the opening of a school to educate children of former slaves. Regular worship services began in 1872, and the

---

[87]W. Glenn Jonas Jr., *Nurturing the Vision: First Baptist Church Raleigh, 1812–2012* (Macon: Mercer University Press, 2012) 135.

[88]Minutes of the Session, 5 January 1857. The poor handwriting makes the first name difficult to read. The last name "Lam" is clear. The notation indicates that he had been the church Sexton for "25 or 30 years." He apparently died within two months after receiving membership in the church, as a note at the bottom of the page in the sessional records states that he died on 7 March 1857.

[89]Ibid., 6 November 1864. The owner's name appears to be "Mr. Wright Hunt," but the handwriting is difficult to read.

[90]Ibid., 5 April 1866. A reference in the sessional records dated 9 January 1867 states that Williams and his wife were dismissed to join "2nd Presbyterian (Colored)" in Statesville, North Carolina.

[91]Ibid., 31 March 1874. The handwriting makes the first name "Sugar" difficult to decipher.

group took the name "Presbyterian Church, Colored." The name later changed to "First Presbyterian Church, Colored." Rev. James Crestfield became the first pastor of the church. The first building was located on the southeast corner of Davie and Haywood streets. Eventually, the church moved several blocks west on Davie Street and is known today as the Davie Street Presbyterian Church.[92]

The sessional records, particularly the annual reports to the Orange Presbytery, reveal interesting data about First Presbyterian Church and the war's impact. When the war began, the church reported 120 members in its annual report to the presbytery. The church was also on solid financial footing as the war began, contributing $85.55 [$2,330] to domestic missions; $77.55 [$2,060] to foreign missions; $41 [$1,120] to education, $32.50 [$887] to publications; $19.50 [$532] to church extension, and $1,016 [$27,700] for congregational needs.[93] The first report to the presbytery following the war appeared in 1866 with the church reporting 110 members.[94] There is no financial data included with this report, but the following year, the church reported 112 members and the following financial data: $89.60 [$1,460] for domestic missions; $8 [$130] for foreign missions, $73 [$1,190] for publications; $2.50 [$40.60] for education; $16 [$260] for the presbytery; and $1,620 [$26,300] for congregational needs.[95] The church lost 8 percent of its membership during the war years but, on the other hand, the budget

---

[92]Murray, *Prehistory*, 620. There is no mention of the organization of this congregation in either the records of the Session or of the Diaconate of the First Presbyterian Church of Raleigh. The minutes of the session recorded for 16 September 1867 do contain this reference: "The subject of the officers of the Freedman's Bureau Building, a school house for the education of people of color to be under the control of the session of this church was referred to the Board of Trustees of this church and Misters Crow and Taylor were appointed a Committee to lay it before them and report to this session." No doubt, this was a reference to the building that would become the Peace Institute. But, it may have some bearing on the origination of the first African-American Presbyterian congregation in the city as well.

[93]Minutes of the Session, 11 April 1861. The annual report to the presbytery is contained in this entry.

[94]Ibid., 1 April 1866.

[95]Ibid., 1 April 1867.

grew by 70 percent. It appears that the church emerged from the war in a relatively strong position.

Extensive renovation to the building in 1867 represents more evidence that the church emerged from the war in good condition. The renovations encompassed the entire building and the Lecture Room, to the extent that "the whole interior of the building [was] changed."[96] As a part of the changes, the pulpit was lowered, a modern furnace replaced the stove, the pews and other woodwork in the church were refinished, carpet was placed on the stairways, "and the walls of the building [were] plastered and painted to represent stone."[97]

The Civil War seems to have had a highly negative impact on one congregation in the Orange Presbytery, the Milburnie Church. The church, which was first constituted in 1855, had dwindled in membership by 1871 to three members: Mr. Richard B. Seawell (sp?), Mrs. S. Kirkland, and Miss Sallie Litchford. Those members had their memberships transferred to First Presbyterian Church upon the dissolution of the church by the presbytery. Not much is known about this church, but it seems to have struggled since its founding.[98] The war could only have made matters worse. The Milburnie section of the city, to the northeast near the Neuse River, had been an area of growth before the war. A post office opened there in the antebellum years. The Milburnie Paper Mill provided jobs but was destroyed by Union forces as they occupied the city. The mill provided newsprint for multiple North Carolina newspapers of the day and also provided newsprint to the *New York Times.*[99] Following its destruction, the Neuse Manufacturing Company operated a grist mill in the area. The Milburnie section became a popular location for recreational gatherings. The site of the burned paper mill became the location for the Wake County's first hydroelectric plant in 1903. Unfor-

---

[96]*North Carolina Presbyterian,* 29 January 1868, 2.

[97]Ibid.

[98]Minutes of the Session, 5 July, 10 August, and 7 November 1871; Stone, *History of Orange Presbytery*, 113, 359.

[99]Murray, *Prehistory*, 282.

tunately, there was not enough Presbyterian growth in the area to warrant keeping the church in operation.[100]

By 1875, Joseph Atkinson was in his fifty-fifth year. Thirteen years earlier he had expressed to the session that he intended to resign, although no reason is given.[101] Perhaps he believed that his involvement in the war effort demanded more time than he was able to give. Whatever the reason for the proposed resignation, it never materialized. In 1873, the relationship between the pastor and the church seemed to be very strong. The standard notation found each year in the sessional records regarding the pastor's work during the previous year and his reciprocal response contained this statement: "The pastor reports that his salary promised has always been paid and during the year past, he has received *more* than the sum guaranteed. He thinks it proper to add that the members of the congregation have given him repeated testimonies of respect and affection."[102]

By the end of the church year in 1874, the pastor's salary of $1,200 [$25,300] was noted as paid in full.[103] A few weeks later, however, the elders reported communication from some of the deacons who were concerned about the financial affairs of the church and even threatened resignation. The elders responded with a plea that no deacon should resign and a statement that Atkinson planned to preach a sermon "on the subject of systematic giving to the cause of the Lord."[104]

In February 1875, the session reported that J. B. Burwell, one of the deacons, had resigned. His letter of resignation evidently perplexed the

---

[100]Ibid., 563–64, 661–62.

[101]Minutes of the Session, 19 February 1862.

[102]Ibid., 31 March 1873. It was traditional, according to the records, that at the end of the church year (31 March for the nineteenth century), the elders would pass a resolution of approval for the pastor's work the previous year. The pastor then would write his own response in the record book and would indicate whether or not his salary had been paid in full.

[103]Ibid., 3 April 1874. The proposed salary for the year was $1,000. Atkinson was paid an additional $200 that year, as in the previous year.

[104]Ibid., 7 May and 9 May 1874. It should be noted that the United States economy fell into a depression in 1873. This may have been the cause of the church's discussion about finances here.

elders. The entry into the minutes says: "This letter not being fully and satisfactorily understood by all the members of the session it was laid upon the table for future action after the Clerk of the Session could obtain the exact meaning of the language employed."[105] That meeting of the session also reported that J. M. Atkinson had submitted his letter of resignation. No reason for the resignation is given. Did it relate to the resignation of J. B. Burwell from the diaconate. Did the entire episode have to do with financial problems? There is certainly no solid evidence of financial problems in the records, except the fears mentioned above by the diaconate. There was, however, some reason, some issue in the church that promoted Atkinson's resignation. His letter of resignation stated: "In view of the circumstances recently brought to my knowledge I consider it my duty to offer to you my resignation of the pastoral oversight of this church. The resignation if accepted to take effect six months hereafter."[106]

Interestingly, the following month, J. B. Burwell withdrew his letter of resignation from the diaconate, which was accepted by the elders.[107] But Atkinson's resignation continued as planned and he left the church six months later. A problem was present within the fellowship of First Presbyterian Church, although there is no direct description of it. The evidence of it, however, would become manifest within just a few months. For that part of the story, we turn to the next chapter.

---

[105]Ibid., 22 February 1875.
[106]Ibid.
[107]Ibid., 24 March 1875.

the adding machine became necessities in business. European capital began to flow into American corporations, adding to the massive wealth Americans were accumulating.

The City of Raleigh during the Gilded Age

Like the rest of the nation, Raleigh experienced a transformation in the last quarter of the twentieth century as the "sleepy state capital surrounded by remote farming communities in the 1870s was by 1900 transformed into a center of industry, higher learning, consumerism, and social activism."[5] The nationwide financial Panic of 1873 created a depression for a period of time, which kept the Civil War generation in a struggle to survive. Nevertheless, a new generation began to see the world differently in Raleigh. They began to see that through industry the city of Raleigh, as well as the entire South, could be changed. The key to the city's industrial growth was the railroad. The railroad provided new markets for farmers and new products to help reinvigorate their lands. The commercial success of the railroads also brought advantages to merchants and bankers as they found their places in the new economy. Finally, railroads brought new people to the city, which added diversity to the population. It became clear by the end of the century that Raleigh residents "were gradually abandoning an isolated agrarian way of life in favor of one that was increasingly industrial and urban."[6]

First Presbyterian Church of Raleigh

Clement Read Vaughan. The resignation of Joseph M. Atkinson became effective by autumn 1875. On 14 December 1875, the church voted unanimously to call Dr. Clement Read Vaughan to be supply minister for one year beginning on 1 January 1876.[7] The salary agreed upon was $150 [$3,360] per month with use of the manse as well as one month vacation in the summer.

---

[5]K. Todd Johnson and Elizabeth Reid Murray, *Reconstruction to 1920*, vol. 2 of *Wake: Capital County of North Carolina* (Raleigh: Wake County, 2008) ix.

[6]Ibid.

[7]Minutes of the Session, 16 December 1875.

Clement Read Vaughan was born in Charlotte County, Virginia, on 15 July 1827. The records do suggest that Vaughan performed well in his role as supply minister. By the time that the church gave its annual report to the Orange Presbytery, it reported a total of 216 members, 108 children in Sunday school, and the pastor's salary of $1331.13 [$29,800] was paid in full. The church seemed to be healthy just a decade following the Civil War and only two years from the 1873 national economic crisis.[8]

For most of 1876, the elders seemed to have been mostly preoccupied with church disciplinary matters. Little else is mentioned in the sessional records.[9] There is, however, one reference in the sessional records that indicates that trouble could have been in the making within the fellowship of the church. The entry in full reads,

> A committee of three were [*sic*] then elected to wait upon two of our members who had resorted to the courts to settle by litigation a disputed title of property. This committee was Rev. C. R. Vaughan, D. D; Leo D. Heartt, and W. H. Crow. The Session desired they should use their best efforts to prevail upon these brethren to desist from this course and try if possible to settle by arbitration of friends.[10]

Within ten days, the committee reported back to the elders that they were "not successful" in their attempt to prevent the two members from resorting to legal action against one another.[11] There is no further mention of the matter for the rest of the year, nor are the two members named. In October, Vaughan indicated to the session that since his time of employment would be expired by 1 January 1877, he thought it would be advisable for the church to hold a congregational meeting "at some early time to take some action on the subject."[12]

Evidently, a congregational meeting occurred following the 24 October meeting of the session. The purpose of this meeting, however, was

---

[8]Ibid., 2 April 1876.

[9]See, for example, the cases of George Ennis and J. M. Tant in the Minutes of the Session, 9 June, 13 June, 7 July, 3 October, 6 October, 24 October 1876.

[10]Minutes of the Session, 17 March 1876.

[11]Ibid., 27 March 1876. The phrase "not successful" is underlined in the record, no doubt for emphasis.

[12]Ibid., 24 October 1876.

to elect deacons and elders. The record of the meeting is confusing as there seems to have been some disagreement as to the number of elders that should be elected. A. M. McPheeters moved that two elders should be elected. Leo D. Heartt moved to amend the motion by striking the word "two" and substituting the word "one." Debate ensued, and Heartt subsequently withdrew his amendment, and the motion to elect two elders prevailed. William S. Primrose and John B. Burwell were elected by the congregation, and the attention of the meeting turned to election of deacons. William S. Primrose moved that three deacons should be elected. A. M. McPheeters offered an amendment calling for the election of four deacons rather than three. The church voted to approve the amendment, and B. R. Hardaway, Leo D. Heartt, E. R. Stamps, and S. W. Whiting were elected. Following the deacon election, John B. Burwell moved to reconsider the previous vote that declared that two elders should be elected. After some debate about whether the church needed more elders, Burwell moved again that the whole matter should be postponed until the evening of 30 October.[13]

The congregation came back together on 30 October. The stated purpose of the meeting was to make arrangements for the supply of the pulpit beginning on 1 January 1877. Vaughan indicated to the church that he believed that he was physically prohibited from being able to accept a call from the church to be the pastor although he did not specify what his infirmity was. The church then suggested that Vaughan could continue for another year as the supply minister. The church's support and positive feeling for Vaughan are expressed in the resolution that was approved unanimously: "[w]e take this occasion to express our warm regard for Dr. Vaughan personally and our high appreciation of his character and ministerial service in our midst and we invoke upon him the continual blessing of the Great Head of the Church that he may be enabled hereafter and heretofore to declare unto us the whole Gospel of God."[14] The congregation then turned its attention to the issue about the number of elders that needed to be elected. E. R. Stamps's motion to lay the matter on the table lost. H. M. McPheeters asked if it was appropriate to

[13]Ibid., 26 October 1876.
[14]Ibid., 30 October 1876.

conduct such business in a meeting that had originally been called for the purpose of dealing with the impending pulpit vacancy. The moderator decided that the meeting had been duly authorized and plenty of notice given. The way was then cleared to proceed with the election of another elder. After some debate, Burwell surprisingly withdrew his motion to elect a new elder.[15]

The disagreement about the number of deacons and elders to elect, along with the matter of the two members who resorted to the courts to settle their dispute, would all seem to suggest that by 1876 the church was experiencing some internal dissension. The next year would prove to be pivotal in the history of First Presbyterian Church.

Second Presbyterian Church. The first mention of a fracture in the congregation came in spring 1877. On 24 March, the session discussed "the circulation of a report that a Second Presbyterian Church was to be established in Raleigh." The elders were displeased not only that there were plans within the Orange Presbytery to approve the establishment of the church but also that there were members of First Presbyterian Church who were actively involved in raising financial contributions for the effort. The session was opposed to the enterprise, and it was the "unanimous and deliberate judgment of the session that this movement in its conception and working was unwise to say the least." The discussion led to the unanimous passage of a resolution of opposition to the matter that was to be presented by Elder John Primrose at the upcoming meeting of the Orange Presbytery.[16] It should be noted that the membership of First Presbyterian Church at the time was 204 members with 174 children attending Sunday school regularly. The pastor's salary of $1,746 [$40,100] had been paid as well.[17]

A letter from the former pastor J. M. Atkinson was presented to the elders at the meeting of the session in April. In light of the impending annual meeting of the Orange Presbytery, Atkinson wanted to inform the elders that he planned "to ask the sanction of that body to the establishment of a sister Presbyterian Church in this city to be under my pas-

[15]Ibid.

[16]Ibid., 24 March 1877.

[17]Ibid., 29 March 1877.

toral care." Atkinson continued, saying that he anticipated that approximately twenty members from First Presbyterian would join with him in the establishment of the new church. He also informed the elders that "several will join in the application to the Presbytery who will not sunder their connection with your church and several in your own and in other churches will contribute to sustain this enterprise who [*sic*] will retain their relation to their own churches."[18] The elders appointed a committee of two to draft a response to Atkinson's letter and deliver it to him the next day. It was also ordered "to be spread upon the minutes," but it was never recorded in the sessional records.[19]

The annual meeting of Orange Presbytery occurred during the last week of April 1877. One account indicates that "a lengthy discussion on the feasibility of the movement took place" concerning the matter.[20] Though First Presbyterian disagreed, the final vote of the presbytery approved the petition to organize the church, and J. M. Atkinson "was duly authorized to organize the church and officiate as its pastor."[21] The minutes of the Orange Presbytery, reported in the *North Carolina Presbyterian*, contain a very simple reference to the event: "Rev. J. M. Atkinson presents memorial, praying the organization of a 2d church in Raleigh. The church in Raleigh, through its representative and its stated supply, most earnestly deprecates any such action at the present peculiar juncture

---

[18]Ibid., 23 April 1877. An example of Atkinson's contention that there would be members from First Presbyterian who would help with the endeavor although not leave the mother church is found in the fact that William Nathan Harrell Smith was listed among the first trustees of Second Presbyterian Church, but there is no evidence that he ever left the membership of First Presbyterian. See Minutes of the Session (Second Presbyterian Church), 28 May 1877. All references to the sessional records from Second Presbyterian Church will be designated as such by "Minutes of the Session (Second Presbyterian Church)…"; "Minutes of the Session…" will refer to the sessional records from First Presbyterian Church.

[19]Minutes of the Session, 23 April 1877.

[20]*News and Observer* (Raleigh, NC), 29 April 1877, 3.

[21]Ibid.

of circumstances. Discussion of the subject set for 1st order of the day on Saturday morning at 8 ½ o'clock."[22]

The First Presbyterian elders strongly disagreed with the action of the presbytery as evidenced in a long resolution of opposition included in the sessional records. As a matter of principle, they believed that the process had not been properly followed. They had received "no official or direct information in regard to this project."[23] Of course, there was the letter discussed above sent by J. M. Atkinson, but that was not an official notification from the presbytery. The resolution then presented the reasons why the elders believed establishing a new church was a bad idea.

The elders indicated that First Presbyterian Church was one of the smallest churches in the city. The church's records, likely due to the Civil War and its aftermath, had been "thrown into unusual confusion for several years past," and discerning the exact number of members had been a daunting task. At the time of writing, they believed that the church had 209 members, but of that "probably 50 are not to be found, in this community at least."[24] Therefore, the actual number of active members was closer to 150–160, and the church was not strong enough numerically to be able to part with any of its active members for a new endeavor.

Second, the elders declared that although there had been conflict in the congregation previously, they believed that the breach had been healed. Attendance had been good. The "Spirit of God had been poured out and a number of persons brought into the church." The evidence of a new spirit, they indicated, was the recent renovations to the buildings. As a result, "in this state of prosperous progress the church was suddenly startled by the rumor that an active effort was in progress to divide the church by an indefinite draft upon its members."[25]

Third, they believed that the cause of Presbyterianism in the city in general might suffer as a result of dividing First Presbyterian. In their

---

[22]*North Carolina Presbyterian* (Wilmington, NC), 2 May 1877, 2. There is no further information reported except a short note saying that the church establishment was approved.

[23]Minutes of the Session, 11 June 1877.

[24]Ibid.

[25]Ibid.

opinion, if Presbyterianism were established as strongly as some of the other denominations in the city, "we should be most heartily in favor of a movement to establish a second church."[26] Because that was not the case, they believed that it was "impolitic" to establish a new Presbyterian church in such close proximity to First Presbyterian Church, which would threaten to divide the denominational influence and allow the real possibility that the churches might become competitive rather than co-operative with each other.

Finally, the elders addressed the actual cause for the split: a conflict between members. As discussed above, on 11 March 1876, the sessional records reveal that a legal dispute occurred between two members. Unfortunately, the two members were not named. Could the conflict discussed in this resolution a year later stem from the same matter? More than likely it did, and this resolution suggests that the matter had grown from a dispute between two members to an issue that had encompassed others within the congregation: "Every effort has been made, every person has been approached whom there was the least prospect of influencing…the feeling produced by a personal difficulty and conflict in the courts between certain members of the church, has been seriously embittered."[27] The fact that the impetus for organizing a new church was a conflict between members at First Presbyterian Church made the reason for the new church start even less justifiable: "It would crystallize these hostile feelings, give them organic life and render them permanent for an indefinite time in the future. It would create two feeble churches, not coordinate but rival institutions, necessarily antagonistic to each other, and a permanent source of irritation."[28] They acknowledged that there might indeed come a time when "these malcontent members cannot be persuaded to remain quiet in the communion of this church and wait for time and the grace of God to heal the breech [*sic*]." If so, it might "be expedient to let them go." But, the elders strongly believed that "for Presbytery to give them an organization and then crystallize the unhappy feelings which exist, into a permanent form and create a rival and hostile

[26]Ibid.
[27]Ibid.
[28]Ibid.

organization to this church, would be…not only an injury to them, but a permanent and indefinite one to us."[29]

The Orange Presbytery recognized the contentiousness that existed over the decision to organize Second Presbyterian Church. During the discussion at the meeting of the presbytery, they counseled the committee tasked with carrying out the organization of the church (1) "To do all they can to remove all alienation of feeling that may exist between the parties;" (2) "To do all they can to enlist the hearty concurrence and co-operation of the first church in this movement;" and (3) "To assure both parties of the deep interest and sympathy of the Presbytery with all concerned or affected by these trials and of our prayers to God for his blessing upon both."[30]

Looking back from the perspective of more than a century removed, obvious questions surround the names of the hostile disputants and the specific issue that brought them to court. Was it a business dispute, or a property dispute? Was it an internal family crisis? Or, was it a dispute between two different families in the church? Because there are no names given in the record, these questions are almost impossible to answer unless an account is found someday in the personal papers of one of the disputants in an archive somewhere.

From the perspective of the communicants of the new Second Presbyterian Church in Raleigh, the future seemed bright. They included an account of their organization into a church at the beginning of their sessional records. According to their account, earlier in the year some members of First Presbyterian Church "united in proposing to the Rev. J. M. Atkinson the formation of a 2nd Presbyterian Church in Raleigh with Mr. Atkinson as its pastor."[31] Following approval of the Orange Presbytery, Rev. J. Henry Smith, Rev. Archibald Currie, and ruling elder J. A. Womack of the Presbyterian Church in Pittsboro were appointed to constitute the new church. On 15 May 1877, Smith preached a sermon to

---

[29]Ibid.

[30]Minutes of the Orange Presbytery, 28 April 1877, accessed 29 July 2014, https://archive.org/stream/presbyterianchur00pres_20.

[31]The handwritten account appears at the very beginning of the sessional records book for Second Presbyterian Church.

the group from 1 Corinthians 12:22, and the names of the twenty-eight charter members were read.[32] James M. Towles and C. H. Scott were elected as ruling elders while A. D. Taylor and J. M. Monie were chosen as the first deacons. Towles already had ordination as an elder from First Presbyterian Church, but an ordination ceremony was held for the others.[33] Ironically, and perhaps as a gesture of goodwill, the Session of First Presbyterian Church granted the new church use of the building for its organizational services.[34]

---

[32]Ibid. The text from the New Revised Standard Version reads, "On the contrary, members of the body that seem to be weaker are indispensable." Unfortunately, a manuscript of the sermon does not exist. Was the verse interpreted to apply to the members of the new church? Were they the "weaker" members in the sense that their new church had fewer members than the mother church? The members' names were the following: James M. Towles, Mary A. Towles, Mary C. Towles, Sallie B. Towles, Robert H. Towles, M. Alice Towles, James M. Towles, Jr., A. D. Taylor, Sallie L. Taylor, Hannah Johns, H. H. Yarborough, Eliza L. Hope, J. M. Monie, Mrs. J. M. Monie, T. A. Kingsley, M. H. Kingsley, Mary E. Wetherall, John Whitelaw, Mrs. J. D. Primrose, Mr. L. Prempert, James Kennedy, Sally P. Atkinson, Jane P. Atkinson, Mary A. Scott, C. H. Scott, J. P. Valentine, Martha Valentine, Ann P. Smith. Twenty-five members were Caucasian, and three were African-American although there is no distinction between the races identified in the list.

[33]Ibid.

[34]Minutes of the Session, 7 May 1877. The *North Carolina Presbyterian* (23 May 1877, 2) contains an account of the service and a description of the atmosphere that evening: "services took place in the First church, in the presence of a good congregation, a number of persons from other denominations being in attendance and seeming to be deeply interested.... The whole proceeding was conducted very smoothly and in excellent taste, and was as impressive and systematic as if it had been done by a ritual. The prayers at its various steps were especially tender, and the interest, to the close, was deep and solemn. It was the general feeling that Presbytery had made a happy selection for this important and delicate mission, and I cannot but believe that other denominations were impressed with the simplicity and apostolic character of the Presbyterial order. Dr. Vaughan, who is supplying the First church, and Rev. J. M. Atkinson who will probably be called by the Second, were present, as were, also, officers and leading members of First; and the indications seemed to point to greater zeal and consecration on the part of the members of both organizations and to a

Almost immediately, Second Presbyterian Church began planning for the future. A congregational meeting was scheduled for 28 May 1877 for the election of trustees and the establishment of a building committee. Charles H. Scott was appointed to be the church's first Sunday school superintendent.[35] In November 1878, the church received into membership the person who became its most notable member, Governor Zebulon Baird Vance. Vance was received "on examination of profession of his faith in Christ...he having received the sacrament of baptism in infancy was requested to present himself on the coming Sabbath morning for public profession of his faith."[36]

Zebulon Vance was one of the most important political figures in North Carolina history. He was born in Buncombe County just north of Asheville on 13 May 1830. Following his basic schooling, he attended classes for one year the University of North Carolina to continue study in law, which began under the tutelage of John W. Woodfin, an Asheville lawyer, in 1850. In 1852, he was licensed by the State of North Carolina to practice law in the county courts. He returned to Asheville, was elected in 1853 as solicitor for Buncombe County, and the following year granted license to practice in superior courts.[37] Vance made his name in North Carolina politics, becoming a pivotal figure during the crucial years of the Civil War and Reconstruction. He was elected to the General Assembly at age twenty-four and the United States House of Representatives at twenty-eight. He served as an officer in Company F, 14th North Carolina Regiment in the Civil War when he was thirty-one. In 1862, he was elected governor of the state, an office he held on three occasions (1862–1864; 1864–1865; 1877–1879); and four times elected as a

---

greater emulation in the one work, multiform in its parts and in the gifts bestowed for it, of the One Divine Master and Head."

[35]Minutes of the Session (Second Presbyterian Church), 21 May 1877.

[36]Ibid., 27 November 1878.

[37]*Dictionary of North Carolina Biography,* ed. William S. Powell (Chapel Hill: University of North Carolina Press, 1979–1996) s.v. "Vance, Zebulon Baird."

United States senator, serving from 1879 until his death on 14 April 1894.[38]

While Vance's career as a politician is interesting, the more immediate interest for this book concerned his religious views and more specifically why he chose to join Second Presbyterian Church. Of course, there is no way to understand his full motivation unless he left a diary or some autobiographical account to explain his decision to join. Speculation leads to the conclusion that his motive was related to the two most influential women in his life: his wife and his mother. Vance's mother, Mira Margaret Baird Vance, died on 4 October 1878. Margaret was a remarkable woman who through difficulties raised Vance and his six siblings following her husband's death in 1844. She instilled a love of books and reading in her children. A few weeks after her death, Vance described her influence on his life and her devotion to literature: "She was the most correct and impressive reader…and I am satisfied that whatever of elocution I have came from her."[39] His mother imparted a seed of religious faith to her son Zebulon although it did not blossom until many years later. She was a devout Presbyterian according to Vance's earliest biographer. She remained a Presbyterian in her theological outlook all of her life, but because there was no Presbyterian church in proximity to her home, she found herself attending the local Methodist church "for whose traveling ministers her house had long been a hospitable home."[40] The mixture of Presbyterianism and Methodism was reflected in a favorite remark Vance used to make regarding his brother's religious views and

---

[38]Ibid. See also *NCpedia*, s.v. "Zebulon Baird Vance," accessed 21 July 2014, http://ncpedia.org/biography/governors/vance. For a complete biography of Vance, see Clement Dowd, *The Life of Zebulon B. Vance* (Charlotte, NC: Observer Printing and Publishing House, 1897); Glenn Tucker, *Zeb Vance: Champion of Personal Freedom* (Indianapolis: Bobbs-Merrill Company, 1965); Gordon B. McKinney, *Zeb Vance: North Carolina's Civil War Governor and Gilded Age Political Leader* (Chapel Hill: University of North Carolina Press, 2004).

[39]Frontis W. Johnston, ed. *The Papers of Zebulon Baird Vance, Vol. 1* (Raleigh: State Department of Archives and History, 1963) xxii, cited by Joe A. Mobley, *War Governor of the South: North Carolina's Zeb Vance in the Confederacy* (Gainesville: University Press of Florida, 2005) 14.

[40]Dowd, *Life of Zebulon B. Vance*, 213.

his own: "Bob is a Methodist and believes in falling from grace but never falls. I am a Presbyterian and don't believe in falling from grace but am always falling."[41] Grief over his mother's death, no doubt, influenced Vance's religious perspective on life in the weeks following her death.

The religious influence of his wife, Harriett Espy Vance, however, may have been behind Vance's decision to join Second Presbyterian Church. Harriett Espy was the love of his life. She was born in Salisbury, North Carolina, on 11 July 1832, the daughter of Rev. Thomas Espy, pastor of the First Presbyterian Church in the city. At the age of sixteen, she made a personal commitment of faith and "adhered until the moment of her death."[42] During their courtship, however, Vance "was forced to acknowledge to Harriett that he was not as committed to the church as she was."[43] Harriett gave great attention to her faith, even to the extent of writing down her own "covenant of personal religious faith which she periodically updated" and was "an exceptionally pious person…recognized as such by all who knew her, including Zeb."[44] While he had a great knowledge of the Scriptures and occasionally gave some attention to theological speculation, he was not nearly as devout, as evidenced by the fact that he had never united formally with a local Presbyterian church.

It was her death on 3 November 1878 that finally brought Zebulon Vance to the point of personal faith. Autumn 1878 was a particularly stressful time for Zebulon Vance. His mother had died in early October. He and Harriett had four sons, but three of them (Zebbie, David, and Thomas) had problems ranging from bad grades in school to the early

---

[41]Kemp P. Battle, *Memories of an Old Time Tar Heel* (Chapel Hill: University of North Carolina Press, 1945) 91, cited by Tucker, *Zeb Vance: Champion of Personal Freedom*, 204.

[42]Dowd, *Life of Zebulon B. Vance*, 215.

[43]McKinney, *Zeb Vance: North Carolina's Civil War Governor*, 23. Another biographer Joe E. Mobley concurs: "Harriett Espy's pious nature and strict upbringing as a daughter of a Presbyterian clergyman stood in marked contrast to Vance's playful outlook, raucous behavior, and risqué jokes and yarns that made him so popular among the young wags with whom he liked to cavort" (Mobley, *War Governor of the South*, 15).

[44]McKinney, *Zeb Vance: North Carolina's Civil War Governor*, 23.

signs of alcoholism. His son Charlie, who worked with him in the governor's office in Raleigh, was the most reliable. Because of Harriett's illness, Zebulon, who was governor at the time, was forced to deal with his sons' problems without much help from his ailing wife. The pressures of the governor's office, the family problems, and the fact that he was in the midst of a campaign for the United States Senate almost brought him to the breaking point when she died.[45] These pressures in November 1878 were powerful influences that finally brought him to a profession of faith in Christ and membership in Second Presbyterian Church.[46] One biographer summarizes the situation this way: "The exact nature of the religious experience Zeb had following Hattie's death is unclear, but it induced him to formally join a church for the first time in his life.... Zeb was basically not an introspective person; his conversion was a reaction to the deaths of the two most important women in his life."[47]

The final question surrounding Governor Vance's decision to join Second Presbyterian concerns why he chose that church rather than First Presbyterian. His wife was a devout member of First Presbyterian. She was not listed among the charter members of Second Presbyterian, and there is no evidence that she ever joined. Why would the governor choose to join this new, less prominent congregation? The answer may relate to Harriett's wishes and sentiments, which favored Second Presbyterian. This becomes apparent in the fact that when the Orange Presbytery met in April 1877 to affirm the new congregation, Harriett Espy Vance attended the meeting. The official delegates from First Presbyterian were the stated supply pastor, Clement R. Vaughan, and elder W. H. Crow. According to an account of the meeting published in the *News and Observer*, Mrs. Vance, along with Judge E. G. Reade and his wife, were visitors at the meeting, indicating Mrs. Vance was supportive of the new congregation.[48] Hence, exactly four weeks to the day after his beloved Harriett's death, with family and political pressures upon him, Governor Zebulon B. Vance walked down the aisle of Second Presbyter-

[45]Ibid., 338–39.

[46]Ibid., 339–40.

[47]Ibid., 340.

[48]*News and Observer*, 29 April 1877, 3.

ian Church and made a public profession of his faith in Christ.[49] One more piece of evidence that Harriett's sentiments were with Second Presbyterian rather than First Presbyterian is the fact that her funeral was conducted by J. M. Atkinson, and in the published account of the service, he is listed as her pastor.[50]

The surviving records for Second Presbyterian Church reveal that the congregation never gained significant strength in the city after its founding, despite its best efforts. The notable addition of Governor Vance could not bolster the congregation as he soon moved to Washington, D.C. to begin service as a United States senator from North Carolina. The death of James M. Towles in 1879, just two years after the church's founding, was the most devastating blow to the young church. Towles and his family made up one quarter of the church's charter membership, and as one of the church's first two charter elders, he was one of its most important supporters. In a memorial, the elders called attention to his specific place in the early days of the church's establishment: "During the comparatively short period of his connection with this church, to which…he was most affectionately devoted, these qualities of mind and heart shone with increased brightness, and were of signal and inestimable value to the infant and struggling body."[51]

By April 1879, the church reported to the Orange Presbytery that it had thirty-six members and had paid the pastor a salary of $502 [$12,100]. Included with this report is a statement indicating that due to the construction of a building and paying the pastor's salary, the church did not have the ability to give financially beyond itself to other causes. Although the report mentions the building project, there is barely a mention of it in the minutes other than references on occasion to the building committee.[52] By June 1880, the session adopted a resolution expressing

---

[49]Minutes of the Session (Second Presbyterian Church), 27 November 1878. This date, when he was presented before the elders, was a Wednesday evening. The entry indicates that he was "requested to present himself on the coming Sabbath morning for a public profession of his faith." This would have been Sunday, 1 December 1878.

[50]Dowd, *Life of Zebulon B. Vance*, 216.

[51]Minutes of the Session (Second Presbyterian Church), 28 March 1879.

[52]Ibid., 15 April 1879.

thanks to the North Carolina Institution for the Instruction of the Deaf and Dumb for use of their chapel as a temporary location for worship services, an indication that the building project was completed.[53] The building was constructed at the corner of Blount and Polk Streets with a parsonage erected later on the adjacent lot.

By spring 1882, the session produced a two-page "Report of the 2nd Church Raleigh On the State of Religion In It." Several conclusions can be drawn from the report: (1) it was not a wealthy congregation; (2) some of its members lived "in the country" and were unable to attend regularly; (3) the congregation maintained a sense of optimism, especially among the women of the church, and a movement was afoot to construct a parsonage with land already purchased; (4) although the presbytery would have probably wanted the church to contribute to causes beyond the local level, the elders concluded "they ought rather to be surprised that we have not called upon them to do anything for us."[54]

Despite the seeming optimism of the report, the church did not thrive over the next several years. By April 1883, the sessional records indicate that the church was not "able to support [the pastor] properly in his labors."[55] Another reference to financial problems is found in the sessional record for 26 February 1884, where it mentions that the appropriation expected from the church to the presbytery was lowered because of financial difficulty. The membership had declined that year as well. The church reported forty members in 1881, but by 1884, the number dipped to thirty-three.[56]

In 1884 and 1886, the sessional records of the church contain statements that the elders actively discussed the state of the church's well-being and that on both occasions they continued to remain optimistic.[57] The church then experienced a slight growth in membership over

---

[53]Ibid., 6 June 1880. It is odd that there is no mention of celebration about the building's completion.

[54]Ibid., 24 April 1882.

[55]Ibid., 18 April 1883.

[56]Ibid., 10 April 1881 and n.d. April 1884.

[57]Ibid., 10 August 1884 and 7 March 1886.

the years 1886 to 1888,[58] but by late 1889 and into early 1890, members began to transfer their memberships to First Presbyterian Church, a clear signal that the church was rapidly declining.[59] At some point in late 1889 or early 1890, J. M. Atkinson left the church to become pastor of the Presbyterian Church in Warrenton, North Carolina.[60] On 6 March 1891, he suddenly died at the age of 71.[61] A contemporary account of his death indicates that despite some vision problems, he had been in good health. Atkinson gave more than three decades of his life to serving in Raleigh.

Second Presbyterian Church never called another pastor. On 3 March 1890, a reference in the sessional records for First Presbyterian Church indicates that the membership had declined to about fifteen. A representative from the Presbytery was present with the First Presbyterian elders that evening to request the mother church's help in an assimilation plan for the remaining members. An interesting note appeared in the *News and Observer* several years later: "The lot on which the old Second Presbyterian Church stands on Blount Street has been sold to Miss McVea. The building will be removed and a handsome residence built."[62]

A New Pastor at First Presbyterian. Despite the establishment of a second Presbyterian congregation in the city, First Presbyterian Church continued to thrive in the years between the end of Reconstruction and the turn of the century. This was due in large part to the good, stable leadership provided by a new pastor. In February 1878, C. R. Vaughan informed the session that he wanted the congregation to begin taking steps toward finding a replacement for him. The church held a congregational meeting on the afternoon of 18 February in which Vaughan informed the church that he would not be able to continue as their stated supply. He believed that it was in the church's best interest to secure the

---

[58]Ibid., 11 April 1886 (thirty-seven members), 13 April 1887 (forty members), and 24 April 1888 (forty-four members).

[59]Ibid., n.d. November 1889, n.d. January 1890.

[60]Ibid., 27 April 1890. The minutes state, "Mrs. J. M. Atkinson, Miss Jane Atkinson and Mrs. C. H. Scott were at their own request dismissed in good and regular standing to unite with Mr. Atkinson's church in Warrenton."

[61]*News and Observer*, 8 March 1891.

[62]Ibid., 27 January 1895, p. 5, accessed 23 July 2014.

services of a regular pastor. Given all that had happened with the organization of Second Presbyterian, it is not difficult to see his reasoning. A contemporary account of the meeting indicates that Vaughan had developed a love for the church during the period that he had served them: "He spoke very feelingly of the pain it had cost him to make up his mind to sever his connection with the members of the church…among whom he had formed many warm personal friends."[63] The feeling was mutual as it was reported that "he would be the unanimous choice if he would consent to become the pastor of the church."[64] Nevertheless, Vaughan decided that it was best for both him and the church to sever their connection with one another.

The following month, the church unanimously voted to issue a call to Dr. William T. Hall, who for five previous years had been pastor of the First Presbyterian Church in Lynchburg, Virginia. A native North Carolinian, Hall found the opportunity to return to his native state attractive. Upon his return to Lynchburg, however, following his visit to Raleigh, he changed his mind and informed the Raleigh congregation that he would not be accepting the call.[65] On 27 May, the church unanimously issued a call to Rev. John Sims Watkins.[66] A few months later Elder J. B. Burwell was selected to attend the Roanoke Presbytery in Virginia in order to "consummate the call of Rev. John Sims Watkins as pastor to our church."[67]

Watkins was installed as the pastor of the congregation on 23 October 1878. Rev. L. C. Vass of New Bern preached the installation sermon from 2 Corinthians 3:17. The *North Carolina Presbyterian* reported on the event and made special notation of the fact that Drury Lacy, the beloved former pastor of the congregation, was present for the service: "He said he wished, feeble as he was, to be present at what would be the last service of the kind he would ever have the pleasure of attending."[68] Also,

---

[63]"Raleigh Letter," *North Carolina Presbyterian*, 27 February 1878, 2.

[64]Ibid.

[65]"Raleigh First Church Calls a Pastor," *North Carolina Presbyterian*, 13 March 1878, 2; "Raleigh Letter," *North Carolina Presbyterian*, 10 April 1878, 2.

[66]"First Church, Raleigh," *North Carolina Presbyterian*, 5 June 1878, 2.

[67]Minutes of the Session, 4 February and 5 July 1878.

[68]"Installation," *North Carolina Presbyterian*, 30 October 1878, 2.

it is noteworthy that whatever differences and animosity may have existed the previous year with the split and formation of Second Presbyterian Church, the membership of the new church was present at Watkins's installation service. That afternoon, Vass preached a sermon at Second Presbyterian Church attended by Watkins and the members of First Presbyterian. It seems from this report that the rift between the two groups had begun to heal.[69]

Watkins was a native of Virginia and was born on 4 January 1844 in Halifax County to Richard Venable and Mary Ann Baskerville Watkins. He attended school at Dinwiddie Preparatory School and was a student at Hampden-Sydney College from 1860 to 1861, but his schooling was interrupted by the Civil War. He served in the Confederate Army and finally graduated from the University of Virginia in 1867. Following graduation, he was a teacher at Kenmore School for Boys in Fredericksburg from 1867 to 1869 and then enrolled at Union Theological Seminary, where he graduated in 1872. During his time at Union, he married Mary Ludwell Coleman in 1871. He was licensed and ordained by the Roanoke Presbytery. Watkins served as pastor of the Presbyterian church in Roanoke from 1872 to 1878, where he had been serving before accepting the call to First Presbyterian Church in Raleigh. During the period that he served as pastor of First Presbyterian Church in Raleigh, he was also an instructor in moral philosophy at Peace Institute from 1880 to 1890. Also during his time in Raleigh, he received the honorary DD degree from the University of North Carolina. Watkins remained in Raleigh until 1892, when he accepted a call to be the pastor of First Presbyterian Church in Spartanburg, South Carolina. He died in Spartanburg on 29 April 1930. In addition to his legacy as a pastor and teacher, Watkins also authored a book titled *Hand-Book for Ruling Elders*, which was used quite frequently in Presbyterian circles during his lifetime.[70]

---

[69]Ibid.

[70]Scott Eugene Crampton, *Ministerial Directory of the Presbyterian Church, U.S., 1861–1941* (Austin, TX: Von Boeckmann-Jones Co, 1942) 753, http://bbel.hathitrust.org/cgi/pt?id=wu.89067533174;view=lup;seq=5. See John S. Watkins, *A Hand-Book for Ruling Elders* (Richmond, VA: Presbyterian Committee of Publications, 1895).

If numbers are any indication, Watkins's tenure as pastor of First Presbyterian Church was successful. The church reported to the Presbytery a total of 188 members the year that Watkins accepted the call as pastor. The membership grew steadily throughout his tenure. In 1883, there were 270 members, and although the next several years saw a slight decline, in 1888 the session reported 303 members. Finally, during Watkins's last year as pastor of the church, the session reported a total of 343 members.[71]

Another sign of the congregation's health was the establishment of a mission chapel in another part of the city. The first reference to the chapel is found in the sessional record for 8 February 1887. During that meeting, E. R. Stamps moved that a committee composed of L. D. Heartt, L. W. Whiting, and B. R. Harding be formed "to solicit necessary means to erect a mission chapel near the Raleigh and Gaston R. Road Round House, to secure a lot for the same and to take all necessary steps for the establishment of a mission chapel."[72] The committee provided periodic reports throughout the year. By September 1888, the sessional records indicate that the chapel had been erected and that there was "great interest" in the work there. The next month, the elders approved establishment of a "Sabbath School" at the mission chapel. Leo D. Heartt was elected as the superintendent, and Seymour W. Whiting was chosen as assistant superintendent. They were instructed to work together to secure teachers for the work.[73] By April 1891, the work was prospering. The annual report to the presbytery indicated that the "Mission School" (the Sabbath school at the mission chapel) had seventy students enrolled.[74] Unfortunately, there is little information given about the work of the chapel except another reference the next year in the report to Presbytery, indicating that again the Mission School had an enrollment of seventy students.[75]

---

[71]Minutes of the Session, 3 April 1878, 5 April 1883, 18 April 1888, 3 April 1892. In 1886 the session began distinguishing between "resident" and "non-resident" numbers in the annual reports to presbytery.

[72]Ibid., 8 February 1887.

[73]Ibid., 5 September and 10 October 1888.

[74]Ibid., 1 April 1891.

[75]Ibid.

First Presbyterian Women and Missions. Another sign of strength in the church during Watkins's tenure relates to the women of the church and their organization for mission support. The Ladies Foreign Missionary Society was organized on 15 September 1875, three years before Watkins became the church's pastor. But it grew in popularity among the women, and its work became integral to the church's life and outreach during the last two decades of the nineteenth century. The organizational meeting of the society occurred at the home of Mrs. William Crow. The twenty-five women present declared that "their hearts [were] stirred up to take part in hastening the glorious fulfillment of God's promise that the heathen shall be given to Christ for an inheritance to the uttermost parts of the earth." Mrs. Mary Rice Lacy, the wife of former pastor Drury Lacy, was selected as the society's first president and Mrs. Rachel Wildes was appointed as secretary-treasurer.[76] The organization grew rapidly. By the second month of its existence, the minutes report that the membership had grown from the original twenty-five to fifty-one.[77]

During the nineteenth century, especially following the Civil War, American women found avenues of empowerment outside of the home. Organizing for mission support within their churches was one such means. This was especially true in Presbyterian, Methodist, and Baptist churches as "[f]emale supporters thrilled to the courage and heroism of young missionary women who accompanied their husbands to the jungles of Asia and Africa, and who suffered and perished nobly there."[78] By 1888, Methodist, Presbyterian, and Baptist women in the South had organized nationally to support missionaries within their respective denominations.[79]

---

[76]Minutes of the Ladies Foreign Missionary Society, 15 September 1875.

[77]Ibid., 6 October 1875. See also "The Ladies Are Moving," *North Carolina Presbyterian*, 25 June 1879, 2.

[78]Jane Hunter, *The Gospel of Gentility: American Women Missionaries in Turn-of-the-Century China* (New Haven: Yale University Press, 1984) xiii, cited in Robert R. Mathisen, *Critical Issues in American Religious History: A Reader* (Waco, TX: Baylor University Press, 2001) 427.

[79]For a good discussion of the evolution of female involvement in missionary support through the nineteenth century and its impact on American culture,

The records of the Ladies Foreign Missionary Society from the last quarter of the nineteenth century show an emphasis in three areas. The first is associated with a female missionary to China named Helen Kirkland. She was born in Scotland in 1828 but immigrated to the United States with her family. Evidently, she had traveled extensively before leaving for mission work in China. She arrived in China on Christmas Day 1874 and remained there until her death in 1895.[80] Early on, the Raleigh women seemed to be captured by Helen Kirkland's sacrificial commitment to missions. She was unmarried and middle-aged when she arrived in China. In November 1875, the record reflects that the women decided that they would support "Miss Kirkland's school in Hang Chow China" as a specific target of their efforts.[81] Eventually, the women began to refer to Kirkland as "our own" missionary.

The minutes from the society during the years 1875 to 1892 contain numerous references to Helen Kirkland. Occasionally, the women received a letter from her that was read to the group. On other occasions, they read letters from her that had been sent to other people and somehow passed along to the women in Raleigh.[82] Sometimes they displayed pictures sent by Kirkland from China, which always interested the women in Raleigh.[83] In the modern age of Internet and social media, it is often difficult to imagine how awe-inspiring actual photographs of foreign lands and people would have been to women in nineteenth-century America.

In 1884, Rev. G. W. Painter was a guest speaker to the Ladies Foreign Missionary Society. Reportedly, there was a "large attendance" at this meeting because Painter had worked with Kirkland in China. "He

---

see Barbara J. MacHaffie, *Her Story: Women in Christian Tradition* 2nd ed. (Minneapolis: Fortress Press, 2006) 171–78.

[80]A. T. Graves, "In Memoriam: Miss Helen Kirkland," in *Woman's Work in the Far East* (Shanghai: Presbyterian Mission Press, 1895) 139. The source is available through Google Books.

[81]Minutes of the Ladies Foreign Missionary Society, n.d. November 1875.

[82]See for example the record from Minutes of the Ladies Foreign Missionary Society, 1 March 1876, in which a letter that she had sent to her pastor in Virginia was read by the group.

[83]Ibid., n.d., April 1876.

spoke of Miss Kirkland in terms of affectionate praise, saying she was the life and soul of the mission, indefatigable in her labors among the women and children and had done more to remove the prejudice against foreigners than anyone else."[84]

Second, the Ladies Foreign Missionary Society placed great emphasis on missions education. They studied the lives of Presbyterian missionaries in numerous countries around the world. They were interested in the missionaries and their families, how they lived their lives on the mission field, the challenges they faced and the ministry successes they were able to secure. They were also captivated by missionary reports of the different cultures and religions encountered. Each month, the women had a designated topic for their meeting that usually focused on a particular country. They read aloud an article about the missionary in that country and his/her work there. On other occasions, they read letters from the missionaries that described firsthand the ministry performed. The women were particularly captivated by the missionaries' difficulties from living in a different culture. Additionally, they studied missionaries from other denominations.[85] Also, despite the fact that their society carried the name "Foreign," the women studied the mission work taking place within the North American context. For example, in May 1890, the topic of the meeting was the mission work being done among the Sioux nation in the American West.[86]

The final emphasis apparent in the minutes of the Ladies Foreign Missionary Society gives evidence of a nascent feminism. This mirrored the trend in the nation as women in subtle ways began to discover new possibilities of service and leadership.[87] In particular, the women at First Presbyterian found themselves captivated with the lives of women in the other countries that they studied and the trials suffered by some of them. This can be seen in several places in the records. For example, on 7 June 1882, the women discussed Presbyterian mission efforts in Greece. The discussion eventually centered on women in the Greek culture, and the

---

[84]Ibid., n.d. February 1884.

[85]Ibid., 4 November 1885 and 13 October 1886.

[86]Ibid., 5 June 1885 and n.d. May 1890.

[87]Hunter, *Gospel of Gentility*, xiii.

she retained until her death in 1896. Records reveal her importance to the organization when in 1892 it recorded, "To her the Society owes its existence, and through her efforts it has been kept alive."[94]

The Reades were a prominent family in Raleigh in the late nineteenth century. Edwin, an elder in the church, was one of the most important politicians in the city, whose career spanned the complicated politics of the Civil War and Reconstruction era. He served in the United States House of Representatives and also for a brief period in the Confederate Senate, as well as in a number of appointed political positions. In 1865, he was elected as an associate justice of the North Carolina Supreme Court, a position he retained until 1879, when he transitioned to a banking career. Following the death of his first wife, Emily Ann L. Moore, in 1871, Reade married Mary Parmele, herself a widow.[95]

The meetings of the Home Missionary Society were conducted in a similar fashion to those of the Foreign Missionary Society. The meetings were called to order, and the requisite business for the meeting was addressed. While the records are not as detailed as those of the Foreign Society, the meetings frequently had a guest speaker or a discussion about some item related to the local work of Presbyterians that served as the meeting's program. The stated work of the society from its inception was to "do Home Mission work within the bounds of our own Presbytery, as far as practicable."[96] During its first fifteen years, the society's largest contribution was $129 [$3,220] to the Presbyterian church in Wilson for construction of their church building. Two gifts (one of $100 [$2,500] and the other for $75 [$1,870]) were given to liquidate the "evangelistic debt of Orange Presbytery."[97] Most of the gifts, however, totaled $10-$25 [$250-$625] and went to various struggling churches throughout the Orange Presbytery. The women also utilized some of their funds for projects related to their own church. Two gifts of $50

---

[94]Minutes of the Ladies Home Missionary Society, n.d. October 1892.

[95]See *NCpedia*, s.v. "Reade, Edwin Godwin," accessed 9 September 2014, http://ncpedia.org/biography/reade-edwin-godwin.

[96]This is quoted form a short history of the Society contained the Minutes of the Ladies Home Missionary Society, n.d. October 1892.

[97]Ibid. No further explanation is given for use of this contribution.

[$1,260] each (one in 1887 and the other in 1888) were given toward the Mission Chapel building discussed above. And, a gift of $50 in 1886 went toward retiring the debt of First Presbyterian's building renovation.[98]

Church Music Enhancement. An important improvement in the worship atmosphere of the church occurred in the 1870s. From the church's inception through the Civil War and Reconstruction eras, the worship atmosphere relied upon non-instrumental music. That changed when the church purchased an organ in 1871 and then, a few years later, secured the services of Professor Albrecht Baumann to direct the choir and serve as the church organist when a "suitable" organ was purchased.[99] Baumann served the congregation in this capacity until 1891 when he began to receive a salary for his services.[100]

Albrecht Baumann was a native of Germany born in 1830. He immigrated to the United States in 1857. Baumann moved to Charlotte in 1863 and was hired by Rev. Robert Burwell to be the music director at the Female Institute in the city. In 1872, when Burwell moved to Raleigh to assume the leadership of the Peace Institute, he brought Baumann with him. Baumann became the director of the Musical Department at the school and remained in that position for twenty years until

---

[98]Ibid. According to the records, churches (other than First Presbyterian) receiving funding from the Ladies Home Missionary Society in its first fifteen years were Wilson ($129 [$3,220]); Caleh ($10 [$250]); Ebenezer ($10); Chapel Hill (three gifts of $25 [$625] each); Shiloh (two gifts of $10 each); Gulf ($15 [$375]); the Presbyterian church at Davidson College ($20 [$500]); Dallas ($5 [$125]); Lumberton ($10); Scotland Neck ($10); Lagrange ($25); Leggetts ($29.93 [$748.00]); Greenville ($5); Granville ($25).

[99]Johnson and Murray, *Reconstruction to 1920*, 583; Minutes of the Session, 3 February 1873.

[100]See Alexander B. Stronach, "The Old Presbyterian Church," *News and Observer*, 22 March 1908, 3. Alexander B. Stronach, who was born in 1847, recalled that in his childhood growing up at First Presbyterian Church, there was no instrumental music. The sessional record for 3 February 1873 indicates that an organ was about to be purchased and that a letter was to be written to Baumann to secure his services as organist. In 1891, the session voted to begin paying him a regular salary. See Minutes of the Session, 3 February 1873 and 2 February 1891.

his death in 1892.[101] The church thought so highly of Baumann that he was elected to be an elder in 1888. In a very touching memorial resolution to Baumann's life, the elders recalled,

> His place in the sanctuary and weekly meetings for prayer was never vacant, except where detained by sickness or other cause.... No congregation was ever more fortunate in their Choir Director. An accomplished and enthusiastic musician and with it all, an humble and devoted Christian, he threw his whole soul and heart into this important part of our worship and thus added...to the solemnity and interest of our services.[102]

One other seemingly minor improvement in the worship services at the church occurred in 1890. The session passed a motion to consult with the deacons to see if funds were available to print what they called a "pastor's indicator" that could be placed in the pews each Sunday. This printed document contained the hymns to be sung as well as the pastor's text from which he would preach. This may have been the first church bulletin provided to the congregation.[103]

Resignation of John Watkins. In the early 1880s, Watkins began to have health problems that necessitated several periods where he needed to be away from his pastoral duties. The exact nature of these problems is not revealed in the record. In 1881, he announced to the congregation that "owing to his continued bad health he would take advantage of the rest they had kindly offered him, and would leave for the mountains during the week to be gone for several months."[104] The issue seems to have been chronic because three years later the elders refer to his being absent again. They stated that as his health seemed to be "improving," they

---

[101]"Death of Prof. A. Baumann," *News and Observer,* 24 September 1892, 1.

[102]Minutes of the Session, 7 November 1892.

[103]Ibid., 8 October 1890.

[104]"First Church—Raleigh," *North Carolina Presbyterian,* 6 July 1881, 2. See Minutes of the Session, 22 June 1881, where the granting of the leave of absence is recorded but no specifics are given about the nature of the illness: "Leave of absence having been granted to the pastor to ____ [unintelligible] his health, the Rev. W. W. Downey of Parkersville, W. Va. was invited by the session and pastor to fill the pulpit during his absence."

should send a letter to him which allowed him to "prolong his absence so as to receive the fullest benefit therefrom."[105] There is no other reference to Watkins's health in the sessional records.

In 1888, however, there is recorded a fascinating letter that Watkins addressed to the elders. He presented them with the letter, requested that they read and discuss it, and then left the room. Basically, the letter says that since he was coming to the end of a decade of service to the church, he wanted to know if the elders thought that he should continue in the role as pastor. He believed that the church ought to have the opportunity to evaluate his work and make a change if it were deemed appropriate. He requested that the elders each vote "yes" or "no" and that no one vote anonymously. Furthermore, he requested that no permanent record be kept of anyone's vote so as not to bring embarrassment on anyone. He continued,

> I wish you to understand distinctly that I give this opportunity to make a change in the pastorate not because of any unpleasantness in the relation which exists between myself and the church, or any individuals, not because I am dissatisfied in any way, not because I have any plan in regard to other positions, but solely and only because I am persuaded that every pastor ought to open the way for a change, if the people desire it, at least every ten years.[106]

Watkins's letter provides a measure of deep insight into his character. Significant humility and a genuine love for the members of First Presbyterian are expressed in the letter. There seems to have been nothing that triggered the need for the pastor to write the letter as he states, "Nor do I ask you to take the vote on the question of my remaining because I have heard of any dissatisfaction in the church with my work."[107] This also does not seem to have been a standard practice among the pastors of the Orange Presbytery of the time. Most likely, it is the genuine intent of a loving pastor to allow his congregation to gauge what is best for its future in an era of great change. He even states, "Times have

---

[105]Minutes of the Session, 21 August 1884.

[106]Ibid., 9 May 1888. The letter is reproduced in the minutes of the meeting. It encompasses three pages in the record book.

[107]Ibid.

changed very much in the last 30 or 40 years and churches are becoming more restless and more inclined to make changes than formerly."[108] Because a genuine love existed between Watkins and the church, it is not surprising that the elders responded to Watkins that "it was the opinion of the Session without a dissenting voice that no change in the pastorate is desired."[109] In their response to Watkins, recorded in the minutes, the elders state, "It is the sense of the Session that dissolution of our existing relations would in no manner be conducive to the interests of the church, but would in all probability work the opposite result."[110]

During the decade that he had been pastor of the congregation, Watkins was successful by any measure that could be used to determine success. This exchange with the session indicates that affection existed between pastor and parish. The concern and patience during Watkins's periods of illness also suggest a harmonious relationship. When Watkins first became the pastor of the church, the annual report to the Presbytery indicated that the church had 188 members. Ten years later, that number had grown to 303 members. Watkins assumed the pastoral duties during the difficult period when Second Presbyterian Church had just been organized, and there must have been challenges in the relationship between the two congregations although there is nothing in the record indicating such.

Watkins remained as the pastor of the church for several more years. In December 1891, he informed the session that "his eyes had been giving him renewed trouble and that he was considering a call to the Presbyterian Church in Spartanburg, S.C."[111] He told the elders that his physician advised him that "rest for his eyes was absolutely necessary."[112] In a moment of frankness, he admitted to the elders that if he accepted the new position in South Carolina, he would be able to gain rest for his eyes from intense study in sermon preparation "by using his accumulated material while if he remained here he must continue to study and thereby

[108]Ibid.
[109]Ibid.
[110]Letter from Elders to Watkins, Minutes of the Session, 14 May 1888.
[111]Minutes of the Session, 7 December 1891.
[112]Ibid.

use his eyes."[113] The elders pleaded with Watkins to consider the matter further, which he agreed to do. Within two weeks, however, he made the decision to resign and requested the session to call an congregational meeting for the following Sunday so that he may inform the membership. It is noteworthy that the session, in seeking to keep him as their pastor, at first refused to comply with his request. The next month, however, his letter of resignation was presented to the church. In the letter he mentioned "protracted sickness," indicating that his health problems were chronic.[114] In the session's annual report to the presbytery in April 1892, the following message relating to the reciprocal duties between pastor and parish is recorded: "Owing to the resignation of our pastor, no record of reciprocal duties can be presented, but it is right to say that he parted from his people with mutual affection and esteem."[115]

The First Presbyterian Church of Raleigh stood poised for the next century but needed new pastoral leadership in 1892. Other matters began to need attention as well, as shall be seen in the next chapter.

---

[113]Ibid.

[114]Ibid., 7 December and 23 December 1891, and 24 January 1892.

[115]Ibid., 3 April 1892.

6

Poised for a New Century

The Context

By the last decade of the nineteenth century, Americans were able to look back upon a nation that encountered monumental change throughout the century and look forward to a new century of promise. Industrialism brought economic prosperity to a few but brought misery to the working classes, especially in the large urban centers. The promise of the "American Dream" brought waves of new immigrants from Europe to the shores of America. But without any government regulation of business or the workplace, workers were often subjected to long hours and difficult conditions in the factories, not to mention occupational safety hazards. To make matters worse, the tenement housing complexes created horrible living conditions in which disease could spread rapidly. Confronted by those circumstances, not all social theorists accepted the status quo.

Thorstein Veblen became a noted social critic, and his *Theory of the Leisure Class* (1899) was one of the most important studies of the late nineteenth century to challenge the assumptions made by the Social Darwinists. Churches also began to address the social ills of the large cities. The Social Gospel Movement, led by the German Baptist pastor Walter Rauschenbusch, sought to "Christianize" the social structures of society. Rauschenbusch believed that individual conversion through revivalism alone would not cure the nation's ills. He called for a "Christian socialism" whereby the wealth in society could be redistributed more evenly. Rauschenbusch laid out his vision in three books that soon made him a household name: *Christianity and the Social Crisis* (1907), *Christianizing the Social Order* (1912), and *A Theology for the Social Gospel* (1917).

In addition, labor unions began to organize for workers' rights. For instance, the year 1869 saw the organization of the Knights of Labor.

The American Federation of Labor was founded in 1886. Famous labor strikes from the period included a nationwide railroad workers' strike in 1877, the Homestead steelworkers' strike in 1892, and the Pullman railroad workers' strike in 1894. By 1900, labor and management had become willing partners at times and, at others, bitter enemies.

Corruption and conflict characterized the politics of the Gilded Age. Political campaigns (much like today) were riddled with personal attacks. Political bosses, such as the legendary "Boss" William Tweed in New York City, were effective in manipulating the vote at the local level. At the national level, the Republicans dominated the presidency from 1876 to 1884 with Rutherford B. Hayes, James Garfield, and Chester A. Arthur. During those years, conflict between those who advocated an expanded money supply and those who did not led to fights over the gold standard. The specific needs of farmers led to the formation of the Populist Party in the 1890s, which promoted affordable transportation, lower taxes, price controls, and cheap credit. The economic crash of 1893 served to strengthen the Populists, who were successful in electing several congressmen and senators. In 1896, Populism reached its crescendo as it brought its support alongside of the Democrats in nominating William Jennings Bryan to be the Democratic candidate for president. His "Cross of Gold" speech, one of the greatest political speeches in American history, electrified the convention. Despite his oratorical skills, Bryan lost the election, marking the gradual decline of the Populists. Nevertheless, they were successful in achieving some reforms, such as direct election of senators, the income tax, and an improved money and credit system.[1]

As westward expansion continued during the 1890s, Americans dominated the continent and began to compete with European nations for territories in other parts of the world. The territory of Alaska was purchased from Russia in 1867, and Hawaii became an American territory in 1898. America also showed interest in the Caribbean, Central and South America, the South Pacific, the Philippines, and China. Following the Spanish-American War in 1898, America emerged as a world power.

---

[1]Winthrop D. Jordan and Leon F. Litwack, *The United States*, 7th ed. (Englewood Cliffs, NJ: Prentice Hall, 1991) 493–94. William Jennings Bryan was an active and dedicated Presbyterian throughout his life.

The City of Raleigh at the Close of the Nineteenth Century

The Gilded Age and the Progressive Era in Raleigh, along with economic successes, brought sociological division. With the end of Reconstruction, racial tensions began to grow in the capital city. In September 1898, a race riot erupted in the city between some white soldiers stationed in Raleigh and some of the African-American population in the eastern portion of the city. Two skirmishes took place over a Saturday night and Sunday afternoon, resulting in a tense atmosphere but no significant injuries. By the beginning of the twentieth century, the joy of the freed slaves had turned into the misery of a segregated city.[2]

First Presbyterian Church of Raleigh

Eugene Daniel. During the last decade of the nineteenth century, Raleigh's First Presbyterian Church was faced once again with the need to select a new pastor. John S. Watkins had served the congregation for fourteen years and by all accounts was greatly loved and admired. With a new century on the horizon, the selection was a critical decision for the church.

Several months after the Watkins's resignation, the church called Rev. Eugene Daniel to serve as stated supply. On 25 December 1892, the church unanimously elected him to serve as its pastor.[3] Daniel was born on 25 March 1849 in Sumter County, Alabama. He received his education at Oakland College, Davidson College, and Columbia Theological Seminary.[4] Following his graduation from Columbia in 1871, he

---

[2]Ibid., 18–20. See *Farmer and Mechanic*, 3 January 1878, cited by ibid. on p. 32. Governor Zebulon B. Vance, speaking to an Emancipation Day celebration on New Year's Day 1878, expressed the white sentiment: "You cannot, of course, expect me to join with you in celebrating this day, the anniversary of that emancipation which I struggled so long to prevent, and which I, in common with almost all the people of my race in the South, regarded as an act of unconstitutional violence to the one party and as an injury to the other." See pp. 32–46 for a discussion of race relations in Raleigh and Wake County during that era.

[3]Minutes of the Session, 2 January 1893.

[4]Edgar Sutton Robinson, ed., *The Ministerial Directory: Of the Ministers in "The Presbyterian Church in the United States" (Southern), and in "The Presbyterian Church in the United States of America" (Northern), Together with a Statement of the*

was licensed to the ministry by the Harmony Presbytery in South Carolina. Also, in 1871, he married Susannah Witherspoon in Camden, South Carolina. Evidently, he moved west during 1871 because records show that he was ordained by the Ouachita Presbytery of the Cumberland Presbyterian Church and served as a pastor in Camden, Arkansas, from 1871 to 1875. From 1875 to 1893, he served as pastor of the First Presbyterian Church in Memphis, Tennessee. Following his tenure in Raleigh, he moved to Lewisburg, West Virginia, where he served from 1903 to 1910 as pastor. Following a brief return to North Carolina to serve First Presbyterian Church in Shelby, he spent ten years as a stated supply pastor in Fernandina, Florida (1912–1922). He died in Eatonton, Georgia, on 14 January 1935.[5]

During the first few months after Daniel became the church's pastor, the story of the Second Presbyterian Church finally concluded. In April 1893, the sessional records indicate that Mary Ann Towles presented a letter to the elders written by J. M. Monie, a deacon at First Presbyterian but formerly an elder at Second Presbyterian, indicating that she was a member in good standing at Second Presbyterian. She requested and was "received upon her own application there being now no officer to said church and upon the session's cognizance of her Christian standing."[6] Several more people from the defunct church also pre-

---

Work of the Executive Committees and Boards of the Two Churches, with the Names and Location of Their Educational Institutions and Church Papers (Oxford, OH: The Ministerial Directory Company, 1898) 37, http://babel.hathitrust.org/cgi/pt?id=njp.32101076517547;view=1up;seq=49. Oakland College was located near Lorman, Mississippi, about eighty miles south of Jackson. The school was originally founded in 1830 by Dr. Jeremiah Chamberlain with the support of the Mississippi Presbytery. Initially, the college saw growth. Chamberlain, however, was a Unionist and a Whig and was assassinated on the campus in 1851 by a secessionist. The school closed in 1860. Following the Civil War, the property was purchased by the state of Mississippi and is known today as Alcorn State University. See "History," Alcorn State University, accessed 11 December 2014, http://www.alcorn.edu/discover-alcorn/history/index.aspx.

[5]E. C. Scott, ed. *Ministerial Directory of the Presbyterian Church, U. S., 1861–1941* (Austin, TX: Von Boeckmann-Jones Co., 1942) 169, http://babel.hathitrust.org/cgi/pt?id=wu.89067533174;view=1up;seq=181.

[6]Minutes of the Session, 7 April 1893.

sented themselves for membership that spring.[7] In July, the session discussed the property owned by Second Presbyterian Church. Evidently, an inquiry was made to First Presbyterian to see if the church would be interested in buying the property. The elders declined the offer, saying that the issue is "one between the committee and the trustees of Albemarle Presbytery on the one hand, and the trustees holding the legal title to the said property, together with such other person or persons as may hold over equitable interest in the said property."[8] It may be recalled from the previous chapter that the First Presbyterian Session was originally opposed to the presbytery's support for the formation of Second Presbyterian Church. The elders now were in no mood to take on the problems associated with assuming control of the property.

The New Church Structure. Without a doubt, the most important event to occur during the pastorate of Eugene Daniel was the construction of a new building. By 1893, the church building, first constructed in 1818, was no longer adequate for the needs of the congregation. Evidence of this first appeared in the sessional records for 19 September 1893. During that meeting a subcommittee composed of elders S. W. Whiting, J. B. Burwell, and H. M. McPheeters submitted a written report, specifying five areas of importance related to the congregation.[9]

The first item mentioned in the report concerned the church structure. It concluded that "the most prominent fact confronting us is the insufficiency and suitableness of the church building for meeting the demands of the congregation in public worship; for supplying the conveniences required by the various boards and societies of the church and especially for providing rooms for the Sabbath School and Bible Classes and for the general development of the youth of the congregation."[10] The subcommittee believed that the "Providence of God" was leading the

---

[7]Ibid., 8 and 15 April 1893.

[8]Ibid., 3 July 1893.

[9]Ibid., 19 September 1893. For a detailed account of the history of the building process for the church's second sanctuary, see David H. Permar, "The Building of the Second Sanctuary of the First Presbyterian Church Raleigh, North Carolina, 1892–1900" (paper presented upon the ninety-fifth anniversary of the Vanguard Class, Raleigh, NC, 4 July 1999).

[10]Minutes of the Session, 19 September 1893.

congregation "to the greatest work which the church has had before it for more than half a century—that of erecting a suitable edifice for the worship of Jehovah."[11]

The second item in the report mentioned the "young men (not less than forty)" who were members of the church. The subcommittee believed that "latent possibilities of usefulness too great to be overestimated" existed within this group, "the development of which depends in large measure the future prosperity of the church."[12] The report mentioned the organizational opportunities available for the young women in the church and suggested "that the young men should be speedily called together for organized training in public prayer and in Christian work."[13]

The third item mentioned in the report related to the church's sense of mission. The subcommittee believed that whatever needs existed within the congregation "our interest in missionary work must not be destroyed but to the extent of our ability as indicated by the circumstances of the congregation at the time we must do what we can towards giving the Bread of Life to the Perishing."[14] As seen in the previous chapter, the women of the church, by this time, had two thriving organizations devoted to the promotion of both domestic and foreign missions. Furthermore, they were committed to providing for the physical needs of some of the less fortunate people within their own city. The elders were aware that a church focused only on its internal needs was unable to carry out the command of Christ to be a witness within its community and beyond.

Although the fourth item in the report is not discussed as thoroughly as the previous three, it was nevertheless important and concerns the music and worship of the congregation. The elders were "of the opinion that the time has come when the edification of the congregation will be promoted by the introductory of a hymn and tune book."[15] This matter was attended to quickly, as it was reported a few months later that the

---

[11]Ibid.
[12]Ibid.
[13]Ibid.
[14]Ibid.
[15]Ibid.

book *Hymns of the Ages* was adopted as the church hymnal.[16] Then, the following month, a "scheme for bettering the music of the church and Sabbath School" was approved by the session whereby a "competent teacher of music" was to be paid by voluntary subscriptions to teach music, twenty-four lessons in all.[17]

The final item in the report to the session involved creating opportunities for fellowship among the members. By 1893, the church had grown to 243 resident members.[18] The elders were aware that the members needed opportunities to socialize with one another. Therefore, they suggested "to the ladies of the congregation that social gatherings of the members of the church and their friends in the Lecture Room or other convenient place" be held every three months. This they believed "would conduce to mutual acquaintance and thus draw the members nearer together in public worship."[19]

Eugene Daniel became quite ill during the last three months of 1893, and although the sessional records do not specify the type of illness, it was so severe that he could not conduct worship services or his pastoral duties. An entry in the records at the end of 1893 reports that the session did not meet during the last three months of the year, "but the Elders met often together informally for consultation." In addition, worship services were held as scheduled on Sundays and Wednesdays and were led by several elders and one of the deacons. The reference concludes, "These services were far better attended than might have been expected and the congregation was held together united in a common bond of sympathy and love."[20]

By spring 1894, the pastor's health had improved. Residential membership grew to 300. The session also noted that a decision was made to hold services every Friday evening at the Mission Chapel, beginning on 11 May, and there were plans to organize a Sunday school there. Elder C. P. Wharton was elected to be superintendent of the work

[16]Ibid., 24 January 1894.
[17]Ibid., 5 February 1894.
[18]Annual Report to the Presbytery, 24 April 1893.
[19]Minutes of the Session, 19 September 1893.
[20]Ibid., n.d. 1893.

at the chapel.[21] Evidence that there were firm plans to build a new building is seen in an entry in the *News and Observer* on 22 August 1894: "The design for the new Presbyterian church to be built in this city by the congregation of Dr. Daniel is on exhibition in Mr. Bruner's office. It is the creation of our local architect, Mr. A. G. Bauer, and is a charming blending between the Eastern and Gothic styles. The lines and angles are a rest to the eye and the effect is impressive. Work will begin right away and pushed with due diligence."[22]

Further progress toward erection of a new building came the following year. On 28 August 1895, the sessional records show that "quite an amount of interest was manifested in the matter of church and Sunday school Room building improvement." The moderator reportedly gave "a quiet invitation" the previous Sunday morning for all men interested in the matter to meet the next day. At that meeting, the report adopted by the session in 1893 (mentioned above) was unanimously approved by those who had gathered. A request then was extended to the session for a congregational meeting to consider the matter the following month.[23] The congregation adopted the plan on 15 September 1895. Also at the congregational meeting, $9,000 [$258,000] was pledged toward the project, and two committees were appointed, financial and building, chaired by A. A. Thompson and Julius Lewis, respectively.[24] With the leadership of Thompson and Lewis, pledges toward the new building increased to approximately $18,000.[25]

---

[21]Annual Report to Presbytery, 16 April 1894; Minutes of the Session, 7 May 1894.

[22]*News and Observer* (Raleigh, NC), 22 August 1894, cited in Permar, "Building of the Second Sanctuary," 2. According to Permar, "Mr. Bruner" is T. K. Bruner, a church member and secretary of the North Carolina Board of Agriculture at the time.

[23]Minutes of the Session, 28 August 1895; Permar, "Building of the Second Sanctuary," 2.

[24]Permar, "Building of the Second Sanctuary," 2.

[25]William McClanahan White, *Directory and Historical Sketch of the First Presbyterian Church of Raleigh, N.C.* (Raleigh, NC: Edwards and Broughton Printing Co., 1910) 6.

At the end of the year in 1895, the session discussed matters related to the mission chapel. The elders determined that it had become "impracticable to continue work there" because it was no longer considered to be "suitable mission ground." The session decided to inform the deacons of the matter and requested that the property be sold or rented.[26] The property was sold by the following spring.[27]

The following year, 4 November 1896, the contract for the building was given to George W. Waring, a contractor from Columbia, South Carolina, for a cash payment of $20,000 [$579,000].[28] The projected cost was only for the building itself. It did not include furnishing, carpet, lighting, etc. Waring was known in the city at the time as the contractor that designed the administration building at Shaw University. In early spring 1897, the project finally commenced.[29]

If the congregation gave approval to erect a new building in 1894, why did it take until 1896 to contract with a builder? The answer can be found in the Panic of 1893, which led to an economic depression in the nation that lasted for several years. That would have impeded the congregation's confidence and ability to begin the project immediately.[30] One hint that the church may have been concerned about finances and the economy is seen in the action of the session on 12 October 1896. In that meeting, the church approved a recommendation from the deacons "with the deepest regret" and "after a long and painstaking review of the financial condition of the church" that the pastor's salary had to be reduced beginning in January 1897 from $2,000 [$57,900] per month to $1,600 [$46,400]. The action was "mutually agreed upon between the pastor and the Session," and the elders "most heartily wish that the in-

[26]Minutes of the Session, 2 December 1895.

[27]Ibid., 10 April 1896.

[28]White, *Directory and Historical Sketch*, 6.

[29]*Raleigh* (NC) *Daily Tribune*, 5 March 1897, 2.

[30]For a brief article about the Panic of 1893 and its impact, see "Panic of 1893," accessed 15 December 2014, http://www.u-s-history.com/pages/h792.html.

come of the church could be so increased as to allow us to escape so disagreeable a recommendation."[31]

There is an interesting story related to the architectural design of the building. Originally, as mentioned above, Adolphus Gustavus Bauer, a well-known Raleigh architect, was selected for the project. He was born in 1858 in Martinsburg, West Virginia, the son of German immigrants. He graduated from Bethany College in West Virginia and spent two years in Pittsburg, Pennsylvania, studying at the Iron City Business College. He subsequently enrolled at the Philadelphia Academy of Fine Arts, where he met Samuel Sloan, an architect in the city, who hired him as a draftsman. The two men moved their business south to Raleigh, where Sloan set up an office in 1884. Sloan was the chief architect for the executive mansion in Raleigh, Memorial Hall in Chapel Hill, and the Western North Carolina Hospital for the Insane in Morganton. In a private memoir, Bauer claimed to have drawn the plans for all three of these buildings.[32]

Upon the sudden death of Sloan to a stroke, Bauer took over the business in 1884. Three years later he moved to Wilmington, where he became the architect for St. Andrews Presbyterian Church among other projects. A few years later, he left Wilmington for a six-month tour of Europe. Upon his return to the United States, he worked as a draftsman in various cities, including New York, Chicago, Cincinnati, Atlanta, and Lexington (Kentucky). He finally returned to North Carolina in 1891, where he began designs for some of his more famous buildings, such as the North Carolina School for the Deaf.[33]

---

[31]Minutes of the Session, 12 October 1896. See also Minutes of the Diaconate, 21 September 1896.

[32]Biographical information on Bauer's life taken from *North Carolina Architects and Builders: A Biographical Dictionary*, s.v. "Bauer, Adolphus Gustavus (1858–1898)," accessed 15 December 2014, http://ncarchitects.lib.ncsu.edu/people/P000040. For a thorough analysis of his life and work, see William B Bushong, "A. G. Bauer, North Carolina's New South Architect," *North Carolina Historical Review* 60/3 (July 1983): 304–332.

[33]*North Carolina Architects and Builders: A Biographical Dictionary*, s.v. "Bauer, Adolphus Gustavus (1858–1898)."

In 1891, Bauer met and fell in love with Rachel Blythe, the daughter of a Cherokee Indian mother and a white father. Blythe had been raised in the Oxford Orphanage and came to Raleigh in 1890, where she became a teacher at the Raleigh Business College of Stenography and Typing. The couple was secretly married because at the time North Carolina law forbade intermarriage between whites and Native Americans. A few years later, Rachel became pregnant so they traveled to Washington, D.C., and were married in a public ceremony in June 1895. Rachel gave birth to their daughter Owenah on 17 October 1895. She became pregnant with their second child the following spring.[34]

Life for the family took a tragic turn on 2 May 1896. Bauer was riding in Durham in an open carriage with Charles Norton, en route to a building site when their carriage was struck by a passenger train. Both men suffered critical injuries. Bauer suffered head injuries and required recuperation at the North Carolina Hospital for the Insane (Dorothea Dix Hospital). Even after his release, he suffered from bouts of dizziness and was unable to concentrate for long periods of time. This had a detrimental effect on his work, and he soon developed the reputation for being unable to fulfill his responsibilities. In July 1896 in a letter to his sister, he wrote,

> Last May, when the accident occurred, it seemed to me I was going to do a better years business than ever. I had a great many orders on hand, but when people read from the papers that I was dying, or if I did not die, I would never be able to do work again, they all went to other Architects, and so when I got well enough to get out and try to do work, there was nothing to do but a couple of jobs. If I had them on hand, however, I [would] not feel competent or able to attend to them.[35]

To make matters worse, Rachel gave birth to their second child on 27 December 1896 but died from complications of childbirth on 9 January 1897. She had been ill for much of the fall before the child's birth, no doubt weakened from caring for both Bauer and their infant born the previous year. Rachel's death proved to be a terrible blow to Bauer. He

---

[34]Ibid.; Permar, "Building of the Second Sanctuary," 11.

[35]*North Carolina Architects and Builders: A Biographical Dictionary*, s.v. "Bauer, Adolphus Gustavus (1858–1898)."

was forced to send his two children to live with relatives. He settled a suit against the railroad company for the accident and with the money constructed a remarkable marker for Rachel's grave in Oakwood Cemetery. A year later, having finally completed all of his projects, on 11 May 1898, alone in his room, Bauer died from a self-inflicted gunshot wound.[36]

Given the tragic events in Bauer's life, it is understandable that the church turned to another architect Charles E. Cassell to design the building. A contemporary account indicated that Cassell designed the building but Raleigh architect Charles Pearson was the "supervising architect." How much influence from Bauer remained in the work of Cassell is difficult to determine.[37]

By early 1897, the project was ready to commence. The building committee included Julius Lewis (president), George Allen (secretary and treasurer), W. S. Primrose, J. M. Moore, C. P. Wharton, Dr. J. H. Crawford, and Professor D. H. Hill.[38] The project was divided into two phases. The first phase was to complete a new Sunday school space. Once that phase was completed, the worship services would be held in that space until the main sanctuary was completed. In January 1897, Julius Lewis and George Allen headed up an effort to prepare the Sunday school building to be demolished by transferring the furniture to the sanctuary portion of the campus.[39] The first phase of the project was completed a year later, and the new Sunday school building was occupied on 26 January 1898.[40] The cost of that phase of the building project was close to $10,000 [$290,000] and was completed with no debt.[41]

---

[36]Ibid.; Permar, "Building of the Second Sanctuary," 11–12.

[37]*Raleigh Daily Tribune*, 5 March 1897, 2. For a comparison of the architectural styles of the two architects, see *North Carolina Architects and Builders: A Biographical Dictionary*, s.v. "Bauer, Adolphus Gustavus (1858–1898)" and *North Carolina Architects and Builders: A Biographical Dictionary*, s.v. "Cassell, Charles E. (1838–1916)," accessed 16 December 2014, http://ncarchitects.lib.ncsu.edu/people/P000042.

[38]*Raleigh Daily Tribune*, 5 March 1897, 2.

[39]Minutes of the Session, 4 January 1897.

[40]*The Raleigh* (NC) *Times*, 27 January 1898, 3; Permar, "Building of the Second Sanctuary," 4.

[41]*The Press-Visitor* (Raleigh, NC), 21 April 1898, 1.

By June, the congregation was in the process of financial planning for the second phase of the project, the new sanctuary.[42] By spring 1899, the old sanctuary had been demolished, and discussions occurred about laying the cornerstone of the new building.[43] In the meantime, the membership continued to grow. The annual report to the presbytery in 1898 indicated a total membership of 378. The enrollment number increased to 391 the following year.[44]

The cornerstone for the new building was laid on 28 June 1899 with full Masonic rites, and the ceremony was held with a large number of people present. The cornerstone included a copper box containing the following items of historical interest to the church:

- a list of names of the pastor, officers, and members of the church
- the names of the superintendent, officers, teachers, and students listed by classes in the Sunday school
- a statistical statement of the church and Sunday school, which had been submitted to Albemarle Presbytery
- a financial statement of the church for the year ending 31 March 1899
- a copy of the *Westminster Catechism*
- a photograph of the first church structure, which sat on the property originally built in 1818
- a photograph of the Sunday school room built in 1825
- a list of the officers and members of the Ladies Home and Foreign Missionary Societies
- names of members of the senior and junior divisions of the Busy Bee Band
- a list of the officers and members of the Ladies Aid Society

---

[42]*The Raleigh Times*, 27 June 1898, 1. The article here indicates that a joint meeting with the building and finance Committees had been planned for the evening of 27 June 1898.

[43]Minutes of the Session, 8 June 1899.

[44]Annual Report to Presbytery 1898 and 1899, in Minutes of the Session, 4 April 1898 and 3 April 1899.

- historical sketch of the Ladies Aid Society written by the president, Mrs. E. E. Moffitt
- a list of the officers and members of the Young Ladies Aid Society
- a list of the officers and members of the Junior Presbyterians
- a list of the members of the Westminster League of the church
- a list of the members of the building and finance committees for the new building
- a list of names that formed the committee that planned the cornerstone laying ceremony
- a list of the Masonic officers participating in the ceremony
- a list of the members of the Raleigh Chamber of Commerce
- a silver dollar contributed by George C. Jordan, the first gift received for the new building project and a matching gift of another silver dollar given by Chester G. Whiting, a deacon at First Presbyterian Church
- a collection of various newspapers, pamphlets, as well as Presbyterian and other Christian denominational papers[45]

Following the laying of the cornerstone, construction on the sanctuary continued, and the work was completed in July 1900, five years after the first pledges were solicited toward the project. The main sanctuary had seating for 600, which could increase to 750 when moveable_chairs were utilized. The Sunday school area seated 400. The church had a new organ and furnishings as well. Total cost for the entire project was approximately $36,500 [$1,040,000].[46]

The congregation occupied the new sanctuary in September 1900. The accomplishment represented a high point in the church's history as it closed out the nineteenth century. Earlier that spring, the session reported to the Albemarle Presbytery a total membership of 454 members (414 resident, forty non-resident).[47] A three-day celebration during the

[45]*The Morning Post* (Raleigh, NC), 29 June 1899, 6.

[46]White, *Directory and Historical Sketch*, 7.

[47]Annual Report to Presbytery included in Minutes of the Session, 9 April 1900. Also contained in the entry in the sessional records for this date is a refer-

weekend of 14–16 September marked this historic moment in the church's history. On Friday evening of that week, William McPheeters, grandson of the church's first pastor, delivered the sermon during a special worship service. The following evening, John S. Watkins, pastor of the church from 1878 to 1892, delivered the sermon in another special worship service. On the following morning, "the people by the hundreds" came to the dedication service, which also included representation from "every congregation from every denomination in the city."[48] Pastors from the other churches in the city attended and delivered brief words of congratulations. Dr. Walter W. Moore of Union Theological Seminary in Richmond, Virginia, preached the sermon, prompting one witness to write that "an abler, more eloquent discourse has seldom been heard in Raleigh."[49] Following the sermon, A. A. Thompson, chairman of the finance committee, reported that the church had borrowed $7,000 [$200,000] in order to complete the project and as of the time of the dedication celebration, $3,000 [$85,900] of debt still remained. A special offering was collected during the service, which garnered $1,500, cutting the debt in half. In 1907, the church's debt was completely paid off.[50] Dave Permar concludes that a portion of the Devereux property had been leased in 1900 for ninety-nine years and the proceeds from that transaction were applied to the remaining debt.[51] A communion service was held on Sunday afternoon, and the celebration weekend concluded with a

---

ence to seven memorial windows that were purchased for the new sanctuary. The entry reads, "One each for Judge Edwin G. Reade and his wife, placed by Mr. John W. Hardee; One each for Judge W. N. H. Smith and his wife by their children, Mr. E. C. and Mr. W. W. Smith and by arrangement of Mrs. M. O. Smith while in her last sickness; one for Professor Albrecht Baumann by a fund in hands of Mrs. Addie Daniels and Miss Fannie McPheeters; and one to the memory of Rev. Robert Burwell, D. D. by his children. A large memorial window is also being prepared to the memory of Dr. William McPheeters by his children." The large window given by the McPheeters children is the large Tiffany window at the center and back of the current sanctuary.

[48]*News and Observer*, 18 September 1900, 5.

[49]Ibid.

[50]Annual Report to Presbytery included in Minutes of the Session, 12 April 1907.

[51]Ibid., and Permar, "Building of the Second Sanctuary," 7.

service on Sunday evening, during which Dr. Watkins preached a second sermon.

One final thing about the construction of the new building needs recognition. Permar points out that the church faces neither Morgan nor Salisbury Streets. Instead, the sanctuary opens directly to the corner, "facing the Capitol, acknowledging the role of Presbyterianism in the history of State government in North Carolina."[52] Permar recounts that the North Carolina Supreme Court met in the Session Room of First Presbyterian Church in 1831 after fire destroyed the old statehouse. In 1835, the North Carolina Constitutional Convention met in the church's sanctuary. And, the church boasts a long list of governors, state and national legislators, and judges and justices who have been members of the church. The very design of the building symbolizes the long tradition of cooperation between First Presbyterian and the state government.

Alfred Harrison Moment. First Presbyterian Church opened the twentieth century with strength. A new building project was completed. By April 1902, the membership had grown to 456 members (402 resident, fifty-four non-resident).[53] When Daniel's tenure as pastor began in 1893, the church had a total membership of only 326 (243 resident, 83 non-resident).[54] In autumn 1902, Daniel offered his resignation in order to accept a call to a church in Lewisburg, West Virginia.[55] The church immediately began the process of seeking a new pastor.

Initially, the church extended a unanimous call to Rev. W. E. Cave of Paducah, Kentucky, and 4 January 1903 was to be his first Sunday as pastor.[56] Cave, however, experienced a few personal misfortunes just before his move to Raleigh. In late January 1903, the session, on behalf of

---

[52]Permar, "Building of the Second Sanctuary," 14.

[53]Annual Report to Presbytery included in Minutes of the Session, 10 April 1902.

[54]Ibid., 24 April 1893.

[55]Minutes of the Session, 15 September 1902.

[56]Ibid., n.d. 1902. (This undated entry falls between October 1902 and January 1903).

the church, expressed sympathy upon the death of Cave's wife.[57] Also at that meeting, the session granted Cave an indefinite leave of absence because he was "suffering from nervous trouble."[58]

The following month, the sessional records report that Rev. Alfred Harrison Moment was temporarily filling the pulpit in the absence of Cave.[59] Cave did eventually travel to Raleigh. However, his stay was not very long at all. In February 1904, the *News and Observer* reported that he had arrived in the city and preached at the church. The article, however, mentioned that his permanent move to the city had been delayed, not only because of his wife's illness but also because of an "illness in the family." It reported that he planned to return to Kentucky after a stay of only a few days in the city and that he would resume his pastoral duties later.[60] By late spring, Cave was still in Kentucky and unable to move to Raleigh.[61] Finally, in January 1904, a local newspaper reported that Cave and his children were expected to arrive in Raleigh the following week.[62] Upon his arrival on 15 January, the local news reported that his delay was due both to his wife's death and his own illness.[63] The only hint to the type of illness that he suffered came in a cryptic statement in the newspaper account: "He says that he has not yet fully recovered from his sickness and that his nervous system is out of order."[64] But the following week, it was reported that Cave was going to Philadelphia for a consultation with a specialist about his condition. Once again, his illness was not identified.[65] On 12 February 1904, the session read a telegram from Cave, who was referenced as "pastor elect of the church." It stated that

[57]Ibid., 25 January 1903. "It was decided to officially convey to our pastor elect by letter our expression of the deep sympathy of the church and Session with him in the heavy bereavement he has sustained by the death of his wife."

[58]Ibid.

[59]Ibid., 27 February 1903.

[60]*News and Observer*, 22 February 1903, 2.

[61]Ibid., 12 May 1903, 8.

[62]*The Morning Post*, 8 January 1904, 8.

[63]Ibid., 16 January 1904, 2.

[64]*News and Observer*, 19 January 1904, 5.

[65]*The Morning Post*, 26 January 1904, 6.

his illness required him to resign his call from the church as its pastor.[66] Alfred Moment had filled the pulpit throughout the year as the church anticipated Cave's arrival. When it became apparent that Cave would be unable to serve, the church turned to Moment and extended a call in March 1904.[67]

Alfred Moment was born on 22 January 1844 in Clarke, Ontario, Canada. He came to the faith at age twenty-one, making confession of his faith in the Presbyterian church in Newtonville, Canada. He graduated from Hanover College in Indiana in 1872 and entered Princeton Theological Seminary a few months later. He attended seminary for one year, then spent a year preaching in Maine. He returned to Princeton the following year and graduated in 1876. He was licensed by the Presbytery of New Brunswick on 25 April 1876 and was then ordained by the Presbytery of New York on 9 July 1876. Following ordination, he was installed as the pastor of the Spring Street Presbyterian Church in New York City, a position he held until 1884. For a year he served the Seventy-seventh Street Presbyterian Church in New York, followed by a nine-year pastorate at the Westminster Presbyterian Church in Brooklyn. In 1894, he left for a trip abroad, which lasted for two years. When he returned, he spent several years doing editorial work for several Presbyterian publications until finally moving to Raleigh in 1903. He received the honorary DD degree from both Hanover College and Lennox College in Iowa in 1886. He was married twice. The first marriage to Magdalena Wurst lasted for a little more than a year until her death on 11 July 1880. His second marriage was to Julia Wilson, who died in 1885, leaving him with one daughter. Moment spent only three and a half years as pastor of First Presbyterian Church in Raleigh, succumbing to typhoid fever on 5 October 1907.[68]

---

[66]Minutes of the Session, 12 February 1904.

[67]Ibid., 3 April 1904. Cave's resignation was accepted by the congregation on 28 February. The call was extended to Moment on 6 March, and he accepted the call the following week.

[68]Joseph H. Dulles, ed. *Necrological Report Presented to the Alumni Association of Princeton Theological Seminary at its Annual Meeting May 8th, 1900* (Princeton: C. S. Robinson and Co., 1900) 554–55.

During Alfred Moment's short tenure at the church, several important things happened. First, the Sunday school experienced tremendous growth. In April 1904, the session's annual report to the Albemarle Presbytery listed 324 students in the Sunday school with twenty-six teachers.[69] In the spring before his death in 1907, the Sunday school grew to 464 students with thirty-five teachers.[70] Although the records do not give a reason for the explosion in growth, no doubt the new facilities designed specifically for the Sunday school contributed. Furthermore, Moment was an excellent teacher of the Bible and taught a men's Sunday school class, posthumously named after him, which existed for more than fifty years after his death.[71] The Alfred H. Moment Class was organized under that name on 4 July 1909 although the class itself had existed as the Men's Bible Class for several decades before. One account indicates that Moment's "learning, and great knowledge of both the Bible itself, and the Bible lands, combined with a charming and attractive personality, at once brought the class to a hitherto unknown prominence, and attracted many of the leading men in the church to join it."[72]

A second important development during Moment's short tenure involved the reorganization of the women's missionary programs. In November 1904, the Ladies Society for Christian Work was organized, bringing the various missions auxiliaries all under one umbrella. Prior to this action, the women of the church had both foreign and home missions organizations, as well as the Busy Bee Band, which was composed of the children of the church and originally organized in 1877.

Alfred Moment provided the suggestion for the new organization. The Ladies Society for Christian Work was divided into three "departments," each of which had a particular outreach focus. The Foreign Mission Department gave attention to Presbyterian missions outside of the United States. The Home Mission Department devoted attention to

[69]Annual Report to Presbytery included in the Minutes of the Session, 17 April 1904.

[70]Ibid., 12 April 1907.

[71]The information about Moment's teaching ability was taken from an unpublished biographical account with no author listed. It is found in the church's archives.

[72]White, *Directory and Historical Sketch*, 15.

mission endeavors within the United States. Finally, the Local Department concerned itself with outreach within the city of Raleigh. Mrs. W. S. Primrose, longtime advocate for mission action and education at First Presbyterian Church, was elected president of the organization with Mrs. L. P. Duncan as secretary, Mrs. B. R. Lacy as treasurer, and Mrs. J. W. Scott as assistant treasurer. Each department also had its own officers.[73]

The organization met monthly. One of the three departments had responsibility for the program each month thereby ensuring that all of the women would become aware of Presbyterian efforts in missions globally, domestically, and locally. Following the program each month, each of the three departments conducted its own monthly meeting. A typical example of a monthly meeting can be seen from the record of the March 1905 gathering. The Foreign Mission Department had responsibility for the program that day. It presented a report on the names and locations of missionaries from the Southern Presbyterian Church around the world. Finally, the society was hosted by "four young ladies from Japan who dispensed Japanese hospitality" with a reception and who also shared articles about Japanese culture. There is no indication as to who these young Japanese women were or why they were in the city of Raleigh at the time.[74]

In November 1905, a Presbyterian missionary from China, Rev. W. F. Jenkins, who was in the city of Raleigh at the time, was the guest speaker. This meeting was held on Sunday afternoon rather than on Monday (the typical meeting time). There is also a notation in the minutes that the women from the other churches in the city were invited to hear Jenkins speak.[75] In February 1906, the Foreign Mission Department had the program responsibility again and invited Mrs. H. B. Price, a missionary from Japan who happened to be in the city visiting relatives, to be the guest speaker. Again, women from other churches were invited to attend. As was also typical at the meetings, following the program and business portion of the agenda, the women moved to the church parlor for a reception. On this particular occasion, the minutes indicate that the "women retired to the parlor which had been made very attractive with

[73]Minutes of the Ladies Society for Christian Work, 3 November 1904.
[74]Ibid., n.d., March 1905.
[75]Ibid., n.d., November 1905.

shaded lights and beautiful flowers and tables set with glittering…and dainty china."[76]

In the previous chapter, the suggestion was made that the women's organizations at First Presbyterian Church signified a growing presence of women in leadership and influence in the church in the late nineteenth century. Further evidence of this could be seen in the minutes from the society's meeting in April 1906. At that meeting, "Mrs. Moffitt suggested the advisability of the ladies taking up the matter of the church trying to purchase the property on the other side of the church building. She thought this ought to be done and advised appointing a committee to confer with the officers of the church."[77] Mrs. Moffitt's motion was well received with the result that she was appointed chair of the committee she suggested. The session took up the matter later in the month and made plans to approach the owner of the property to see if he would be willing to sell.[78] It is unclear whether the women initiated interest among the elders in the property or if the idea had already been discussed among others in the church and the women were just expressing their wish to pursue the matter. Either way, it is significant that the women wanted to express their opinion to the elders about the matter.

The organization of the Vanguard Sunday school class represents another significant event that occurred during the short tenure of Alfred Moment's pastorate. The founder of the class was Edmund Burwell Crow, born in 1874 and the grandson of Robert Burwell, the first president of William Peace University. Crow worked his entire career as a successful banker with the Commercial National Bank. He was also active in civic affairs, being involved with the organization of the Rotary Club of Raleigh in 1914, the first civic club in North Carolina. Crow served as the primary teacher of the Vanguard class from its beginning in 1904 until 1932.[79]

---

[76]Ibid., n.d., February 1906.

[77]Ibid., n.d., April 1906.

[78]Minutes of the Session, 25 April 1906.

[79]David H. Permar, "History of the Vanguard Class of Raleigh," (n.p., 2004) 1–2. A copy of this short unpublished history is located in the church archives.

The roots of the Vanguard class can be traced back to six young men who graduated from the Primary Department in the First Presbyterian Church Sunday school. Crow, then only seventeen years old, organized them into a class in 1892. Three years later, when Crow's mother, Nannie Burwell Crow, died, the class of six students that she taught was blended into Crow's class. By 1904, most of these young men were high school graduates. On 3 July 1904, the class formally organized into the Vanguard Class, a name suggested by Alfred Moment. David I. Fort was elected the first president of the class with Louis D. Womble, Jr. as secretary and Carey K. Durfey as treasurer.[80]

The Vanguard Class became an institution within the church. In its early days, it provided social opportunities for the young men who were members. For example, within just a few weeks of its organization, a "Moonlight Picnic" was held at Milburnie on 21 July 1904. A voluntary collection was taken to cover the expenses of the evening. If a boy wanted to invite a girl to accompany him, plans were made for that: "Agreed…that all the boys would suggest at the meeting the following Sunday the girl that they would like to invite and a list of those be made out and given to the chaperone and let them invite the girls, and ask them to bring a small lunch."[81]

Throughout the twentieth century the class provided men of the church with opportunities for Bible study, service, and fellowship. The Vanguard Class continues to be a strong presence at First Presbyterian Church.

A final important event that occurred during Alfred Moment's pastorate was the purchase of the Peace Institute by the Presbyterians. First Presbyterian Church led the way in this endeavor. In 1907, the health of the president of Peace, James Dinwiddie, was failing. He had been at the helm of the school since 1890. The sessional records from 20 February 1907 report that Dinwiddie wanted to sell the school's stock and property for $50,000 [$1,280,000] in order to keep it in Presbyterian hands.[82]

---

[80]Ibid., 2.

[81]Ibid., 3, quoting from the records of the Vanguard Sunday school Class.

[82]Minutes of the Session, 20 February 1907.

The session formed a committee, which reported back on 12 April 1907, and the action was deferred to a future date.[83]

Dinwiddie, an elder at First Presbyterian Church, had a remarkable life as an educator. He was born on 29 June 1837 in Campbell County, Virginia. He was educated at Hampden-Sydney College and the University of Virginia, earning the MA degree in 1861. He served as an officer in the Confederate army during the Civil War.[84] Following the war, he served as principal of Sayre Institute in Kentucky for one year and then became professor of mathematics at Southwestern Presbyterian University in Clarksville, Tennessee, for ten years. He followed that with a five-year stint as professor of mathematics at the University of Tennessee. In 1885, he purchased the Central Female Institute in Gordonsville, Virginia, and ran the institution until 1890, when he came to Raleigh to take over the leadership of Peace Institute. During his seventeen-year tenure at Peace, he purchased most of the school's stock and became the owner of the school and the property. His leadership was pivotal, helping the school to transition from a preparatory institute into a college-level institution.[85]

Following Dinwiddie's presentation to the session in February, the Albemarle Presbytery eventually took up the matter upon the suggestion and prompting of First Presbyterian Church. The Presbytery met that year in Goldsboro. Governor Robert Brodnax Glenn, himself a North Carolina Presbyterian, attended the meeting to provide encouragement for the presbytery to purchase the school.[86] In a twenty-five minute speech to an audience "crowded to its utmost capacity," Glenn said, "Every moment of my time is occupied, but nothing has ever appealed to me more than the subject with which I now present."[87] He indicated that Peace Institute could be purchased for $45,000 [$1,150,000] whereas its actual value was $100,000 [$2,560,000]. Following the governor's

---

[83]Ibid., 12 April 1907.

[84]*NCpedia*, s.v. "Dinwiddie, James," accessed 24 December 2014, http://ncpedia.org/biography/dinwiddie-james.

[85]Ibid. For more information about the Dinwiddie years at Peace, see Sidney Ann Wilson, *Personae: The History of Peace College*, (n.p., 1972) 21–31.

[86]*News and Observer*, 24 April 1907, 4.

[87]Ibid., 25 April 1907, 5.

speech, the Presbytery gave unanimous approval for the purchase on behalf of the North Carolina Synod. The resolution stated,

> Whereas a committee of the First Church of Raleigh has, for the Presbyterian Church of North Carolina, purchased Peace Institute for the sum of $45,000, and
>
> Whereas, eighteen thousand dollars have been pledged, thereby leaving a balance, therefore be it
>
> Resolved, first, that this Presbytery endorse the purchase of Peace Institute by said committee.
>
> Second, that a committee of three members of the Presbytery be appointed to co-operate with the aforesaid committee in raising the necessary amount of money for the full payment of Peace Institute,
>
> Third, it is recommended that the Pastors and Sessions urge their congregations to take part in this praise-worthy work of securing Peace Institute.[88]

The plan for Peace provided that each presbytery in the state of North Carolina would have a direct interest in the school, an arrangement identical at the time to that of Davidson College. Each presbytery would elect two trustees to form a board for the purpose of governing the school.[89] The plan ensured that Peace would remain in Presbyterian control, a fulfillment of Dinwiddie's wish.

Unfortunately, Dinwiddie did not live very long after the action of the Albemarle Presbytery. During the summer, he developed "bronchial trouble" and hoped that a trip to visit his son in San Francisco might bring improvement. He died on 2 July 1907. His body was returned to Raleigh, and he was buried at Oakwood Cemetery nine days later.[90]

The death of James Dinwiddie was a blow to the congregation of First Presbyterian Church. But the death of Alfred Moment to illness was the worst loss of the year. Moment became ill in August 1907 with typhoid fever and died on 5 October. In a memorial recorded in the sessional records, the elders expressed the deep sense of loss felt by the congregation: "He loved his people with a strong devotion, and his people

---

[88]Ibid., 26 April 1907, p. 1.

[89]*The Raleigh Times*, 27 April 1907, 2.

[90]*The North Carolinian* (Raleigh, NC), 11 July 1907, 2.

loved him too. His last thoughts were for them; and his last prayer, uttered with great clearness and fervor, filled with thankfulness and love...shortly before his death, was in their behalf." The memorial continued, "We scarcely realize how much we need each other until one of our beloved number is promoted to higher usefulness and joys. It is good to have had in our midst so sweet a Christian character as Dr. Moment, and sad indeed to have them taken from us."[91]

It is noteworthy that in a little more than four years of ministry, Moment made such a lasting impact on the congregation of the First Presbyterian Church that, a few weeks after his death, the Sunday school class that he taught on a regular basis requested from the elders that it be allowed to place a memorial tablet to his memory in the back of the church. The tablet remains there presently.[92] As mentioned above, on 4 July 1909, the class was reorganized under the name "Alfred H. Moment Class."[93]

The period from 1893 to 1907 was eventful for First Presbyterian Church. The coming decades would force the church to deal with national issues and problems the likes of which had not been seen since the 1860s. Strong, steady pastoral leadership, along with effective lay leadership, was required to help the church navigate those turbulent times.

---

[91]"Memorial" (unpublished document, n.d.), contained in Minutes of the Session, 23 October 1907.

[92]Minutes of the Session, 28 October 1907.

[93]White, *Directory and Historical Sketch*, 15.

7

Growing into a New Century

The Context

Americans had every reason to be optimistic as the twentieth century dawned. The horrors of the Civil War and the challenges of Reconstruction were by then decades in the past. The Industrial Revolution and a seemingly unlimited supply of natural resources made the nation the richest on earth as American wealth almost doubled in the decade between 1890 and 1900. The natural resources of the nation, as well as its technology, were being exported around the world by the beginning of the new century.[1] The average American in 1900, looking ahead to the new century, could not have imagined the changes that would come in the next three decades. The twelve-second flight piloted by Orville Wright at Kitty Hawk, North Carolina, in 1903 began an aviation revolution, and within three decades, planes were crossing the Atlantic Ocean. Henry Ford's Model T and assembly line production of automobiles soon made the horse and buggy obsolete. Trolley cars made mass transit in cities much simpler. Electricity reached many rural areas by the 1930s. America was becoming "modernized."

The nation's optimistic spirit was evident in its newly elected president in 1900 William McKinley, who said, "I can no longer be called the President of a party. I am now the President of the whole people."[2] A year later, on 6 September 1901, McKinley's assassination brought the nation back to reality. There were still large problems that needed serious attention. Industrialism had produced a rich nation, but Americans were not equally wealthy. One percent of the population controlled 40 percent of the wealth. Blacks, women, and immigrants were still far from being treated as equal to white men. Unchecked capitalism created monopolies

---

[1]Winthrop D. Jordan and Leon F. Litwack, *The United States*, 7th ed. (Englewood Cliffs, NJ: Prentice Hall, 1991) 569.

[2]Quoted in ibid.

and corporations, which vanquished all competition. Crime and misery festered in the large urban centers. The American worker, for all of his efforts, had still not achieved the "American Dream."[3]

Great social changes also occurred in the first three decades of the new century. The Sixteenth and Seventeenth amendments to the Constitution were ratified by the states in 1913, creating the federal income tax and the direct election of senators, respectively. The Eighteenth Amendment, ratified in 1919, finally brought the era of Prohibition, of which organizations such as the Anti-Saloon League and the Women's Christian Temperance Union had dreamed for decades. Most significantly, the Nineteenth Amendment, guaranteeing women's suffrage, was ratified in 1920.

During the decade dubbed the "Roaring Twenties," Americans celebrated the new economic prosperity and security of the times in spite of Prohibition. Yet the celebratory mood came to an abrupt halt on 29 October 1929 with the crash of the stock market. Following the crash, the nation plunged into its worst economic depression. The nation elected Franklin Delano Roosevelt in 1932, and the following year Prohibition was repealed by the Twentieth Amendment to the Constitution. Roosevelt's New Deal helped to foster economic recovery as Americans gradually returned to work.

Christians in America, especially Protestants, experienced change in the first three decades of the twentieth century as well. In 1906, William J. Seymour, an evangelist and thirty-four-year-old son of former slaves, began a revival in a small mission on Azuza Street in Los Angeles, California, giving rise to the Pentecostal tradition—arguably the most important Christian movement of the twentieth century.[4] The Edinburgh Conference of 1910, originally intended as an effort to bring various Christian denominations together for interdenominational missionary support, led to the creation of the ecumenical movement. (The idea of finding common ground among all Christians still occupies the thoughts

---

[3]Ibid., 570.

[4]See Grant Wacker, *Heaven Below: Early Pentecostals and American Culture* (Boston: Harvard University Press, 2001) for the definitive history of that important movement.

of many theologians and ministers today.) Fundamentalism developed as a conservative reaction to the rise of critical methodology in biblical studies, as well as to the optimism of nineteenth-century liberalism. Fundamentalism made its way into the mainstream of American culture, and the nation found itself engrossed in a trial of a high school teacher in Dayton, Tennessee, who broke Tennessee law by teaching the theory of evolution in his biology class. The "Scopes Monkey Trial," as it was dubbed, pitted the great agnostic ACLU attorney Clarence Darrow against guest prosecutor William Jennings Bryan. Darrow's surprise move of calling Bryan to the stand as a witness humiliated Bryan (who died of a stroke later that week in Dayton), but more importantly it shed light on the reactionary literalism of the fundamentalists, forcing the movement to lose popularity for decades.[5]

The City of Raleigh and the Road to Growth and Development

Advances in technology made life easier for citizens of Raleigh in the first three decades of the twentieth century. By 1900, the telegraph had given way to the telephone. In 1907, there were seven small telephone companies serving Wake County, including three in Raleigh. During that year, Southern Bell, Wake's largest phone company, merged with Inter-state Telephone and Telegraph, creating a new company called Capital City Telephone Company. The name changed five years later to Southern Bell Telephone Company.[6] As a further sign of development, the railroad and streetcars were joined by a new form of transportation by 1900. Within the first three decades of the twentieth century the automobile became the preferred means of transportation in Raleigh. The popularity of the car necessitated good roads, so in 1903,

---

[5]See Ray Ginger, *Six Days or Forever: Tennessee v. John Thomas Scopes* (New York: Oxford University Press, 1988) for a good presentation of the trial and the circus atmosphere that came to Dayton that year. See George M. Marsden, *Fundamentalism and American Culture: The Shaping of Twentieth-century Evangelicalism 1870–1925* (New York: Oxford University Press, 1980) for a classic interpretation of fundamentalism.

[6]K. Todd Johnson and Elizabeth Reid Murray, *Reconstruction to 1920*, vol. 2 of *Wake: Capital County of North Carolina* (Raleigh: Wake County, 2008) 521–22.

Wake County implemented a tax to provide funding for better roads. Four years later, H. G. Holding, the county road superintendent, recommended that the county replace all wooden bridges with steel.[7] Raleigh resident Fred A. Olds caught the spirit of the transportation revolution on New Year's Eve 1912 when he said, "The first concrete road in the South has been built, as an object lesson, and there has become set in the minds of all thinking men a high purpose to take Raleigh's streets out of the mud and make them what they ought to be, and Raleigh men are joining with those outside to end forever the reproach of bad roads in Wake."[8]

First Presbyterian Church of Raleigh

William McClanahan White. The death of Alfred Moment in 1907 once more created a need for a new pastor. The church thrived during the last quarter of the nineteenth century and entered the twentieth century with strength. The annual report to the Albemarle Presbytery that year indicated a membership of 424 with 464 registered as members of the Sunday school. Most importantly, the report included this sentence: "During the past year the entire balance of the indebtedness of our church building has been cancelled. This has been done at a sacrifice to many, but done most cheerfully."[9] The growth in membership, Sunday school participation, and finances in such a prominently located capital city church provided an attractive possibility for a new pastor. It did not take the congregation long to settle on a pastor from Virginia, who proved to be a perfect match for the church.

On Sunday, 23 February 1908, the church extended a unanimous call to Rev. William McClanahan White from Petersburg, Virginia.[10] White was born on 20 June 1861 in Glade Springs, Virginia, to H. M.

---

[7]Ibid., 231–41.

[8]*The Raleigh* (NC) *Times*, 1 January 1913, n.p.; Olivia Raney Library Scrapbook, 176, as cited by Johnson and Murray, *Reconstruction to 1920*, 241.

[9]Annual Report to the Albemarle Presbytery contained in Minutes of the Session, 12 April 1907.

[10]White's middle name "McClanahan" in church records, as well as in the local Raleigh newspapers, is usually abbreviated as "McC."

and Blanche McClanahan White. His father was also a Presbyterian minister and well known in Virginia Presbyterian circles. He attended college at Washington and Lee University and following his graduation, taught for three years at Fishburne Military School in Waynesville, Virginia. He followed a call to ministry and enrolled at Union Theological Seminary in Richmond, where he graduated in 1893. The year before his graduation from seminary, he married Susie Lorentz from Christiansburg, Virginia. White's ministerial pathway from seminary to First Presbyterian Church in Raleigh began with Mizpah Presbyterian Church in Richmond. From there he served the Old Stone Presbyterian Church in Lewisburg, West Virginia, and then Second Presbyterian Church in Petersburg, where he served for five years before the call to Raleigh.[11]

Gaining and Losing Prominent Members. During the early years of White's pastorate, the church gained a prominent member and lost a longtime, faithful member. Robert Brodnax Glenn was a well-known name in North Carolina politics at the beginning of the twentieth century. He was born on 11 August 1854 in Rockingham County, North Carolina, to a tobacco planter and lawyer, Chalmers L. Glenn, and his wife, Annie S. Dodge Glenn. His father died at the Battle of South Mountain, Maryland, in 1862 while serving in the 13th North Carolina Regiment in the Civil War.[12]

Glenn enrolled at Davidson College in 1871 and studied there for three years. He moved to the University of Virginia, where he took a preparatory law course for one year and then enrolled in Judge Richmond Pearson's law school in Richmond Hill, North Carolina. In 1877, he was admitted to the bar in Rockingham County. He had a distinguished law career for a few years serving as general counsel for Western Union Telegraph Company and for Southern Railway. His political career began in 1880 when he was elected to the state legislature from Stokes County. He served as one of the Democratic presidential electors from North Carolina in both 1884 and 1892. President Grover Cleveland appointed him as the U. S. attorney for the western district of North Carolina from

---

[11]*News and Observer* (Raleigh, NC), 23 February 1934, 1–2.

[12]*NCPedia*, s.v. "Glenn, Robert Brodnax," accessed 12 May 12, 2015, http://ncpedia.org/print/6057.

1893 to 1897. In the midterm elections of 1898, Glenn was one of the proponents for the Democratic efforts in North Carolina to regain white supremacy in the state's political arena. The next year, Forsyth County elected him as its state senator.[13]

In 1904, Glenn was elected to serve as governor of North Carolina and served in the office until 1909. During this time, among other accomplishments, he was most noted for becoming the state's "prohibition governor."[14] Glenn was a faithful Presbyterian and was a strong advocate of prohibition. In 1908, North Carolina voted for prohibition largely due to the political efforts of Glenn.[15]

When he moved to Raleigh to assume office as governor, Glenn and his family joined First Presbyterian Church. He became active in the congregation and was ordained an elder on 31 May 1908. Glenn's ordination as an elder marked the first time in North Carolina history that a sitting governor had been ordained to such a role.[16] Following his term as governor, Glenn remained active as a leader in Presbyterian circles. He used his giftedness as an orator on behalf of the Board of Home Missions of the Presbyterian Church, the Lyceum Bureau, as well as on the Chautauqua circuit. He died on 16 May 1920.[17]

The death of William Stuart Primrose in 1909 was also a serious blow to the First Presbyterian Church. Primrose was one of Raleigh's most prominent citizens. He was born in Raleigh on 12 November 1848, professed his faith and became a member on 7 July 1864, and served the

---

[13]Ibid.

[14]Ibid. See also Margaret L. Chapman, "The Administration of Governor Robert B. Glenn" (master's thesis, University of North Carolina, 1956).

[15]*NCPedia*, s.v. "Glenn, Robert Brodnax."

[16]*News and Observer*, 2 June 1908, 5. It is noteworthy, that J. R. Young, the state's insurance commissioner, and Franklin McNeill, chairman of the state's Corporation Commission, also assumed duties as an elder at the service. They had previously served the church as elders and therefore did not need to be ordained with Glenn. The *News and Observer* noted that it was "unusual that three State officers took the vows [at the same time] to serve First Presbyterian Church here as Elders in it."

[17]*NCPedia*, s.v. "Glenn, Robert Brodnax."

church as an elder for thirty-nine years.[18] Additionally, Primrose served the church as clerk of the session and superintendent of the Sunday school for many years. Primrose was a prominent businessman in Raleigh, making his mark in the insurance business. He was also an early supporter of the North Carolina Agricultural and Mechanical College, known today as North Carolina State University. He was a faithful supporter of Peace Institute and involved in the leadership of that institution as well. His obituary declared, "The people of Raleigh, irrespective of class or condition, recognized his high worth, his disinterested patriotism, his fine Christian character, and his unselfish devotion to the best interests of his city."[19]

On 22 July 1915, the congregation lost one of its most dedicated women, Miss Bettie Penick.[20] She was deeply involved in the Ladies Society for Christian Work and in 1885 founded the Busy Bee Band Society, an organization with the purpose of teaching children in the church the importance of foreign missions. She also taught the Pilathea Class for Young Women, which was renamed the Bettie Penick Bible Class after her death.[21]

The Vanguard Class and Local Missions. White's leadership at Raleigh's First Presbyterian Church produced unprecedented growth. During his twenty-six-year pastorate, the primary emphasis was evangelism and local missions. Early in his Raleigh tenure, the session approved a resolution to create a "Men's Association for Christian Work in Wake County," an organization for adult men to carry out the work of local missions. The elders encouraged all the men of the church to join in the endeavor. The clerk further reported in that meeting that Mr. William B. McIlwain Jr., a student at Union Theological Seminary, had been employed during the summer vacation period of that year "to assist and investigate the religious conditions in the various parts of Wake Coun-

---

[18]His ordination as an elder occurred on 12 November 1876. See "Memorial" contained in Minutes of the Session, 2 May 1909.

[19]*The Raleigh* (NC) *Times*, 12 April 1909, 1.

[20]*News and Observer*, 24 July 1915, 6.

[21]William P. McPherson, ed., *The History of First Presbyterian Church, Raleigh, North Carolina: 1816–1991* (Raleigh: Commercial Printing, 1991) 98–99.

ty."[22] He visited and preached in Falls Neuse, Wendell, Apex, Zebulon, Millbrook, McCullers, Willow Springs, and Fuquay Springs. The elders deemed it "advisable" for the church to conduct services on a regular basis at all the locations except Falls Neuse, Wendell, and Zebulon.[23]

The reference to William McIlwain revealed the key strategy employed by White in the effort to establish mission congregations that would eventually become self-sustaining. McIlwain was but the first of a number of seminary students that came to work under the tutelage of White.[24] Another assistant pastor during White's pastorate was J. Edwin Hemphill. Hemphill began his work in fall 1911. The sessional records give special notice that on 22 October 1911 he was ordained by the Albemarle Presbytery and installed as assistant pastor of the church. He left Raleigh in 1914 to become the pastor of Pryor Street Presbyterian Church in Atlanta, Georgia.[25] Hemphill remained in Atlanta for several years before moving to Petersburg, Virginia, where he spent the remainder of his career as the pastor of the Tabb Street Presbyterian Church from 1924 to 1942.[26]

During the early years of White's term as the church's pastor, the most significant event to occur on the national level was the American involvement in World War I. Woodrow Wilson's efforts to steer a course of neutrality were successful for the first few years of the war, but America's isolationism changed in April 1917 after Germany resumed its unrestricted submarine warfare in the Atlantic Ocean. World War I was a devastation that brought twentieth-century technology to the battlefield to be used upon troops still trained in nineteenth-century tactics. When the war concluded in 1918, more than fifty thousand American soldiers

---

[22]Minutes of the Session, 5 October 1908; McPherson *History of First Presbyterian Church*, 41.

[23]Minutes of the Session, 5 October 1908.

[24]See McPherson, *History of First Presbyterian Church*, 41–43. White's strategy is also described in *First Presbyterian Church Raleigh, NC, 1816–1941* (Raleigh, NC: First Presbyterian Church, Raleigh, North Carolina) 8. This small pamphlet was produced by a committee of members for the church's 125th anniversary celebration.

[25]Minutes of the Session, 9 August 1914.

[26]*Progress-Index* (Petersburg, VA), 3 May 1953, 4.

were dead—numbers that pale in comparison to the losses of Russia (1.7 million), Germany (1.8 million), France (1.4 million), Great Britain (0.9 million), and Austria-Hungary (1.2 million).[27] Given the tragic consequences of World War I, the hope was that the leading nations of the world would see that such devastation never happened again. The Treaty of Versailles did provide for a League of Nations to be formed (Woodrow Wilson's dream) so that local grievances could be settled by neutral nations to prevent war. Unfortunately, partisan politics in the United States Congress never allowed for American ratification of the peace treaty or the League of Nations. Without American participation, the League of Nations failed, and only a few decades later, the world was at war once again.

When America became involved in World War I in 1917, the city of Raleigh did its part to support the war effort. Wake County provided a total of 1,647 men to the army, 352 to the navy, and nine to the marine corps. Twelve women from the county served in the nursing corps. A causality list published in December 1918 indicated that 256 Wake County soldiers were killed in action, 84 died from wounds, 140 died of disease, and 74 were wounded.[28] Furthermore, Raleigh was home to the military base Camp Polk during the War. The camp, located near the State Fairgrounds, was one of the army's first tank training bases. Construction on the base began in fall 1918 and the war ended before its completion. In spite of the efforts of many citizens to keep the base in Raleigh permanently, the army decided to relocate. Nevertheless, during its short existence, Raleigh citizens were by and large supportive of the soldiers and the operations of the base.[29] Despite the efforts of the city as a whole, not all of its residents supported America's involvement in the war. In one particular case, Floyd E. Simpkins, son of Primitive Baptist minister Elder W. A. Simpkins, was arrested on 9 August 1917 for threatening the life of President Woodrow Wilson. Allegedly, the younger Simpkins, while delivering bread to a store in Smithfield, said,

---

[27]Jordan and Litwack, *United States*, 616–17.

[28]Johnson and Murray, *Reconstruction to 1920*, 416. See pp. 397–420 for a full discussion of Wake County and Raleigh during World War I.

[29]Ibid., 410–14.

"There ain't a damn bit of use of this war." He went on to say that if he were drafted he hoped that Wilson would be the first person he "got a crack at." According to accounts, his father appeared at the hearing before John Nichols, the U.S. commissioner, arguing that his son was only joking. The case was sent to a federal court but was dismissed.[30]

Two of the church's assistant pastors were direct participants in the war. The first, Benjamin Rice Lacy Jr., was a native of Raleigh, born 30 July 1886, and grew up at the First Presbyterian Church. His father, Benjamin Rice Lacy Sr., was North Carolina commissioner of labor (1893–1897 and 1899–1901) and served as the state treasurer of North Carolina from 1901 to 1929. The elder Lacy was a strong proponent of organized labor in the state. His grandfather was Drury Lacy, who served as pastor of First Presbyterian Church from 1837 to 1855, when he left to become the president of Davidson College. The mother of the junior Lacy was Mary Burwell Lacy, whose father was president of Peace Institute from 1872 to 1890.[31]

Lacy attended the Raleigh Male Academy and then entered Davidson College. He graduated with a degree in history, was awarded a Rhodes Scholarship, and studied abroad at Oxford University from 1907 to 1910. Following his study at Oxford, Lacy returned to the United States. The session, meeting on 11 September 1910, recommended for him to be under the care of the Albemarle Presbytery as a candidate for the ministry.[32] That same year, he enrolled at Union Theological Seminary, earning a bachelor's degree in theology three years later. Following graduation, he remained at the seminary for a year as the Moses D. Hoge Fellow and taught church history.[33]

Albemarle Presbytery ordained Lacy, and he became assistant pastor at First Presbyterian Church in 1914.[34] The Women's Society of Chris-

[30]*News and Observer,* 10 August 1917, 1, and 16 August 1917, 5, as cited by Johnson and Murray, *Reconstruction to 1920*, 401.

[31]*Dictionary of North Carolina Biography,* ed. William S. Powell (Chapel Hill: University of North Carolina Press, 1979–1996) s.v. "Lacy, Benjamin Rice, Jr."

[32]Minutes of the Session, 11 September 1910.

[33]Ibid.

[34]Ibid., 5 October 1914.

tian Work made special mention of Lacy's return to his home church at their monthly meeting in September 1914: "It is with satisfaction that we again have his services as Dr. White's Assistant in our very encouraging work in Wake County."[35] Like the other assistant pastors under White's tenure, Lacy had mission responsibilities among several fledgling congregations in Wake County birthed by First Presbyterian. Unfortunately, American involvement in World War I interrupted Lacy's work at the church. In 1917, he became a chaplain with the 113th Field Artillery of the army's 30th Division. Expressing their support for him, the Women's Society of Christian Work presented Lacy with a small "gold piece" as a token of their support and appreciation for "the work he has so nobly done for His Master in our midst the past three years."[36]

Lacy served with distinction as a chaplain from 1917 to 1919. Returning home, he married Emma Elizabeth White, the daughter of William McC. White, and for a brief period of time served as a pastor in Johnston County. In 1920, he accepted a call as pastor to the Central Presbyterian Church in Atlanta, where he remained for six years. In 1926, he became the president of Union Theological Seminary, a position he held until his retirement in 1956. During those decades, Lacy served the Presbyterian denomination in numerous capacities, most notably in 1948 as a U.S. representative to the International Conference on Theological Education in Geneva, Switzerland. In 1950, he was chosen as moderator to the General Assembly of the Presbyterian Church of the United States. Through the years, he also received honorary degrees from Davidson College, Duke University, Hampden-Sydney College, the University of Richmond, and the University of North Carolina. He died on 3 August 1981.[37]

Another assistant pastor whose ministry at the church was cut short by the war was Edward Smith Currie. He was born in Pittsboro, North

---

[35]Minutes of the Women's Society of Christian Work, 13 September 1914. The record reflects the name of this organization prior to 1914 as "Ladies Society of Christian Work." The minutes from 1907 to 1914 are missing, and presumably the name change occurred during that period.

[36]Ibid., 10 September 1917.

[37]*Dictionary of North Carolina Biography*, s.v. "Lacy, Benjamin Rice, Jr."

Carolina, on 28 September 1888 and grew up near Fayetteville. He attended Davidson College, graduating in 1912. Five years later, he graduated from Union Theological Seminary and embarked upon a career in ministry.[38] Prior to his graduation, First Presbyterian Church called him as an assistant pastor on 14 December 1916.[39] Like Lacy, he joined the United States Army as a chaplain in 1918. Before he left for duty, he married Gay Vaughan Wilson of Richmond, Virginia, on 19 July 1918. As a chaplain, Currie was popular with the soldiers under his charge. He was assigned to the 316th Field Artillery unit of the 81st Division, earning the nickname "the wrestling parson" from a story that supposedly he issued a challenge to the men of his unit that any man who could best him in a wrestling match would not have to attend chapel. But, if he was able to defeat the challenger, the soldier would be required to attend chapel.[40]

Following his discharge from the army, Currie and his wife sought appointment as missionaries to China. First Presbyterian Church was supportive in that effort. William McC. White reported to the session on 9 September 1919 that Currie "was very anxious to enter the missionary field as our representative and that the proper authorities had advised that it would require about $2,600 [$35,000] to provide for him and his wife in the foreign field."[41] The elders discussed how the funding might

---

[38]This information is taken from an unpublished account of Currie's life and work titled "Edward S. Currie: Vanguard Missionary to China." The scrapbook is contained in the records of the Vanguard Class at First Presbyterian Church, Raleigh.

[39]Minutes of the Session, 14 December 1916. Currie was licensed to the ministry in July 1917 by Fayetteville Presbytery and ordained by the Albemarle Presbytery in August 1917. The biographical sketch contained in the Vanguard Class records titled "Edward S. Currie: Vanguard Missionary to China" (unpublished document, n.d.) reports that Currie was ordained by Albemarle Presbytery. Another source, indicates that his ordination occurred in the Granville Presbytery: "Presbyterian Church U.S. Missionaries to China 1900–1920," accessed 20 April 2015, http://www.phcmontreat.org/bios/Bios-Missionaries-China-1900-1920-PCUS.htm.

[40]See *News and Observer*, 21 September 1919, 8, and "Edward S. Currie: Vanguard Missionary to China."

[41]Minutes of the Session, 9 September 1919.

be secured, deciding finally to appoint a subcommittee to study the matter. Several days later, the session met once again to discuss the matter. It was reported that a church in Richmond agreed to pay half of Currie's salary of $2,400 [$32,300] and First Presbyterian would pay the other half with the Vanguard Class in the church paying half of that. By November of that year, Currie and his wife embarked for China.[42] The following year, the elders assured the continued support for the Curries by designating the first Sundays in June and November for special missions emphasis called "Currie Sundays." On these Sundays, special offerings were collected for the Curries' salary.[43]

The Vanguard Class faithfully supported the Curries throughout their career as missionaries, considering the couple to be "their" missionaries. They served in China from 1920 to 1952, with the exception of the years 1937 to 1938, when Chinese current events forced their brief return to the United States. From 1952 to 1959 they served in Taiwan. In 1959, they retired to Montreat, North Carolina, where they lived the remainder of their lives. Gay Currie died in October 1980, and Edward died 25 February 1981.[44]

First Presbyterian Church rallied behind the war effort. The first mention of the war effort among the Women's Society of Christian Work came on 3 December 1917 at the group's monthly meeting. The planned program for the meeting was cancelled so that the women could hear an appeal from an officer home on furlough named John Boushall. He spoke to the women on behalf of the YWCA and its campaign to raise money to build "Hostess Houses" in the military camps as well as other matters related to the work of the organization during the war effort.[45] At their monthly meeting in September 1918, the topic of the war

[42]Ibid., 25 September, and 11 November 1919. According to "Edward S. Currie: Vanguard Missionary to China," the Ginter Park Presbyterian Church in Richmond was the other church providing for the Curries' support. This was the home church of Currie's wife.

[43]Minutes of the Session, 12 May 1920.

[44]"Former China Missionary Dead at 92," *The Presbyterian News* 47 (March 1981), contained in "Edward S. Currie: Vanguard Missionary to China."

[45]Minutes of the Women's Society of Christian Work, 3 December 1917.

also surfaced. They discussed their work among the soldiers at Camp Polk, and especially the "nurses who have so willingly given their services to our country and [encouraged that] they be remembered daily in our prayers."[46]

The Vanguard Class was also actively involved in the war effort. In addition to B. R. Lacy and Edward Currie, other Vanguard members serving in the military during the war were Andrew Crinkley, L. M. Fergerson, W. H. Graham, W. J. Hudson, Thomas A. Lacy, R. W. McGeachy, H. D. Taylor, T. H. Redding, W. H. Rogers Jr., Fleming Sherwood, F. W. Sherwood, Cy Thompson Jr., H. A. Thompson, Harry Tucker, Everett Upchurch, E. H. Walderon, Lorens White, and Seymour Whiting.[47] Each of the 150 members of the class at the time agreed to purchase a liberty bond to support the war effort also, making sure that "Those who did not go into active service across the sea did their 'bit' in the Homeland."[48] That was exemplified during June 1917. E. R. Pace, a member of the class, owned four acres of land on Glenwood Avenue and agreed to allow the class members to grow a corn crop. On 5 November, the members, assisted by some of the students from Peace Institute and some others, harvested and shucked the entire crop in one hour and a half. The corn was taken to Lassiter Mill, where it was ground into corn meal. The class sent gift packages of corn meal to President Woodrow Wilson, secretary of the navy and Raleigh native Josephus Daniels, and several others in the Wilson administration. The proceeds from the crop were donated to the American Red Cross.[49] Several weeks later, the Vanguard Class received a letter of thanks from Edith

---

[46]Ibid., 9 September 1918.

[47]These names were taken from page 3 of a short history of the Vanguard Class located in the records of the Vanguard Class. This is different than the history referenced in the previous chapter written by Dave Permar. Hereafter, this history will be cited as "Vanguard History" (unpublished manuscript, n.d.). Seymour Whiting developed pneumonia and died at an army camp in Douglas, Arizona. See *News and Observer*, 17 January 1918, 8.

[48]"Vanguard History" (unpublished manuscript, n.d.) 3–4.

[49]Ibid., 4–5; *News and Observer*, 11 November 1917, 13.

Bolling Wilson, the first lady.[50] The class continued the farming project for the duration of the war, adding other crops and pigs to the work.

Through the influence of E. B. Crow, the Vanguard Class experienced remarkable growth during the White pastorate, and its influence extended beyond Raleigh, even outside of North Carolina. For example, J. Edwin Hemphill organized such a class at Pryor Street Presbyterian Church in Atlanta, Georgia. On 10 April 1920, the *Atlanta Constitution* reported that Hemphill invited E. B. Crow to speak the following Sunday evening at the Atlanta church. The article identified Crow as "one of the most capable laymen of the Presbyterian church" and revealed that the Atlanta class "was organized on the plan of the Vanguard Class in the First Presbyterian Church in Raleigh, of which Mr. Crow is the teacher."[51] By December 1920, the Pryor Street Vanguard Class had "become interested in forms of community service, and [was] having meetings weekly."[52] Classes were also organized in Washington, D.C. and in Richmond and Norfolk, Virginia.[53] An anonymously written poem about Crow contains an explanation for how the Vanguard movement spread:

There was a man named E. B. Crow
He was a regular hummer;
He organized the Vanguard Class
And boomed it all the summer.
And when the summer hot was done
He ran it all the winter;
In fact in Bible Classes he
Became a regular sprinter.
And when a member moved away
He made him start another;

---

[50]"Vanguard History," 5. The letter, dated 14 November 1917, reads "Gentlemen: May I thank you most warmly for your courtesy in sending the corn meal to the President and it will be a great pleasure to use it, accompanied as it was with your good wishes. Very sincerely yours, Edith Bolling Wilson."

[51]*Atlanta* (GA) *Constitution*, 10 April 1920, 7.

[52]Ibid., 18 December 1920, 8.

[53]David H. Permar, "History of the Vanguard Class of Raleigh" (unpublished manuscript, 2004) 6.

And now of Vanguards everywhere
He is the Revered Mother.[54]

Crow was an exceptionally gifted layman and a very successful businessman. At age seventeen, he began working for the Commercial National Bank in Raleigh sweeping the lobby floor each business day. From that inauspicious beginning, he worked his way through the ranks at the bank to the position of vice president. He was so successful as both a lay teacher in the Vanguard Class and a businessman that one writer declared, "it is difficult to determine...whether he wields a bigger influence as a business or religious leader."[55] Crow originally organized the Vanguard Class at First Presbyterian Church in 1904, an outgrowth of a class of boys taught by his mother, who died in 1895. Through the influence of William McC. White's predecessor, Alfred Moment, Crow led the class, whose motto is "Always Ready," to a membership of more than 150 during the 1920s. Crow was described as "an evangelist of tithing."[56] In 1921, the combined income of the 150 men who were members of the Vanguard Class exceeded $200,000 [$2.6 million] annually. Crow inspired 40 percent of the members to sign a pledge to give one-tenth of their income "for God's work and His Kingdom here among men."[57]

Crow regularly issued a challenge to the men of the Vanguard Class that after a year of tithing, if they were not better off financially, he would repay out of his own pocket the amount of tithe given.[58] Crow's philosophy was likely influenced by the famous sermon "Acres of Diamonds," preached thousands of times by Russell Conwell (1843–1925), a Baptist pastor from Philadelphia and founder of Temple University. Conwell is widely regarded as an early originator of the "health and wealth" gospel, popularized later in the twentieth century by names such as Norman Vincent Peale and Robert Schuller. Conwell's central thesis

---

[54]Ibid.

[55]Frank G. Weaver, "Put God in Your Budget," *Young Men* 47 (September 1921): 204.

[56]Ibid.

[57]Ibid.

[58]Ibid.

in "Acres of Diamonds" was that wealth is possible for any Christian and that it is the Christian's duty to become wealthy so that the cause of Christ might be furthered.[59] Conwell was not the only voice on the national scene espousing the success gospel. A contemporary of Conwell with a similar philosophy was Andrew Carnegie. Carnegie, who became extremely wealthy in the steel industry during the late nineteenth century, wrote a famous essay called "Gospel of Wealth." The concept was essentially a religious expression of Social Darwinism. Carnegie's central argument was that morality produces financial success while the poor are immoral and deserve their plight in life.[60] Carnegie's essay was popular among successful businessmen in the early twentieth century, and it would be no surprise that as a fellow Presbyterian his ideas would have also made their way into the thought of Crow.

Crow's leadership in the Vanguard Class became an important aid for local mission work so dear to the pastoral philosophy of William McC. White. White's vision for local missions, coupled with the energy and financial strength of the Vanguard Class, fostered the organization of several new churches in the city. On 4 July 1917, the Vanguard Class dedicated a new chapel built on property given by Karl Hudson and located on East Martin Street. Edward Currie became the first pastor of "East Vanguard Chapel." The venture was so successful that in 1925 the Vanguard Class provided $25,000 [$332,000] for a new sanctuary to be built at the corner of Swain and Martin Streets. One member of the class, H. H. Milner, became an active participant in what eventually came to be called the East Vanguard Church. Because of Milner's support and involvement, the congregation took the name Milner Presbyterian Church and moved to its present location on New Bern Avenue. This congregation produced its own mission church called the Buffalo Vanguard Church located near Lake Wheeler Road. That church is known today as St. Barnabas Presbyterian Church and is now located on Carolina Pines Avenue.[61]

---

[59]*Dictionary of Christianity in America*, ed. Daniel G. Reid et al. (Downers Grove, IL: InterVarsity Press, 1990), s.v. "Conwell, Russell Herman."

[60]*Dictionary of Christianity in America*, s.v. "Wealth, Gospel of."

[61]Permar, "History of the Vanguard Class," 6–7.

In 1918, the Vanguard Class purchased forty acres of land on Whitaker Mill Road. Thirty of the acres were subdivided and sold for single-family residential development. On the remaining ten acres, the North Vanguard Chapel was established. The building was financed through the purchase of $12,000 [$186,000] in bonds by the class. That mission church eventually became Westminster Presbyterian Church, which established its own mission, Neuse Chapel.[62]

The Vanguard Class was also instrumental in the establishment of a few other Presbyterian churches such as the Ernest Myatt Presbyterian Church in Garner and West Raleigh Presbyterian Church. The class also aided in the building of Pullen Memorial Baptist Church located on Hillsborough Street near the campus of North Carolina State University. In 1924, largely because of the fundraising activity and property development, the Vanguard Class was incorporated as a nonprofit organization by the North Carolina secretary of state.[63]

Another important project the Vanguard Class completed during the White pastorate was the erection of a new classroom. The new room was designed by a member of the class Murray Nelson and was constructed by a fellow member James A. Davidson. Construction began in 1919 and was completed by the following year. The entire cost of the construction was $5,469.28 [$73,600]. The formal dedication of the room coincided with the dedication of the class's first memorial window in honor of E. B. Crow's mother, Nannie Burwell Crow, in 1925. One unique feature to the new Vanguard room was an electric roll-call sign, made in the shape of the class emblem. The board contained 216 lights, one for each member. As the member entered the classroom, he threw a switch that lit up the light on the board by his name. The class used the electric sign until its removal in 1972.[64]

E. B. Crow left Raleigh and moved to Richmond, Virginia, in 1933. The class erected a bronze plaque on the back wall of the classroom and dedicated it to his years of service as its organizer and teacher. Crow died on 28 February 1945.

---

[62]Ibid.

[63]Ibid., 8.

[64]Ibid., 11–12.

New Sunday School Building. Within just a few years of White's tenure as pastor, it became apparent that the Sunday school had grown beyond the capacity of the building being used. The first mention in the record of the need to enlarge the Sunday school facilities appears in the records of the monthly meeting of the deacons on 4 April 1910: "Mr. W. R. Smith and E. Bloom [sp?] were appointed a committee to see Mr. Barrett regarding the bill presented by him for the drawing plans for the enlargement of the Sunday school room."[65] The topic was further discussed on and off over the next several months and then, at least in the records that survive, the topic seems to have been tabled.[66] The first mention of the topic among the elders appeared in May 1913 and then again in March 1914.[67] Also in March 1914, the deacons revived their previous discussion of building an extension to the Sunday school. A suggestion was offered that the building committee call for competitive bids for the work to be done. After a considerable amount of discussion and Dr. White's blackboard illustration of what such a building might look like, the deacons approved a resolution that "provisionally approves the plans for the building committee of the Sunday school for an extension of the same, provided the congregation shows willingness to give proper financial support."[68]

Various discussions continued about the need for more educational space over the next several years. On 5 March 1916, the deacons received a letter from Mrs. B. R. Bunch in reference to the need for more adequate space in the Sunday school. The letter was referred to the pastor with a pledge to work with him and the session on the matter.[69] On 1 April 1917, the minutes of the diaconate record that "Mr. Hudson Smith representing the Vanguard Class appeared before the board and showed the necessity of enlarging the Vanguard room immediately."[70] The next month the deacons passed a motion that "Dr. White call immediately a

[65]Minutes of the Diaconate, 4 April 1910.

[66]Ibid., 1 June 1910, 2 July 1911, 6 August 1911.

[67]Minutes of the Session, 8 May 1913 and 18 March 1914.

[68]Ibid., 22 March 1914.

[69]Ibid., March 1916.

[70]Minutes of the Diaconate, 1 April 1917.

meeting of the officers of the church to discuss ways and means for the enlargement of the Sunday school building."[71] From that point forward, the idea seems to have been dropped again. Mission chapels and perhaps more importantly World War I served as interruptions to serious fund-raising efforts for a new Sunday school building.

By 1920, the discussions about a new Sunday school building had resumed. One option briefly discussed involved adding a second story to the current building.[72] The following month, a newly appointed building committee reported that a "modern up to date Sunday school building would cost in the neighborhood of $40,000 [$465,000]."[73] Discussions continued throughout the next year about options for easing the crowded conditions. This led to negotiations to purchase property adjacent to the church property.[74] The property was purchased for $13,750 [$179,000]. By the following month, the church already had subscriptions of $8,000 [$111,000] for payment of the newly purchased property.[75] A firm decision by the church to build a new educational building finally came at the end of 1922.[76] In January 1923, a recommendation was approved that $75,000 [$1.02 million] be raised for the new building by the congregation in cash and pledges on the following schedule: 10 percent immedi-

---

[71]Ibid., 6 May 1917.

[72]Minutes of Joint Meetings Between Elders and Deacons, 12 October 1920. These monthly joint meetings began in January 1919. The meetings continued until January 1926, when it is noted that no further joint meetings occurred.

[73]Ibid., 20 November 1920. It is also noted at this meeting that the crowded condition of the primary department necessitated that its Sunday school exercises be held on Sunday afternoons rather than Sunday mornings because of such crowded conditions within the entire Sunday school.

[74]Ibid., 16 May, 9 August, 8 November, 6 December 1921, 9 January 1922.

[75]Ibid., 9 January and 14 February 1922.

[76]Although there is no record of the congregational meeting where the church approved the project, the Minutes of the Joint Meetings Between Elders and Deacons for 13 November 1922 reveal the following motion: "That the officers of the church recommend that a congregational meeting be called to consider the question of building a new Sunday school building to house our growing Sunday school and they recommend that a suitable building be built if the way be found clear to do so."

ately; 10 percent by 1 April 1923; 10 percent by 1 July 1923; 20 percent by 1 January 1924; 25 percent by 1 July 1924; and 25 percent by 1 January 1925.[77] The following month, $27,783 [$379,000] in cash and pledges was reported.[78] Within a few months, it was determined that at least an additional $10,000 [$136,000] would be needed.[79]

By the end of 1923, the church received four construction bids for the building ranging from $91,000 [$1.24 million] to $110,000 [$1.5 million], all above the amount of $85,000 [$1.16 million] authorized by the congregation. The companies were asked to revise their bids in an effort to cut building costs. The lowest bid, offered by the Harrison Construction Company was eventually accepted for $74,000 [$1.01 million].[80] The new building was completed by 1925.

Communion Controversy. There is an interesting, if only minor, disagreement that appeared in the church records during the White pastorate, which concerned the ordinance of Holy Communion. On 7 April 1913, the sessional records report that a committee of three deacons, Dr. Guy A. Roberts, Professor Henry Stockton, and Professor F. M. Harper, came before the session with a suggestion that the church use the individual cup for communion service, an indication that the common cup or the intinction method of communion had heretofore been used. Likely, the concern of the deacons was hygiene. The record noted that the issue "was favorably discussed and action deferred to another meeting of the Session."[81]

The matter arose later in the year and "was considered most carefully." This time the session voted to adopt a new communion method using individualized cups, but Elder J. M. Monie "desired his name be recorded as having voted against the motion."[82] The vote for the change did

---

[77]Minutes of the Joint Meetings Between Elders and Deacons, 22 January 1923.

[78]Ibid., 15 February 1923. The fundraising continued successfully throughout the year. By 6 August, more than $38,000 [$519,000] had been pledged.

[79]Ibid., 23 April 1923.

[80]Ibid., 7 December 1923. There is a notation that the $74,000 bid did not include heating or architectural fees.

[81]Minutes of the Session, 7 April 1913.

[82]Ibid., 9 November 1913.

not lay the matter to rest, though. By February, the sessional records show that the elders approved a request from the deacons to purchase two more plates for the communion service as well as two additional offering plates. Then, James R. Young made a motion "that arrangements be made to serve the communion to any members desiring it the old way, not with individual cups."[83]

This would hardly classify as a serious controversy. It is interesting that J. M. Monie was insistent that his name be identified as voting against the change. It seems that the church was able to reach a compromise to accommodate any members who desired to receive the Eucharist in "the old way." If hygiene was the issue originally motivating the deacons to suggest the change, it is noteworthy that this controversy occurred four years before the devastating influenza outbreak. The pandemic of Spanish influenza dominated much of the attention of Americans and Raleigh residents from 1917 to 1919. Estimates are that worldwide the pandemic attacked more than one-fifth of the world's population and killed more than fifty million.[84] North Carolina lost more than three thousand people to the disease in 1917, with another twelve thousand the following year. Finally, statewide deaths dropped to 6,000 in 1919. Wake County suffered from the disease more than any other county in North Carolina in October 1918 with 293 deaths reported in that month alone.[85] It would seem that the change in communion method was timely.

---

[83]Ibid., 22 February 1914.

[84]National Archives and Records Administration, "The Deadly Virus: The Influenza Epidemic of 1918," accessed 30 March 2016, http://www.archives.gov/exhibits/influenza-epidemic.

[85]Johnson and Murray, *Reconstruction to 1920*, 483. One Raleigh resident remembered, "[T]he coffins were stacked up like cordwood on the baggage trucks at the old train station. There was a lady in our neighborhood who came around to help. The hospitals were full to overflowing and there were loads of houses with everybody sick. She took soup to the sick, and helped lay out the corpses. When asked wasn't she scared, she said, 'No.' …but most people were scared. So many were sick we even had difficulty getting a preacher to bury a little two-year-old-baby girl." (Quoted by Johnson and Murray, *Reconstruction to 1920*, 483.)

Death of William McClanahan White. In winter 1934, White was stricken with influenza. At first, it appeared that the illness would not be severe. His condition worsened, however, and he died on 22 February.[86] His death ended twenty-six years of fruitful ministry at the First Presbyterian Church. His leadership and commitment to missions provided the church with unprecedented growth at the beginning of the new century. His gentle pastoral way caused one interpreter to say, "When God called him, his death, though a shock to the congregation, was itself like a benediction. His exit was not dramatic, but like someone leaving a room and quietly closing the door behind him. Dr. White came to us quietly and left us in the same way; yet between that coming and that going there stands the unblemished record of a Christian gentleman."[87]

---

[86]*News and Observer*, 23 February 1934, 1.
[87]McPherson, *History of First Presbyterian Church*, 43.

8

Strengthening the Legacy

The Context

Following World War I, American optimism for the new century began to revive. The crash of the stock market in 1929, however, and the onset of the Great Depression transformed American optimism into misery. The spirit of the 1930s could best be characterized in the words of a 1932 song called "Brother, Can You Spare a Dime?":

They used to tell me I was building a dream,
And so I followed the mob;
When there was earth to plow or guns to bear
I was always there, right there on the job.
They used to tell me I was building a dream
With peace and glory ahead;
Why should I be standing in line
Just waiting for bread?[1]

The landslide re-election of Franklin D. Roosevelt to the presidency in 1936 signaled American confidence in his leadership and ability to bring an end to the economic woes through his New Deal, but there were no simple solutions, and for millions the misery would continue for several more years.

Internationally, the 1940s brought further worries to the American people. The devastation of World War I and its aftermath left the German people vulnerable to the promises of Adolf Hitler to restore Germany to greatness. Benito Mussolini extended the fascist threat to Italy. The rise of Stalin in Russia with his blood purges, a Spanish civil war,

---

[1]Yip Harburg (lyrics) and Jay Gorney (music), "Brother, Can You Spare a Dime?" Songs of the Great Depression (1931), Department of History, College of Staten Island of City University of New York, accessed 16 June 2015, http://csivc.csi.cuny.edu/history/files/lavender/cherries.html.

and Japanese aggression in the Pacific all became grave concerns to Americans. For the second time in the century the world was about to be drawn into war. This time Americans were less eager to go to war than they had been during the "Great War." Public opinion polls in 1937 revealed that 70 percent of Americans thought it had been a mistake to enter World War I and that 95 percent thought the nation should avoid European troubles if it came to war.[2] That all changed almost overnight when the Japanese attacked Pearl Harbor on 7 December 1941.

World War II forever altered the course of American history. Hundreds of thousands of young men either volunteered or were drafted for service. When it was over, more than 400,000 American soldiers died in the four years of war, and thousands more were wounded. Back home the war effort brought rationing of almost everything needed for daily life, such as gasoline, sugar, and coffee although that did have the positive effect of uniting the nation behind the war effort. Women by the thousands for the first time in American history were hired by factories to build tanks, jeeps, airplanes, and ships because so many of the men were in the armed forces. African Americans also served heroically in the military, at first in segregated units but eventually alongside white soldiers.

The war ended in Europe in on 8 May 1945, and the American military was then able to focus entirely on the war in the Pacific theatre. An invasion of the Japanese mainland was avoided by the surrender of Japan on 2 September 1945, following the detonation of atomic bombs over Hiroshima and Nagasaki. The atomic bomb was a weapon more powerful than the world had ever seen, and its possession propelled the United States to the status of the leading superpower in the world. The increased productivity of the war effort brought prosperity once again to the American economy. But the war had brought greater hardship to the other Allies, the Soviet Union, Great Britain, and France. Their colonial empires were also threatened by various nationalist actions in Africa, Asia, and the Middle East. Germany and Japan were devastated by the

---

[2]Winthrop D. Jordan and Leon F. Litwack, *The United States*, 7th ed. (Englewood Cliffs, NJ: Prentice Hall, 1991) 695.

war, and China was on the verge of a bitter civil war. The world was still in turmoil following the war's end.[3]

The danger was compounded by 1949 when the Soviet Union exploded its own atomic bomb. The inability of the Soviet Union to cooperate with the other Allies following the war's conclusion in Europe led to the beginning of the Cold War—a war characterized by espionage, subversion of foreign governments, and an arms race. Americans feared the spread of communism, a fear that led to war once again, this time in Korea. The Korean War lasted from 1950 to 1953, costing the United States another 53,000 soldiers. The 1950s became a decade of great patriotism as love of God and country were joined together in the American psyche. The phrase "under God" was inserted into the Pledge of Allegiance in 1954. "In God We Trust," which had been added to American coinage during the Civil War, became the nation's official motto in 1956, the year Dwight D. Eisenhower was elected to a second term as president.

City of Raleigh

The middle decades of the twentieth century were characterized by sustained growth and development in Raleigh. In 1936, the Federal Theatre Project, a New Deal program designed to promote live artistic performances throughout the country, provided the funding necessary for the birth of the Raleigh Little Theatre, which has operated continuously since then. The first performance in the theater was a play promoting temperance called *The Drunkard*, originally written in 1844.[4]

RDU airport, a joint venture between the cities of Raleigh and Durham, was established in 1943. Its precursor, the Raleigh Municipal Airport, established in 1929, provided passenger and mail service beginning in 1932. Business soon outgrew the small airfield, and in 1938, Eastern Airlines president Eddie Rickenbacker convinced city leaders of both Raleigh and Durham to cooperate in building a new airport. Work began in 1941, and the transportation improvement that resulted with

---

[3]Ibid., 729.

[4]David Perkins, ed., *Raleigh: A Living History of North Carolina's Capital* (Winston-Salem, NC: John F. Blair, 1994) 134–35.

the opening of RDU revolutionized the business environment in the Triangle (Raleigh, Durham, and Chapel Hill).[5]

Another important mid-century milestone for Raleigh occurred as developer Willie York overcame opposition from the Raleigh Garden Club and the residents of Cameron Park to create Cameron Village in 1949, Raleigh's first shopping center. It provided 500,000 square feet of retail space and became highly successful. During the later decades of the twentieth century, other shopping centers were built, and eventually enclosed malls were added as additional options, but Cameron Village remains as a symbol of the economic boom in the Raleigh postwar years.[6]

First Presbyterian Church of Raleigh

Patrick Dwight Miller. Upon the death of William McClanahan White on 22 February 1934, First Presbyterian Church began to search for a new pastor, which occupied most of the rest of the year. By mid-December, the church elected Patrick Dwight Miller to be the next pastor.[7] His installation occurred on 10 February 1935.[8] Miller was a native of Carnesville, Georgia. He was born on 13 January 1900, the son of John Calhoun and Florence McWhorter Miller.[9] He was educated at Davidson College, receiving his AB in 1922 and then his BD and ThM at Union Theological Seminary in Richmond, Virginia, completing his work there in 1927. In 1933, Davidson College conferred upon him the honorary DD degree.[10] He was married in 1931 to Lila Bonner, an Atlanta physician. The couple had three children: twin daughters Belle and Mary, and a son Patrick Jr., who became a professor of Old Testament at Princeton Theological Seminary and has had a distinguished career as a biblical scholar, serving in 1998 as president of the Society of Biblical

---

[5]Ibid., 139–42.

[6]Ibid., 180–81.

[7]Minutes of the Session, 16 December 1934.

[8]William P. McPherson, ed., *The History of First Presbyterian Church, Raleigh, North Carolina: 1816–1991* (Raleigh: Commercial Printing, 1991) 44.

[9]Ibid.; "Rev Patrick Dwight Miller," accessed 18 June 2015, http://www.findagrave.com/cgi-bin/fg.cgi?page=gr&GRid=127790423.

[10]McPherson, *History of First Presbyterian Church*, 44.

Literature.[11] Belle served for much of her career as the director of the Social Justice and Peacemaking unit of the Presbyterian Church in the United States and then for a number of years on the faculty at Candler School of Theology at Emory University. Mary became an ordained minister in the United Church of Christ denomination and married Walter Brueggemann, one of America's leading biblical interpreters.[12]

Prior to assuming the role as pastor of First Presbyterian Church, Miller worked for the denomination as educational secretary of the executive committee of Home Missions of the Presbyterian Church in the United States for six years. In this role he coordinated the Home Missions work for the missionaries laboring in the field. He was also editor of the Home Mission section of the *Presbyterian Survey*, the official publication of the Presbyterian Church in the United States.[13]

One of the first issues to surface in the sessional records as Miller assumed the role of pastor was Sabbath observance within the city of Raleigh. Like all Protestants of the era, First Presbyterian Church opposed any kind of "worldly" amusements on Sunday. On 24 February 1935, the session adopted a motion instructing the pastor to convey in writing to the Raleigh Ministerial Association a request that other churches join with First Presbyterian in an effort to prohibit "Sunday movies" from being shown in the city.[14] The following year, the session wrote a letter

---

[11]"SBL Presidents," accessed 18 June 2015, http://www.sbl-site.org/SBL presidents.aspx.

[12]"Brueggemann to Speak at St. John's," *Lubbock* (TX) *Avalanche-Journal*, 23 January 1999, http://lubbockonline.com/stories/012399/052-1060.shtml#. VYMmi1L8IzQ.

[13]McPherson, *History of First Presbyterian Church*, 44. See also undated correspondence between Dr. P. D. Miller and First Presbyterian Church, Raleigh (reproduction of original letter), Minutes of the Session, 14 January 1935. Reproduced for the sessional records is a letter from Homer McMillan to the First Presbyterian Church commending Miller to the congregation. Following a brief description of Miller's work in the area of Home Missions, McMillan said, "There is a genuine regret on the part of everyone with whom he labored that he feels it is his duty to enter the pastorate. It was hoped that he would find here his life work."

[14]Minutes of the Session, 24 February 1935. Other churches joined the effort, according to later references in the sessional records. See Minutes of the

to the General Motors Corporation expressing appreciation that they did not keep their Parade of Progress open in Raleigh on Sunday.[15] In 1936, the "union services" began on Sunday evenings. These services were ecumenical in nature and initially began with cooperation between First Presbyterian Church, Edenton Street Methodist Church, and First Baptist Church. The tradition continued for several decades among those three historic downtown churches.[16] The union services represent tangible evidence of the good will that existed and continues to exist among the historic downtown Raleigh churches.

Another important development during the Miller pastorate was the building of a new manse. The original manse, a gift from Frances Devereux, was no longer in use, and the church was without a suitable home for the pastor. In 1935, Fred F. Harding donated a lot on Caswell Street to the church for the purpose of building a new manse. The elders determined that construction would begin as soon as the church had $3,000 [$50,900] in donations and that the total cost would not exceed $10,000 [$170,000].[17] The four-bedroom, two-story brick structure was soon completed and was used by the church's pastors for the next forty years.[18]

Session, 28 April 1935 and 12 May 1935. The session seemed to have been equally concerned about competition on Wednesday evenings as well. On 30 October 1936, the session requested Dr. Miller to address the Raleigh Ministerial Association concerning its opposition to the YMCA's sponsoring its "High Y" meetings on Wednesday evenings.

[15]Ibid., 1 June 1936. The Parade of Progress was the brainchild of Charles Kettering, director of research at General Motors. The parade began in 1936 and moved from city to city, showcasing various technological advances in the area of transportation. A group of fifty-seven men staffed the parade. They set up an aerodrome with a stage and then produced a show that must have amazed crowds in the depths of the Great Depression. For more information see "1936 Parade of Progress," accessed 24 June 2015, https://gmheritagecenter.com/gm-heritage-archive/Featured_Innovations/1936_Parade_of_Progress.html.

[16]See W. Glenn Jonas Jr., *Nurturing the Vision: First Baptist Church Raleigh, 1812–2012* (Macon, GA: Mercer University Press, 2012) 239.

[17]Minutes of Joint Meetings Between Elders and Deacons, Minutes of the Session, 6 January 1936; McPherson, *History of First Presbyterian Church*, 46.

[18]McPherson, *History of First Presbyterian Church*, 46.

By the time that Miller became the pastor at First Presbyterian Church, the congregation had a long history in the city of Raleigh of caring for the underprivileged. This commitment to local mission work was enhanced in 1936 with a sizable gift from Henry H. Milner, an elder from the First Vanguard Church and former member of First Presbyterian. Milner created what came to be known as The Presbyterian Fund, Inc. with a substantial gift of $125,000 [$2.1 million]. The fund was administered through First Presbyterian Church. Milner determined that the earnings from the principal were to be used for home mission work in Raleigh, ministerial education for young people called to ministry, and general benevolence needs.[19] One of the most significant ministries to be financed by the Presbyterian Fund was the Cary Street Mission, organized and operated by Mrs. Lisette Friedlan Bunch. Originally the church's secretary, she left that position to work among the needy women and children of the city. Eventually known as the "City Missionary," Mrs. Bunch carried on her ministry for several decades in the area known as Halifax Court, the city's first public housing project established in 1939.[20]

Another significant development in the congregation during Miller's ministry was the church's participation in the Minister's Annuity Fund. In the 1930s, no doubt in response to the economic hardships created during the Great Depression, the General Assembly of the Presbyterian Church in the United States implemented a Minister's Annuity Fund; a retirement plan for ministers. During Miller's employment by the denomination he was actively involved in the effort to promote the plan within the denomination. When he began his ministry at First Presbyterian Church in Raleigh, the North Carolina Synod appointed

---

[19]Ibid.

[20]Ibid.; "History of Raleigh," last modified 12 January 2015, accessed 24 June 2015, https://www.raleighnc.gov/government/content/PubAffairs/Articles/Historic.html. At First Presbyterian Church, Bunch organized the Four-Square Class and served as its teacher for the next forty-seven years until her death in 1967. The class was for girls who completed high school and went into the workplace rather than college. The Four-Square Class played an instrumental role in the organization of the Young Women's Christian Association (YWCA) in Raleigh.

him as chairman of the annuity fund drive within the state.[21] Each synod within the General Assembly was given a designated amount of money to be raised from among the presbyteries. In turn, each presbytery within the synods received an assessment that trickled down to the churches. The assessment assigned to First Presbyterian Church was 7.5 percent of the pastor's salary per year for three years for a total of approximately $9,000 [$149,000], a hefty sum given the other financial responsibilities of the church as well as the economic difficulties of the 1930s.[22]

The church eventually approved the plan, but it took some effort.[23] The minutes of the diaconate for March 1938 include a letter from the chair of the board, C. C. Scarlette, to the other deacons concerning the matter. Scarlette had recently received communication from the pastor, who was being pressed to report to the presbytery the church's decision about two matters: (1) Will First Presbyterian Church agree to participate in the Minister's Annuity Fund? (2) Will First Presbyterian Church agree to the assessment assigned to it? Undoubtedly, Miller would have been embarrassed if First Presbyterian Church had rejected participation in the plan, given that he was the chairman of the committee promoting the plan within the Synod of North Carolina.[24] In his letter, Scarlette declared that the "matter of accepting or rejecting the obligation of the Ministerial Annuity together with the assessment necessary, is of such character and magnitude that the Board of Deacons cannot of themselves commit the Deacons in their joint capacity as Trustees of the church to decide, subject to the approval of the Congregation."[25] He indicated that "several years ago" the proposal had been rejected by a joint meeting of both the diaconate and the session because of the extra financial burden it carried.[26]

The session, however, approved the plan on 7 March 1938.[27] McPherson conveys an interesting story of how one elder came to a

---

[21]McPherson, *History of First Presbyterian Church*, 46.

[22]See Minutes of the Diaconate, 8 March 1938.

[23]Ibid.

[24]Ibid.

[25]Ibid.

[26]Ibid.

[27]Minutes of the Session, 7 March 1938.

change of heart about the plan. R. W. Dunn, one of the elders, originally opposed the plan and had difficulty sleeping because "[h]e had never before voted against his minister."[28] Believing that the Holy Spirit had spoken to him during the night, Dunn contacted ten people the following morning and asked for a pledge for the fund of $300 [$4,960] each. The first person contacted was a fellow elder, and reportedly Dunn told him, "I am not going to leave until you give me $300 or a pledge in that amount."[29] The elder, evidently still opposed to the ministerial fund, said, "I am not going to give a penny to the Minister's Annuity Fund, but I'll give you $300 and you can use it as you please."[30] Eventually, Dunn was able to visit the manse and give his pastor $3,000 [$49,600] in cash and pledges, the church's budgeted amount for the plan that year.[31]

For the synod and presbytery, the work remained to achieve the funding necessary for the Minster's Annuity Fund. In November 1938, the session received a letter indicating that Granville Presbytery "stands at the bottom of the Presbyteries of the Synod of North Carolina."[32] The letter revealed that the North Carolina Synod had raised 57 percent of the amount asked of it and that the Granville Presbytery had only raised 21 percent of its assessed amount. The presbytery encouraged its churches that despite the fact "that in every congregation there are local obligations that must of necessity be discharged....this is a task entrusted to Presbyterians, and its success can be attained only by the cooperation and generosity of local congregations within the Presbyterian church."[33]

Also during Miller's pastorate the church celebrated its 125th anniversary in early 1941. The committee selected to plan the event established the goal to challenge the church to retire all of its debt before the

---

[28]McPherson, *History of First Presbyterian Church*, 47.

[29]Ibid.

[30]Ibid.

[31]Ibid.

[32]Undated correspondence between Lawrence I. Stell and J. S. Kennison of Granville Presbytery and First Presbyterian Church (reproduction of original letter), Minutes of the Session, 14 November 1938. Stell served as moderator and Kennison as stated clerk of the presbytery.

[33]Ibid.

anniversary celebration.[34] By the time of the church's anniversary on 21 January 1941, the debt was gone, a significant milestone and also evidence that the church had weathered the Great Depression.[35]

Within just a few days of the church's anniversary, Miller announced to the congregation that he had accepted a call to become the pastor of the First Presbyterian Church in San Antonio, Texas.[36] After a ministry there of several years, he moved to Atlanta, where he served as pastor of the Druid Hills Presbyterian Church. He then became the executive secretary of the Board of Church Extension in the Presbyterian Church until his retirement in 1965. He died on 3 June 1974.[37]

Maurice Omar Sommers. Following the resignation of Patrick Miller and a search that lasted for several months, the church extended a call to Maurice Omar Sommers on 19 October 1941.[38] Sommers was born on 31 March 1902 in Patricksburg, Indiana.[39] He received his bachelor's degree from Purdue University in 1925. He earned his BD and ThM from Union Theological Seminary in Richmond, Virginia, in 1930 and 1932, respectively. In 1931, he became the pastor of Graves Memorial Presbyterian Church in Clinton, North Carolina, where he remained until 1938. He then moved to Marietta, Georgia, where he served the

---

[34]The committee to plan the celebration was appointed in early 1940. See Minutes of the Session, 5 February 1940. The plan to retire the church debt was revealed to the session at its meeting on 11 November 1940.

[35]McPherson, *History of First Presbyterian Church*, 48.

[36]Minutes of the Session, 12 January 1941. The session agreed on 12 January 1941 to call for the congregational meeting for the announcement. The congregational meeting occurred on 26 January 1941.

[37]McPherson, *History of First Presbyterian Church*, 44; "Rev Patrick Dwight Miller," accessed 18 June 2015, http://www.findagrave.com/cgi-bin/fg.cgi?page=gr&GRid=127790423&ref=acom.

[38]Minutes of the Meeting of the Congregation of First Presbyterian Church, 19 October 1941. These minutes are contained in the sessional records for that year.

[39]"Registration Card for Maurice Sommers," accessed 28 June 2015, http://search.ancestry.com/cgi-bin/sse.dll?db=YMDraftCardsWWII&h=168768&indiv=try&o_vc=Record:OtherRecord&rhSource=60525.

First Presbyterian Church before accepting the call to First Presbyterian Church in Raleigh.[40]

Sommers began his ministry at the church on what could be considered the most momentous Sunday in American history, 7 December 1941. Through his leadership the church became quickly involved in the war effort. Even before the attack on Pearl Harbor brought American involvement in the war, the church had already formed a "Committee on Program for Soldiers and Sailors" for the purpose of remaining informed of "boys from our church who go into the service of our country."[41] By February 1942, the church was lending assistance to the YMCA to provide hospitality to soldiers passing through the city.[42] An interesting comment in the sessional records two months later indicates the sense of fear that gripped the nation in the early days of American involvement in the war. It was noted that the church "should place its facilities at the disposal of the Government" in a potential emergency situation where refugees might need to be housed and cared for.[43]

One of the most important ways that First Presbyterian Church supported the war effort was to house soldiers in its facilities as they came through the city. The women's circles provided much of the hospitality, such as keeping the rooms clean and providing snacks, reading materials, and breakfast. The women hosted a Christmas party for soldiers as well. The Vanguard Class contributed by providing hosts for the soldiers each weekend. On average, forty soldiers were housed in the church facility each weekend.[44] By January 1944, a report to the session indicates that more than 2,000 soldiers had used the facility during the previous year.[45] The church facility for the soldiers operated until 31 March 1946.[46]

The church did not forget the spiritual dimension of the war effort. Beginning in December 1942, the church doors were unlocked each day

---

[40]*News and Observer* (Raleigh, NC), 6 December 1941, 14.

[41]Minutes of the Session, 7 July 1941.

[42]Ibid., 8 February 1942.

[43]Ibid., 6 April 1942.

[44]McPherson, *History of First Presbyterian Church*, 49.

[45]Minutes of the Session, 3 January 1944.

[46]McPherson, *History of First Presbyterian Church*, 49.

from nine to five so that anyone who wished may come into the sanctuary and pray.[47] During each Sunday worship service throughout the war, at a designated time, the church organist played "My Country 'Tis of Thee," quietly on the organ for a time of silent prayer for the soldiers. Mamie Wyatt, Luella Corell Metcalf, and Elizabeth Stamps, along with some of the other women of the church, held weekly prayer meetings in the Bettie Penick Sunday school room for soldiers, and during the prayer time, the soldiers from First Presbyterian Church were prayed for by name.[48] The women took seriously the responsibility to pray for the soldiers. During the pastor's vacation period in 1942, the session decided to cancel Wednesday evening services for July and August. Elizabeth Stamps, the president of the Women's Auxiliary, wrote a letter to the session expressing that the women were "disturbed" over the elders' decision to cancel the mid-week services and following "considerable" discussion, the services were continued with the pulpit supply committee providing supervision.[49] The Women's Auxiliary also led the effort to honor each of the church's soldiers at the conclusion of the war. Their service men's committee ordered Bibles to be placed in the pews in honor of each man and woman from the church who served. They also recommended that the Bible class for young business women in the Sunday school should become a class for young couples, both married and unmarried, "thus making a place in the Sunday school for returning men and women."[50]

The founding of White Memorial Presbyterian Church was another important milestone during Sommers's tenure as pastor. The idea for a new church began to be discussed in 1944. That year, the home mission committee of the Granville Presbytery offered to contribute $5,000 [$66,200] for the purchase of a lot in in the Hayes-Barton area of the city so that a new church might be constructed and established. First Presbyterian showed interest in the project and requested that several of the elders on the planning committee take the lead in investigating a

---

[47]Minutes of the Session, 7 December 1942.

[48]Ibid.

[49]Ibid., 6 July 1942.

[50]Ibid., 3 September 1945.

suitable location.[51] Following a survey of the community to assess the need for a new church, the committee reported back to the session that a new church was needed and desired in the area.[52]

On 8 January 1945, R. A. Snow of the planning committee provided a report to the elders that suggested the next step in the process of organizing a new church would be to solicit interest among the membership of First Presbyterian in order to find a group willing to organize the new church. He recommended that matters such as location and the purchase of the property should be left to those who would be organizing the church. The discussion then turned toward the North Vanguard Church, also a mission from First Presbyterian. Could the mother church support both the North Vanguard Church and a new church start? The elders determined that First Presbyterian would continue to assist the North Vanguard Church, "at the same time having in mind the need to develop the responsibility of the church [North Vanguard] to handle its own affairs, and not project its financial policy from this church."[53]

The new church was organized on 19 May 1946 and named White Memorial Presbyterian Church after William McClanahan White, pastor at First Presbyterian from 1908 to 1934. A building was constructed on Oberlin Road. From its organization in 1946 until the sanctuary was completed in 1952, the church met regularly Sunday mornings in the Colony (now Rialto) Theatre on Glenwood Avenue.[54] A total of 236 members from First Presbyterian Church became charter members of the new church, and the first pastor was Dr. Charles Lynnwood Brown, who served from 1946 to 1966.[55]

There were a few other interesting moments during Sommers's pastorate that deserve mention. In 1944, another example of the church's dedication to the Christian Sabbath was once again apparent. The ses-

---

[51]Ibid., 8 September 1944.

[52]Ibid., 11 December 1944 and 8 January 1945.

[53]Ibid., 8 January 1945.

[54]"Who We Are," accessed 29 June 2015, http://www.whitememorial.org/pages/page.asp?page_id=172344.

[55]McPherson, *History of First Presbyterian Church*, 50–51.

sion voted that summer to send a letter to the garage and filling station across the street from the church, requesting that the station close on Sunday mornings from 10:00 a.m. until noon.[56] Within a month, the station complied with the church's request, a gesture that shows how different the cultural values of the 1940s were from those of the early twenty-first century.[57]

As 1948 came to a close, Mrs. C. P. Wharton (Sarah Duncan Wharton) retired after serving as the church organist for approximately fifty years. To show appreciation for her many years of service, the church named her "Organist Emeritus" and designated that she receive a monthly stipend of $35 [$339].[58] She was seventy-one years old at the time and had been a widow for nineteen years.[59] Her husband, Cyrus P. Wharton (1852–1929), had been a prominent photographer in Raleigh and a deacon at First Presbyterian Church. They had been faithful members of the church for years, and the gesture of a stipend in Sarah's later years was a gracious act on the part of the congregation.

Following World War II, some American Presbyterians sought a reunification of the Northern and Southern churches into one General Assembly, an effort to heal the schism that had existed between the two regions since the antebellum years.[60] Reunification efforts eventually stalled as they were met with opposition by many Southern Presbyterian churches, primarily over issues of theology and social matters.[61] Many of the Southern Presbyterian churches considered the Northern Presbyterians theologically suspect. Furthermore, some Northern Presbyterians

---

[56]Minutes of the Session, 5 June 1944.

[57]Ibid., 3 July 1944.

[58]McPherson, *History of First Presbyterian Church*, 52; Minutes of the Session, 13 December 1948.

[59]"Sarah Cornelia Duncan Wharton," accessed 30 June 2015, http://www.findagrave.com/cgi-bin/fg.cgi?page=gr&GRid=44778415.

[60]See Sydney E. Ahlstrom, *A Religious History of the American People*, 2nd ed. (New Haven: Yale University Press, 2004) 648–69, for a general discussion of the division between not only Presbyterians in the antebellum years but also Methodists and Baptists.

[61]Union between Northern and Southern Presbyterian groups did not occur until 1983 with the creation of the Presbyterian Church (U.S.A.).

were also beginning to call for racial desegregation in all areas of American life, an issue that would be placed front and center in the South. The prominence of liberal Presbyterian preachers, such as Harry Emerson Fosdick, whose sermons were broadcast nationwide over the radio and published in magazines and books, caused much suspicion on the part of some in the Southern churches.[62]

---

[62]See *Dictionary of Christianity in America*, ed. Daniel G. Reid et al. (Downers Grove, IL: InterVarsity Press, 1990) s.v. "Fosdick, Harry Emerson"; Robert Moats Miller, *Harry Emerson Fosdick: Preacher, Pastor, Prophet* (New York: Oxford University Press, 1985); Harry Emerson Fosdick, *The Living of These Days: An Autobiography* (New York: Harper and Row, 1956). Harry Emerson Fosdick (1878–1969) was one of the most important religious voices in America in the late nineteenth and early twentieth centuries. Originally from Buffalo, New York, he was educated at Colgate University, where he encountered William Newton Clarke, one of the leading voices of liberalism in America at the time. Fosdick did further study at Union Theological Seminary in New York and Columbia University. Originally, and for most of his life and career, Fosdick was a Baptist. He was ordained to the Baptist ministry, serving his first pastorate in Montclair, New Jersey. His experience as a chaplain in France during World War I, and the horrors he witnessed during the war, made him declare himself a pacifist for the rest of his life after the war, a commitment he held until his death. His growing reputation in New York as an outstanding preacher prompted the First Presbyterian Church in New York City to extend an invitation for him to become their "Pulpit Minister" in 1918. The most famous sermon he ever preached occurred on 21 May 1922, during the height of the Fundamentalist Controversy. It was a direct challenge to fundamentalism called "Shall the Fundamentalists Win?" He gained national attention when the sermon was published by a Presbyterian layman named Ivy Lee. In the sermon, Fosdick denied the necessity of belief in the virgin birth of Jesus and argued that the doctrine of the inerrancy of the Bible could not be squared with the modern worldview. Additionally, he rejected the doctrine of the literal second coming of Jesus. The sermon angered many conservatives, especially in Presbyterian circles. He remained at First Presbyterian Church in New York until 1924, when he was asked to become a member of the Presbyterian Church, a move that would have forced his theology to come under the scrutiny of the denomination. From 1925 to 1930, he was the pastor of the Park Avenue Baptist Church in New York City, which eventually became the Riverside Church, built primarily through the benefaction of its richest member, John D. Rockefeller.

Another factor that made reunification efforts controversial was the Presbyterian support for the Federal Council of Churches, an ecumenical organization created in 1908. The original purpose of the organization, made up of thirty-three denominations, was to promote ecumenical unity and dialogue among Christians. By necessity, the organization avoided specific doctrinal conformity statements in order to allow for as many groups as possible to join comfortably. Only in the preamble to the constitution did a doctrinal statement appear, declaring that the purpose of the Federal Council of Churches was "to manifest the essential oneness of the Christian churches of America in Jesus Christ as their divine Lord and Savior."[63]

Following World War I, the organization began to work for social justice, and as the twentieth century progressed, it became increasingly more progressive in its political activity. The nature of those efforts caused some Presbyterians, particularly in the South, to be suspicious of involvement in the group. By 1947, a number of elders in the Southern Presbyterian Church were especially concerned about the church's participation in the Federal Council of Churches. On 6 August 1947, in Greenville, South Carolina, a group of elders participated by invitation in a dialogue about the organization. The meeting occurred at the behest of Dr. William P. Jacobs, president of Presbyterian College in Clinton, South Carolina, who personally invited the participants and presided. After a discussion of the matter, the group urged the Presbyterian Church in the United States (Southern Presbyterian Church) to withdraw membership from the Federal Council of Churches because of its liberal theology and progressive social and political activities.[64]

The elders at First Presbyterian Church in Raleigh were also concerned about these matters. The issue first appeared in the sessional records on 6 October 1947. The report from the recent meeting of the presbytery was a topic of conversation involving the issues of reunion with

---

[63]*Dictionary of Christianity in America*, ed. Daniel G. Reid et al. (Downers Grove, IL: InterVarsity Press, 1990) s.v. "Federal Council of Churches."

[64]See the pamphlet *Some Reasons Why the Southern Presbyterian Church Should Withdraw from the Federal Council of Churches* (Weaverville, NC: The Southern Presbyterian Journal Company, 1947).

the Northern Presbyterians, as well as withdrawal from the Federal Council of Churches. Following the elders' conversation about the matter, they decided to schedule an additional meeting of the session to discuss the matters further.[65] That meeting occurred the following month when the session voted sixteen to four that the Southern Presbyterian Church should withdraw from the Federal Council of Churches.[66] There is no evidence of a vote by the session regarding reunion with Northern Presbyterians. The matter was discussed again, however, in July 1949 when the elders heard a report and a recommendation that such an action would have negative consequences for the Southern Presbyterian churches.[67]

Sommers's pastorate at First Presbyterian Church concluded in 1949. At a congregational meeting on 22 May of that year, he announced his plans to resign effective 30 June. The church accepted his resignation with regret.[68] Sommers left Raleigh to become the pastor of the First Presbyterian Church in Kingsport, Tennessee, a position he held for several years before moving to First Presbyterian Church in Morristown, Tennessee. He died on 30 March 1990 and is buried in Fort Defiance, Virginia.[69]

James S. Sprunt. The church took more than a year to fill the pastoral vacancy left by Sommers. Initially, the church extended a call to E. B. McGurkin, pastor of First Presbyterian Church in Knoxville, Tennessee, since 1936. McGurkin expressed interest but eventually opted to stay

---

[65]Minutes of the Session, 6 October 1947.

[66]Ibid., 24 November 1947. The General Assembly had instructed the synods to discuss the matter. The Synod of North Carolina had then passed the same instructions along to the presbyteries, which in turned asked their churches to discuss and recommend a course of action. See *Some Reasons Why*, 2.

[67]Minutes of the Session, 11 July 1949.

[68]Minutes of the Meeting of the Congregation of First Presbyterian Church, 22 May 1949 (contained in the sessional record book covering the years 1945–1951).

[69]"Maurice Omar Sommers in the U.S., Find a Grave Index, 1600s-Current," accessed 26 Aoril 2015, http://www.findagrave.com/cgi-bin/fg.cgi?page=gr&GSln=Sommer&GSiman=1&GSst=48&Gsob=c&GRid+1-3-22794&.

where he was.[70] The nominating committee continued its work for several more months, resulting in a congregational meeting on 26 November 1950 for the purpose of extending a call to James S. Sprunt from Tennessee. Sprunt began his duties at First Presbyterian Church on 15 February 1951.[71]

James S. Sprunt was born in Rock Hill, South Carolina, on 24 January 1901 but was reared in Charleston, where his father, Rev. Alexander Sprunt, served as pastor of the First Presbyterian Church for thirty-six years. The younger Sprunt received his BA from Davidson College. He continued his education at Union Theological Seminary in Richmond, Virginia, where he received his BD. He then received his ThM from Princeton Theological Seminary, and later Hampden-Sydney College awarded him the honorary DD degree.[72] Sprunt was an experienced pastor prior to his arrival in Raleigh. He had served churches in Chase City and Boydton, Virginia. He was also the pastor at the Knox Presbyterian Church in Norfolk, Virginia, the Westminster Presbyterian Church in Lynchburg, Virginia, and finally the Lookout Mountain Presbyterian Church in Lookout Mountain, Tennessee.[73]

Sprunt became the pastor of First Presbyterian Church at the beginning of a decade that witnessed the beginnings of remarkable shifts in American society. Among Protestants in the post-World War II era, there remained significant opposition to Roman Catholicism, a sentiment that had roots in the large waves of Catholic immigrants that came to America's shores in the nineteenth century. For example, in 1945, Carl McIntire, a fundamentalist radio preacher, argued that Catholicism was more of a threat to American society than communism: "If one had to choose between the two, one would be much better off in a commu-

---

[70]Minutes of the Meeting of the Congregation of First Presbyterian Church, 26 February 1950 (contained in the sessional record book covering the years 1945–1951).

[71]Minutes of the Session, 18 February 1951; McPherson, *History of First Presbyterian Church*, 55.

[72]"Report of the Nominating Committee, The First Presbyterian Church," (unpublished document, 26 November 1950), contained in Minutes of the Session, 6 January 1957.

[73]McPherson, *History of First Presbyterian Church*, 55.

nistic society than in a Roman Catholic Fascist set-up."[74] Fundamentalists were not the only Protestant group in America suspicious of Roman Catholicism.

Mainstream Protestants were also wary of Catholic power. Franklin D. Roosevelt in 1939 appointed a personal representative to the Vatican, "a move that sparked fierce Protestant opposition."[75] On 20 October 1951, President Harry S. Truman appointed Mark W. Clark to be the first U. S. ambassador to the Vatican. The firestorm of controversy from Protestants in the nation forced Clark to withdraw his name within just a few months. Truman made no further efforts to appoint an ambassador.[76]

In November 1951, the First Presbyterian Session passed a resolution opposing Truman's actions. This resolution represents a very rare occasion in the history of First Presbyterian Church when the church took a public stance on a national political issue. The resolution reads,

> (1) We deeply regret that, at a time when national unity is so imperative, the President of the United States has seen fit to initiate an action in the name of an Ambassador to the Vatican, which is bound to result in unhappy controversy and great division in our country.
>
> (2) We express the hope and the belief that this unwise proposal will be opposed by a large majority of fair-minded Americans of every religious conviction, and that it will be either withdrawn or defeated in the Senate.
>
> (3) We vigorously protest this action as contrary to our blood-bought American heritage of the complete separation of church and state; and we earnestly oppose all diplomatic appointments which recognize any religious entity as a political state.

---

[74]Mark A. Noll, *A History of Christianity in the United States and Canada* (Grand Rapids: William B. Eerdmans Publishing Company, 1992) 537.

[75]Ibid., 439. See also "The Vatican Files," accessed 6 July 2015, http://docs.fdrlibrary.marist.edu/vatican1.html.

[76]"The President's News Conference" (19 January 1950), accessed 6 July 2015, http://trumanlibrary.org/publicpapers/index.php?pid=585. Ronald Reagan finally succeeded in appointing an ambassador to the Vatican in 1984.

> (4) We respectfully but urgently request our representatives in the United States Senate, the Honorable Clyde R. Hoey and the Honorable Willis Smith to vote against the confirmation of this appointment.
>
> Copies of this statement to be sent to President Harry S. Truman and Senators Hoey and Smith.[77]

The postscript to this episode and an interesting example of how quickly things changed in American society regarding Catholics is the election of John F. Kennedy to the presidency in 1960, the first and only Roman Catholic to hold the office. That, however, may in part be attributed to the fact that Kennedy was able to embrace his faith yet dismiss fears that he would be controlled by the Vatican. On 12 September 1960, he made a famous speech before the Greater Houston Ministerial Association in which he indisputably embraced the concept of separation of church and state in order to dispel any fear of Vatican interference.[78] Historians generally agree that this speech was a turning point for the election and for how many Protestants in America viewed Catholics.[79]

One of the church's most important milestones during the Sprunt years was the renovation of the sanctuary. The idea of a full repair and upgrade of the sanctuary facility was discussed as early as 1949, but following the resignation of Sommers, the church decided to delay the project until a new pastor was selected.[80] By July 1951, just a few months

---

[77]Minutes of the Session, 13 November 1951.

[78]For a text of Kennedy's speech, see "Transcript: JFK's Speech on His Religion," accessed 6 July 2015, http://www.npr.org/templates/story/story.php?storyId=16920600.

[79]For example, see Doris Kearns Goodwin, *The Fitzgeralds and the Kennedys* (New York: St. Martin's Press, 1987) 928; Robert Dallek, *An Unfinished Life: John F. Kennedy: 1917–1963* (Boston: Little, Brown, and Company, 2003) 283–84; Thomas J. Carty, *A Catholic in the White House? Religion, Politics, and John F. Kennedy's Presidential Campaign* (New York: Palgrave McMillan, 2004) 139. See also W. J. Rorabaugh, *The Real Making of the President: Kennedy, Nixon, and the 1960 Election* (Lawrence: University of Kansas Press, 2009) 180 ff. Rorabaugh argues that Kennedy's Catholicism won Catholic Republican voters while causing him to lose some Protestant Democratic voters.

[80]Minutes of the Session, 7 November 1949 and 2 October 1950.

after Sprunt's installation, a joint meeting of the deacons and elders had determined to spend up to $1,000 [$9,770] for architectural drawings and plans for sanctuary renovation.[81] McPherson reports that "much discussion" ensued about whether the sanctuary should be "refurbished, remodeled, or rebuilt."[82] The suggestion of moving to an entirely new location was also discussed. Ultimately, the plan for a remodeling of the sanctuary was approved on 22 June 1953.[83] By July 1955, the church accepted bids on the project and began using the Ambassador Theatre for Sunday morning worship services.[84] The plans called for three classrooms and a choir room to be underneath the sanctuary. Along with the sanctuary, the main floor contained a chapel and a classroom to be used by the Bettie Penick Class.[85]

The dedication of the sanctuary occurred on 10 June 1956. The celebratory day began with a new cornerstone placement at 10:15 a.m., followed by the worship service at 11:00 with James Sprunt delivering the sermon. During the afternoon, the church held an open house from 3:00 to 5:00. At 7:30 p.m., Ernest White, a guest organist, performed an organ concert on the new church organ. At 8:00 p.m., the church hosted the traditional union worship service with First Baptist Church and Edenton Street Methodist Church, which featured the First Presbyterian choir singing Mendelssohn's cantata *Hymn of Praise*.[86]

The renovation project featured a new organ, new pews, and a fully air conditioned structure. Within the chancel were two stained-glass windows created by the Willett Stained Glass Company of Philadelphia.[87] Much of the symbolism of the windows was suggested by Sprunt

---

[81]Ibid., 2 July 1951.

[82]McPherson, *History of First Presbyterian Church*, 57.

[83]Ibid. See also Minutes of the Session, 22 June 1953. The vote taken by the congregation was 205 in favor of remodeling and sixty-five in favor of a temporary renovation with a new church to be built in the future.

[84]Minutes of the Session, 10 July 1955. See McPherson, *History of First Presbyterian Church*, 58. The Ambassador Theatre was located one block from the church and was managed by W. G. Enloe, one of the church's elders.

[85]McPherson, *History of First Presbyterian Church*, 58.

[86]*News and Observer*, 9 June 1956, 3.

[87]Ibid.

and based on the passage in John 1:17: "The law indeed was given through Moses; grace and truth came through Jesus Christ." One of the windows represented the Old Testament tradition within Christianity and at the top was the likeness of Moses. The other window, topped by a likeness of Jesus, represented the New Testament. At Sprunt's suggestion, the two windows were dedicated to Mrs. Frances Devereux, who had provided the gift that gave the church its first manse back in the middle of the nineteenth century.[88] The cost for the renovation project was approximately $216,000 [$1.85 million].[89]

Many positive things were happening in the church during the Sprunt years; however, a personal loss in his life brought a cloud of grief over the entire congregation. On 9 September 1952, his wife, Kate, suddenly died. Her death was the result of complications from a recent heart attack. The couple had been married since 1926.[90] From his personal experience of grief, Sprunt preached several memorable sermons to the congregation such as "Not Why, but How?" and "One Foot in Heaven."[91] Following her death, the church established the Kate C. Sprunt Memorial Library in her memory, beginning with a substantial gift from Mr. and Mrs. Alan S. O'Neal.[92] The church selected a library committee to build and maintain the collection.[93] The library's dedication occurred on 15 February 1953, the second anniversary of the Sprunts' arrival at First Presbyterian Church.[94] The library quickly became a successful and integral part of the shared community at the church. By October 1954, the library committee reported that it contained 1,018 volumes and fourteen periodical subscriptions.[95]

---

[88]McPherson, *History of First Presbyterian Church*, 58–59. Sprunt preached a series of sermons for three months following the sanctuary's dedication, which focused on each symbol contained in the chancel windows. The sermons were published by the church in a booklet titled *Windows on the Word.*

[89]*News and Observer,* 11 June 1956, 22.

[90]"Mrs. James Sprunt Passes," *News and Observer,* 10 September 1952, 21.

[91]McPherson, *History of First Presbyterian Church*, 59.

[92]Ibid.

[93]Minutes of the Session, 8 and 19 October 1952.

[94]Ibid., 5 January 1953.

[95]Ibid., 4 October 1954.

Within a few years, Sprunt married Melvina Hobson, who had served the church as director of Christian education. She resigned her position with the church when she married Sprunt although she was not forced to do so. In a letter from the session to her, the elders declared, "We are happy in the thought that we are not losing you, but that we are gaining a worthy companion for our beloved pastor. We realize that you are entering upon a larger field of service and our payer is that you and Dr. Sprunt will be ministering to us for many years to come."[96]

On 17 May 1954, the United States Supreme Court ruled unanimously in the landmark case *Brown v. Board of Education* that the Jim Crow doctrine of "separate but equal" in the public school system was unconstitutional. The court ordered that public school systems all over the nation be desegregated. The ruling signaled the beginning of the end for public segregation in America. On 1 December 1955, in Montgomery, Alabama, Rosa Parks was arrested when she refused to give up her seat on a bus to a white passenger. The civil rights movement was born.

In 1954, North Carolina governor William Umstead created the advisory committee on education to recommend North Carolina's response to the *Brown v. Board of Education* decision. The advisory committee was chaired by Thomas Pearsall, a businessman from Rocky Mount, who also served as speaker of the House in the General Assembly, and was composed of twelve white and three black members.[97] The Pearsall committee recommended several tactics that served to stall desegregation of the schools. It stated that integration could not happen in North Carolina and that it should not be tried and proposed giving local school districts power over pupil assignment to the schools, which would thereby forestall the order from the United States Supreme Court.[98]

In March 1955, the General Assembly passed the Pupil Assignment Act, which gave local school districts control over student school assign-

[96]Undated correspondence between the Session of First Presbyterian Church, Raleigh, and Miss Melvina Hobson (reproduction of original letter), Minutes of the Session, 3 October 1955.

[97]Carl E. Campbell, "Pupil Assignment Act," Ncpedia, accessed 8 July 2015, http://ncpedia.org/pupil-assignment-act. The three black members of the Pearsall Committee were all state employees.

[98]Ibid.

ment, school enrollment, and bus transportation and removed all references to race in the school's laws. It used ambiguous language to administer student transfers between schools and perhaps most importantly set up a very complicated appeals process designed to hinder parental challenge to local board decisions about school assignment. Because any reference to race was eliminated from school laws, the state was able to argue that the Pupil Assignment Act complied with the *Brown* decision, but in reality, it provided a clever way for North Carolina to resist full integration of the state's schools. The law did create a few token examples of African-American students who were able to enroll in predominantly white schools, but it would not be until the late 1960s and early 1970s before schools in North Carolina were fully integrated.[99]

To its credit, the Granville Presbytery resisted the Pearsall action and in 1956 passed the following resolution:

> That the Presbytery of Granville go on record as unqualifiedly opposed to the recommendations of the North Carolina Advisory Committee on Education now being considered before the North Carolina General Assembly on the grounds that these recommendations endeavor to preserve a discrimination which is out of harmony with Christian theology and ethics and clearly contrary to the practice and principles of the Word of God.[100]

Unfortunately, the Session of First Presbyterian strongly opposed the presbytery's resolution. On 27 August 1956, the First Presbyterian Session declared, "The Session of the First Presbyterian Church of Raleigh, North Carolina, believing in the separation of Church and State feels that Granville Presbytery at its meeting on July 24, 1956, erred in adopting the…resolution."[101]

Within the life of First Presbyterian Church there were a couple of other significant events during the Sprunt pastorate. First, the sessional records indicate that by 1952 the Alfred Moment Sunday school class had dwindled to three members and was thereby discontinued.[102] Alfred

[99]Ibid.

[100]Minutes of the Session, 27 August 1956.

[101]Ibid., 27 August 1956.

[102]Ibid., 4 February 1952.

Moment's pastoral tenure lasted for only four years but left an indelible impression upon the congregation of his day. As the reader will recall from chapter 6, he began teaching the Bible to a group of young men while he was the pastor. The class grew to approximately forty members, and he taught it until his death in 1907 when the class was more formally organized into a Sunday school class. It had officers and outreach projects similar in some ways to the larger Vanguard Class. One particular distinctive of the class was its open forum method of Bible study whereby members were expected to study the assigned lesson and then come to the class and express their opinions openly about the text studied.[103]

The other change within the life of the congregation during Sprunt's years was the development of a deacon and elder rotation system whereby each deacon and elder would serve a term then rotate off the respective body for a period of time before being eligible for re-election. Sprunt was in favor of such a system even before he became the church's pastor. In late 1950, while still in conversation with the pastor search committee, he expressed a desire to see such a change and questioned whether the church would be open to it. The rotation system went into effect in 1951.[104]

James Sprunt shepherded the church through the significant years of the 1950s. On 10 May 1957, he announced to the elders that he had accepted a call to the Bethel Presbyterian Church in Staunton, Virginia. In a letter to the session he spelled out four reasons why he felt that he needed to resign: (1) he believed that "reasonably short pastorates are good for a church;"[105] (2) he believed that he had accomplished the goals he set for the church when he began his tenure as pastor; (3) he believed that at age fifty-six, this would be the last opportunity he would have for a move; (4) he saw as a new challenge the call to serve the Bethel Presbyterian Church in Staunton, "a church with a long and honored history of

[103]McPherson, *History of First Presbyterian Church*, 95–96.

[104]Minutes of the Session, 6 November 1950 and 16 April 1951.

[105]James S. Sprunt, "A Statement to the Session of First Presbyterian Church, Raleigh," (unpublished document, 10 May 1957), contained in Minutes of the Session, 10 May 1957.

over two hundred years," but a smaller church with less stress.[106] Ironically, William McPheeters, the founding pastor of First Presbyterian Church, came to Raleigh from the same church.[107] Sprunt served the Bethel congregation from 1957 to 1968 and retired from ministry. He died in Staunton on 21 December 1981.[108]

First Presbyterian Church turned once again to new pastoral leadership. Its next pastor would become the longest tenured pastor in the history of the congregation. That story follows in the next chapter.

---

[106]Ibid.

[107]McPherson, *History of First Presbyterian Church*, 62.

[108]"James Sprunt, D.D.," accessed 9 July 2015, http://www.findagrave.com/cgi-bin/fg.cgi?page=gr&GSln=Sprunt&GSfn=James&GSiman=1&GScid=2133995&GRid=66355518&.

9

Building a Heritage

The Context

In his inaugural address on 20 January 1961, John F. Kennedy said that "the world is very different now." While other words in his speech that day became immortalized, no other phrase captures any better the transformation that the nation was about to experience over the next decade. The "torch has been passed to a new generation" and for those who lived through it, some may have wondered at the end of the decade if the light of the torch had been extinguished.

As Kennedy occupied the oval office, he assumed his predecessor's headaches with Cuba. A botched CIA attempt to overthrow the Castro regime (known as the Bay of Pigs invasion) in 1961 humiliated the young president even though the operation had been planned by the Eisenhower administration. The following year, the Soviet Union, possibly emboldened by the Bay of Pigs fiasco, deployed nuclear missiles on the island of Cuba, which threatened to bring the world to the brink of nuclear holocaust. Most Americans did not know of the crisis until Kennedy's television broadcast to the nation on 22 October 1962, when he declared that any launch of such missiles toward any nation in the Western hemisphere would be regarded as an attack on the United States and would elicit a full retaliatory strike. The crisis was averted following a naval blockade of Cuba and backdoor diplomacy. Kennedy's firm stand against the Soviets established his foreign policy *bona fides,* but his shocking assassination in Dallas, Texas, on 22 November 1963 plunged the nation into mourning and fear for the future.

Lyndon B. Johnson became the thirty-sixth president following Kennedy's assassination and led the nation through the middle years of the 1960s. Elected president in 1964 after defeating Senator Barry Goldwater, Johnson brought important social change to the nation by ushering through Congress legislation dubbed "the Great Society." The

Great Society legislation included expansive social reforms, such as the creation of Medicare and Medicaid, environmental laws, support for public broadcasting and for education, and an initiative to alleviate poverty, which he called the "War on Poverty." Johnson also signed the long-anticipated Civil Rights Act in 1964—arguably the most important social legislation of the 1960s. The public support for Johnson's presidency began to wane after the midterm elections of 1966 because of the continuing escalation of the war in Vietnam. By 1968, Johnson, challenged in the Democratic primaries by Eugene McCarthy and later Robert F. Kennedy, knew that he would not be able to secure the nomination of the party. In a speech before the nation on 31 March 1968, Johnson withdrew from the presidential election, leaving Kennedy, McCarthy, Hubert Humphrey, and George Wallace as the top choices for the party.

Many Americans might have assumed that the nation was coming apart in spring 1968. On 4 April in Memphis, Tennessee, Martin Luther King Jr. was assassinated as he was leaving his motel room to speak at an evening event. When news of King's assassination was reported, riots broke out in scores of cities including Chicago, Washington, and Los Angeles. Robert Kennedy heard the news on his way to a campaign event in Indianapolis and gave an impromptu speech recalling King's commitment to nonviolence and pleading for calm in the midst of the tragedy. But only two months later, after winning the California Democratic primary, Robert Kennedy was assassinated following a victory speech before supporters gathered in the ballroom of the Ambassador Hotel in Los Angeles.

Richard Nixon, the Republican candidate, won the election of 1968 against Hubert Humphrey, who represented a badly fractured Democratic Party, but Vietnam dominated the headlines as the decade closed. By 1970, the Pentagon had long since known that the war was unwinnable. Even after Nixon's attempts to draw down troop numbers, the United States still had more than 300,000 troops in Vietnam. Nixon still achieved reelection in 1972 by a landslide, but by the next year, his administration was embroiled in the Watergate scandal, which ultimately ended with his resignation in disgrace as Congress prepared impeachment proceedings.

The election of Jimmy Carter to the presidency in 1976 brought a wave of optimism to the beleaguered nation after the turmoil of the 1960s, the horrors of Vietnam, and the scandal of Watergate. Carter was the first Southern Baptist ever elected to the presidency. Formerly the governor of Georgia, Carter made a name in Georgia politics by his honesty, integrity, and success as a peanut farmer. His genuine commitment to faith, exemplified by his active membership in the Plains Baptist Church in Plains, Georgia, captured the attention of Americans hopeful for change in Washington. Carter achieved significant milestones during his presidency. One such milestone was the Camp David Accords, which created lasting peace between Israel and Egypt. Other milestones highlighted successful negotiations, such as the SALT II treaty with the Soviet Union (lowering tension even further between the two super powers) and the return of the Panama Canal to Panama. Domestically, he created the departments of education and energy. He also created an energy policy, which encouraged conservation and development of new energy technologies. Perhaps the greatest of his successes related to his promotion of human rights both at home and abroad, which continues to the present through the work of the Carter Center in Atlanta, Georgia. But in spite of his successes, Carter's presidency was ultimately doomed by the inability to negotiate the release of American hostages in Iran, who were taken when the Iranian revolution began in 1979. A failed military rescue effort created a narrative about his administration—that it had weakened America's military—and ultimately led to the landslide election of Ronald Reagan in 1980.

The Reagan administration brought a seismic shift to American politics and culture with its emphasis on free enterprise as opposed to government intervention. Reagan's election also coincided with the rise of the religious right in American politics—a force that would influence political elections for years to come. Reagan emphasized a strong national defense, and many interpreters consider that to be one of the factors that brought an end to the Cold War and the downfall of the Soviet Union. Still, the Reagan administration was not without controversy. The Iran-Contra scandal was the most serious scandal from his presidency and led to indictments of several of his top aides.

City of Raleigh

The city of Raleigh experienced both transformation and growth during that era as well. In 1962, the legislature moved out of the state capitol to new facilities located a few blocks away. The new structure provided 200,000 square feet of space and was not without controversy. The structure ended up costing the taxpayers $6.2 million [$47.7 million], and some critics dubbed it "Baghdad-on-the Neuse," while others lampooned it as the "Taj Mahodges," after Governor Luther Hodges, whose administration conceived the idea.[1]

The business and commerce sector of the capital city received a major boost in 1965 when IBM announced that it would move into the Research Triangle Park. Other businesses arrived in Raleigh in the 1960s, including Exide, Aerotron, Corning Glass, Action Corporation, Athey Products, Duraw Manufacturing, Mallinckrodt, Litho Industries, Crown Zellerback, and Inco Electro Energy.[2]

The state capitol received much-needed repairs in the early 1970s as the General Assembly provided more than $500,000 [$2.16 million] for the project, which gave the old building a complete makeover both inside and out. The goal of the project was to restore the building as nearly as possible to its original appearance. The State Department of Archives and History, as well as architect William A. Dodge III, oversaw the work, which occurred between 1972 and 1975. By 2 June 1975, the work was completed, and the building was declared a National Historic Landmark.[3]

Another important state landmark to receive a makeover was the governor's mansion. For decades, the mansion had been in need of work. For example, in 1925, upon his election, Governor Angus McLean refused to move into the structure because he believed it to be unsanitary. The health department concurred, and money was appropriated for heating, insulation, and plumbing work. By 1971, the legislature began to discuss the possibility of a new structure. Those favoring a complete ren-

---

[1]James Vickers, *Raleigh: City of Oaks, An Illustrated History* (Woodland Hills, CA: Windsor Publications, 1982) 129.

[2]Ibid.

[3]Ibid., 132–33.

ovation of the original structure prevailed, and in 1975, the $575,000 [$2.49 million] project was complete.[4]

For most of the twentieth century, Raleigh had been able to weather the economic storms that created problems in other cities. Because of the large number of state employees, the city came through the Great Depression better than other cities. During the recession that hit the nation in 1975, unemployment figures in North Carolina reached 10.8 percent but reached no higher than 5 percent in Raleigh. The same held true with the larger recession that hit the nation in the early 1980s.[5]

First Presbyterian Church of Raleigh

The most noteworthy twentieth-century pastor at First Presbyterian Church was Albert George Edwards. He was born on 3 December 1916 in Canada to Annabella Donald and William F. Edwards. Due to the death of his mother in childbirth, Albert spent his childhood in Inverbervie, Scotland, where he was raised by his grandparents. During those years, his father moved to Atlanta to become superintendent of transportation for Georgia Power Company.[6] During his high school years, Edwards worked part time for a butcher in Inverbervie and liked the trade so much that he aspired to become a butcher. When his father, however, heard news of it, he insisted that Edwards leave Scotland and come to Atlanta, where he could continue his education instead. His grandfather accompanied him to Glasgow to catch a ship to America, and his parting

---

[4]Ibid., 133. For a complete history of the governor's mansion, see William Bushong, *North Carolina's Executive Mansion: The First Hundred Years* (Raleigh, NC: Executive Mansion Fine Arts Committee and the Executive Mansion Fund, Inc., 1991).

[5]Vickers, *Raleigh: City of Oaks*, 135–36.

[6]"Presbyterian College Report, March 1984," accessed 8 September 2015, https://archive.org/stream/presbyteriancoll371pres/presbyteriancoll371pres_djvu.txt. For other biographical sketches on Edwards's life, see William P. McPherson, ed., *The History of First Presbyterian Church, Raleigh, North Carolina: 1816–1991* (Raleigh: Commercial Printing, 1991) 62–63, and "Albert George Edwards," accessed 8 September 2015, http://www.bryan-leefuneralhome.com/obits/obituaries/albert-george-edwards/.

words to young Albert were, "Laddie, you'll end up in the ministry."[7] Edwards recalled, "I remember laughing inside and saying to myself, 'A fat chance of that happening! That's the most ludicrous thing I've ever heard.'"[8]

Upon arrival in Atlanta, Edwards enrolled at Georgia Tech University and attended for two years. In his second year, he began to attend Westminster Presbyterian Church, where the great Peter Marshall was serving as pastor. Eventually, Edwards changed his career plans from electrical engineering to ministry and transferred to Presbyterian College in Clinton, South Carolina. He received his bachelor's degree in 1940.[9] Three years later, he received his BD from Union Theological Seminary in Richmond, Virginia, and ordination from the West Hanover Presbytery. That same year, he also began his first pastorate at the Orange Presbyterian Church in Orange, Virginia. Edwards then enlisted in the army in 1945, seeking to receive commission as a chaplain, but he was ineligible for an officer's commission because he was not a United States citizen. His citizenship application was not approved until the end of the war. After military duty, he returned to his pastorate in Orange and married Margaret Early, a librarian he had met from Bealeton, Virginia. In January 1948, the young couple moved to Harrisonburg, Virginia, where he accepted a call to the city's First Presbyterian Church, a position he retained until moving to Raleigh in 1958.[10]

Edwards began his pastoral tenure at First Presbyterian Church in January 1958 and remained in that role until June 1986. His steady, wise leadership during that long tenure endeared him to the congregation and the city of Raleigh as well. During those years the church experienced remarkable growth, growing from approximately 1,000 members to more than 2,100 at the end of his pastorate. The church's annual income during those years also grew exponentially from approximately $125,000

[7]"Presbyterian College Report, March 1984."

[8]Ibid.

[9]Ibid. See also McPherson, *History of First Presbyterian Church*, 62. Edwards received honorary doctoral degrees from Davis-Elkins College, Presbyterian College, and Campbell University.

[10]"Presbyterian College Report, March 1984."

[$1.01 million] when he began to more than $1 million [$8.06 million] when he retired.[11] His pulpit delivery and sermon content resonated well with the congregation and the broader Raleigh community. William McPherson, an earlier chronicler of the church's history, estimated that Edwards "probably addressed more high school and college graduates and spoke to more civic clubs and business groups than any man in North Carolina during his time."[12] He served as chaplain to the House of Representatives in the North Carolina General Assembly, spoke more than a thousand times to civic groups and clubs, and delivered nearly 8,000 sermons during his years at First Presbyterian.[13] His preaching was so popular that in 1960 the church began an early worship service on Sunday mornings at 8:45. Even with the two services, crowds filled the sanctuary to capacity and the overflow had to be accommodated in the Vanguard Room and the chapel with the services broadcast over closed circuit television.[14]

During his long pastorate in Raleigh, Edwards initiated numerous ministries to the downtown business community, which helped endear him to the city beyond the walls of the First Presbyterian Church. One of the most popular ministries he began was the Wednesday lunch in the fellowship hall. The church hostess and volunteers prepared lunch for downtown business employees for a nominal fee. After they were served, Edwards led a brief twenty-minute worship service, they were served following a brief, twenty-minute worship service led by Edwards. The "Early Birds," a weekly men's breakfast that first began at the S&W Cafeteria on Fayetteville Street during Lent in 1958 became another popular ministry that gave Edwards contact with the city's business leaders.[15]

---

[11]McPherson, *History of First Presbyterian Church*, 63.

[12]Ibid, 67.

[13]Helen Chappell, "Albert G. Edwards Dies; Led Raleigh's First Presbyterian," *News and Observer* (Raleigh, NC), 10 August 2011, included in "Dr. Albert Edwards," accessed 11 September 2015, http://revfrankhughesjr.org/images/Dr_Albert_Edwards_bio.pdf.

[14]Minutes of the Session, 14 December 1959, 24 January 1960, and 15 May 1960. See also McPherson, *History of First Presbyterian Church*, 64.

[15]McPherson, *History of First Presbyterian Church*, 63–64.

Peace College Lawsuit. Shortly after Albert Edwards assumed his new role as pastor, the church became involved in a dispute and subsequent lawsuit against the Synod of North Carolina concerning the ownership of Peace College. As seen in previous chapters, the history of Peace College is virtually inseparable from the history of First Presbyterian Church. The college's founder and much of its financial support through the years came directly from the church. The close bond between the college and the congregation became apparent in 1953 when the church and the five presbyteries of North Carolina transferred ownership of the college to the synod. Just before the transfer, however, the college added an important amendment to its charter, which stated that the synod could not close the school without providing the original owners (five presbyteries and First Presbyterian Church of Raleigh) the opportunity to resume control.[16]

The fateful scenario played out just two years later. The synod, in attempt to strengthen Presbyterian higher education in eastern North Carolina, devised a plan to consolidate Peace College, Flora McDonald College, and Presbyterian Junior College into a new school to be named St. Andrews Presbyterian College.[17] Despite other possibilities for the school's location, including Raleigh, the synod chose Laurinburg, North Carolina.[18] The consolidation plan meant that Peace College in Raleigh would no longer exist, prompting the school to invoke its charter amendment calling for the pre-1953 owners to assume control. The five

[16]Minutes of the Session, 2 August 1953 and *William Peace University Bulletin* (Fall 2011): 3, accessed 13 September 2015, http://www.peace.edu/ assets/docs/bulletin/WPU_Bulletin_Fall_2011.pdf. The Synod of North Carolina in 1943 requested that all six Presbyterian colleges in North Carolina change their charters and turn ownership over to the synod. Peace complied in 1953. It is interesting that in 1944 Flora McDonald College was hesitant to surrender ownership to the synod for fear that the synod might close the school. The synod responded that the school could change its charter and insert language to the effect that the original owners of the school would have an opportunity to resume operation of the school should a decision to close ever be made. That language, included in the Peace College charter in 1953, saved Peace College from consolidation. See Sidney Ann Wilson, *Personae: The History of Peace College*, 74.

[17]*News and Observer*, 3 July 1957, 2.

[18]Ibid.

presbyteries declined, but First Presbyterian Church stepped forward and assumed complete ownership.[19]

It became quickly apparent that the only way to save Peace College in Raleigh was through legal avenues. Edward Hipp, an elder at the church and an attorney, became the church's legal representative in the matter.[20] The church also enlisted Malcolm B. Seawell as co-counsel. In late 1960, before the church became involved in legal action, a group of five members each from White Memorial, West Raleigh, and First Presbyterian churches presented a compromise proposal to the St. Andrews board of directors. The compromise was an attempt to keep Peace College in Raleigh and proposed that St. Andrews could operate the school as a branch during the 1961–1962 academic year, during which the First Presbyterian Church would establish a foundation made up of the Presbyterians in the Raleigh area, which would take over operations of the school. If the foundation successfully raised the necessary funds to operate the school by 10 June 1962, St. Andrews would release all claim to the school. If, however, the foundation could not raise the funding to support the school in Raleigh, then First Presbyterian would relinquish any claim it had on the school.[21] The St. Andrews board of directors rejected the proposal and pressed forward with its original plans for consolidation.[22] The text of the rejection notice read,

> That after full consideration of the proposals made by the Session of the First [Presbyterian] Church the Board voted that the Session be informed that;
>
> The Board regrets that in view of its responsibility as agent of Synod it cannot accept the recommendations of agreement affecting Peace College and that the physical consolidation in Laurinburg will be executed as scheduled by the Synod and the Board does not intend to

---

[19]Minutes of the Session, 13 March 1957; *William Peace University Bulletin* (Fall 2011): 3.

[20]*News and Observer*, 3 July 1957, 1; Minutes of the Session, 23 February 1959.

[21]Minutes of the Session, 18 December 1960. A copy of the proposal is attached to the minutes of this meeting.

[22]*News and Observer*, 5 January 1961, 21.

> operate Peace College or any branch of St. Andrews College in Raleigh after August 10, 1961.[23]

Supporters of Peace College included more than just the congregation that birthed the school. Dr. Myra Williams Thornton, a former professor at the college wrote the following letter dated 20 June 1961 and addressed to the "Pastor, Elders, Deacons, First Presbyterian Church":

> Dear Friends:
>
> For several years I have thought to write you and others regarding Peace College. The attempt of the Synod of North Carolina to abolish the school has made me heartsick. *Why* would anyone want to abolish a school of the nature of Peace? If the school does what it used to do, and I feel very sure it *still* does, it should never go out of existence.
>
> From 1929 to 1936, a period of seven years, I taught at Peace College. In many ways I consider it one of the finest schools I ever knew. This, to me, is (was) one of the fine things Peace used to do: take girls who were weak and develop strength in them. When I say weak, I mean, in more ways than one: girls who had ability but somehow failed to make use of it have come to Peace and there found the inspiration and guidance necessary to arouse them to their best; girls who perhaps lacked confidence and were enabled to develop it; girls who might be inclined toward careless conduct were so guided and loved at Peace that they grew up right rather than wrong. I never knew a school which did more to help young girls grow into fine young women than Peace College. *Surely* the Presbyterians in N.C.; especially in Raleigh will support this splendid school and enable it to continue meeting the needs of young women! I hope *you folks* will support Peace.
>
> Sincerely yours,
> Myra Williams Thornton, Ph. D.
> (Mrs. James I. Thornton)[24][end block]

The church filed a lawsuit in Wake Superior Court on 12 January 1961, seeking a temporary injunction to prevent the St. Andrews board

---

[23]A copy of the notice, dated 3 January 1961, is attached to Minutes of the Session, 8 January 1961.

[24]Myra Williams Thornton to Pastor, Elders, Deacons, First Presbyterian Church, 20 June 1961. The letter is reproduced in the Minutes of the Session, 25 June 1961.

from interfering with Peace College. Appealing to the 1953 charter change, the church contended that the synod had no authority to close Peace College without first allowing the church the opportunity to assume control.[25] The following month, the court granted First Presbyterian Church the injunction for the continued operation of the college until the final outcome of the lawsuit, denied the St. Andrews board from bringing the Synod of North Carolina into the suit as a co-defendant, and denied the defendants' motion to dismiss the Peace College board of directors as co-plaintiffs.[26] The St. Andrews board appealed the injunction ruling to the North Carolina Supreme Court on 24 May 1961, but the appeal was denied. The injunction remained in place until the full suit could be heard and settled by the courts.[27]

The case was heard in Wake Superior Court by Judge George Fountain in December 1961, and First Presbyterian Church prevailed. The judge blocked all efforts by the Synod of North Carolina to close Peace College but provided that Peace must furnish records of annual audits and budgets to the St. Andrews College board each year, a "pestiferous little thing we wish was not there," according to William McPherson, an elder at First Presbyterian and chair of the Peace College board.[28] The caveat was written by the judge to protect St. Andrews's interests in the school in the event that Peace College should cease to be a church-related institution. The St. Andrews College board of directors again appealed the ruling to the North Carolina Supreme Court.[29]

A few weeks after the superior court decision, another attempt to settle the case materialized. The church proposed that should Peace College ever cease to be a church-related institution, any endowment received by the school after the compromise would not revert to St. Andrews. However, any endowment received by Peace College before the settlement would belong to St. Andrews if Peace ever ceased to operate

---

[25] *News and Observer*, 13 January 1961, 40.
[26] Ibid., 10 February 1961, 36.
[27] Ibid., 25 May 1961, 40.
[28] Ibid., 8 December 1961, 2.
[29] Ibid.

as church-related.[30] The St. Andrews board rejected the compromise, and a few days later, both sides dropped their appeals before the North Carolina Supreme Court.[31] On 10 June 1962, the board of trustees of Peace College of Raleigh, Inc. assumed control of the institution. First Presbyterian Church, now the owner of the college, appointed the twenty-four-member board of trustees as well as a thirteen-member foundation for promoting the school's finances.[32]

Fundraising for the school began—and became successful—almost immediately after the conclusion of the lawsuit. One of the first major benefactors was Grover M. Hermann, a businessman from Chicago who gave an initial gift of $300,000 [$2.31 million] to the school in 1962. William G. Ross, a Peace College trustee and member of First Presbyterian Church, should be credited with connecting Hermann to Peace College. On a business trip to Chicago, Ross and Hermann, who had mutual business interests, began to talk about their respective Presbyterian churches over lunch. Hermann, a member of Fourth Presbyterian Church in Chicago, told of all that his church was doing to better its community. Ross then presented the recent history of First Presbyterian Church in Raleigh and Peace College, as well as the financial needs of the college. Following a trip to Raleigh to visit Peace College, Hermann made the initial gift. Other gifts from Hermann followed, totaling more than $1 million.[33]

The Civil Rights Movement. By the early 1960s, civil rights was one of the dominant public issues in American society. On 16 April 1963, Martin Luther King Jr. was arrested in Birmingham, Alabama, and wrote the famed "Letter from a Birmingham Jail," which criticized the moderate voices in sympathy with the movement. The next month, viewers all over the nation saw televised the horrific images of peaceful protesters (including women and children) in Birmingham being attacked by police dogs and fire hoses under the command of Bull Connor,

---

[30]Ibid., 24 January 1962, 17.

[31]Ibid., 27 January 1962, 5 and 29 January 1962, 18.

[32]Wilson, *Personae*, 75.

[33]Ibid., 76–77. See also McPherson, *History of First Presbyterian Church*, 196.

the city's commissioner of public safety. On 12 June, Medgar Evers, Mississippi's NAACP field secretary, was murdered in his driveway by Ku Klux Klansman Byron De La Beckwith. On 28 August, hundreds of thousands of people gathered in the National Mall in front of the Lincoln Memorial to hear King's "I Have a Dream" speech. Finally, on 15 September, four little girls were killed in the bombing of the Sixteenth Street Baptist Church, just minutes before the morning worship services were to begin.

In the city of Raleigh, the civil rights movement was also one of the main topics of the day. Several years earlier, Bishop Vincent C. Waters of the Raleigh Catholic Diocese took an early step toward civil rights by issuing an order that all of the diocese schools should be fully integrated, following the *Brown v. Board of Education* decision by the United States Supreme Court in 1954. In obedience to the bishop's order, Cardinal Latin High School received eight African-American students for the first time in 1955. It took much longer to desegregate the public schools and the rest of society, but in order to speed things along, African Americans in the city formed the Raleigh Citizens Association to encourage voter registration. Local chapters of the National Association for the Advancement of Colored People (NAACP) and the Congress of Racial Equality (CORE) were also organized in Raleigh. Beginning in May 1963, college students at Shaw University and St. Augustine's College, along with supportive white students at North Carolina State University and other area schools, conducted sit-in demonstrations at numerous local Raleigh businesses, including the S&W Cafeteria, the Sir Walter Hotel, the Ambassador Theatre, Gino's Restaurant, and the statehouse dining room. These demonstrations resulted in arrests of more than 150 protesters during the second week of May. The climax of the May efforts occurred on 10 May when more than 500 protesters marched to the governor's mansion and interrupted a concert performance by the North Carolina Symphony. Governor Terry Sanford refused to discuss the civil rights issue that evening but made a promise to meet with the protest leaders in his office at a later date. On 26 July, William G. Enloe, the city's mayor and member at First Presbyterian Church, who also owned the Ambassador Theatre, created a community relations committee to facilitate the gradual integration of the city's facilities.[34]

The sessional records of First Presbyterian Church during the 1960s offer glimpses of the congregation slowly coming to terms with the national conversation about race. On 27 March 1960, the session, by a split vote, refused to grant a request that the Third Raleigh Conference on Faith and Human Relations be held in the church.[35] The conference was sponsored by four different organizations: the Raleigh Ministerial Association, the Interdenominational Ministerial Alliance, the Raleigh Council of Church Women, and the Raleigh Chapter of the Fellowship of Southern Churchmen, all organizations with progressive agendas. The fact that the session refused to allow the meeting to occur in the church could indicate that First Presbyterian was not quite ready to take the lead on civil rights matters. The fact that the vote among the elders was split likely indicated differences of opinion about civil rights and the church.[36]

The volatility of the civil rights issue for the church can be seen in another reference in the sessional records to a letter from a person named L. M. Smith. Smith wrote to the session "in opposition to integration of the church."[37] Why would he feel inclined to send such a letter unless he was concerned that the session was wrestling with the issue of integrating the church?

One of the most famous episodes in the church related to civil rights occurred in May 1963. In the context of the city's struggle over integration of public facilities, Albert Edwards stepped into the pulpit on 5 May

---

[34]Vickers, *Raleigh: City of Oaks*, 131. Enloe was an elder at First Presbyterian Church and was considered to be a moderate on integration.

[35]Minutes of the Session, 27 March 1960.

[36]Ibid. The record indicates that three elders voted against the majority. See *News and Observer*, 22 April 1960, 20. The conference occurred on 22 April 1960 at Pullen Memorial Baptist Church. The keynote speaker for the conference was Dr. Edwin T. Dahlberg, president of the National Council of Churches. The conference was advertised as "interracial" and "interdenominational."

[37]Minutes of the Session, 18 September 1960. The letter is not attached to the record of the meeting. There is simply a statement that the letter was "received as information" and that the "Clerk was ordered to acknowledge Mr. Smith's letter."

and preached a sermon about integration, telling the congregation that they needed to "take a stand and speak, write, or in some manner be in touch with those who were publicly trying to solve the problems."[38] The following Sunday, as he entered the pulpit, he asked for a show of hands from those who had accepted his challenge the previous week. No one raised a hand, prompting Edwards abruptly to pronounce the benediction and leave the sanctuary to the stunned silence of his congregation.[39] Two days later, the session called a special meeting so that Edwards might explain his unexpected action. Following a "lengthy discussion," William G. Enloe "moved that Dr. Edwards be given a vote of continued confidence in his pastorate."[40] The following week, "Miss Helen Andrews" wrote a letter to the session "expressing her whole-hearted support and admiration for Dr. Edwards's stand on integration."[41]

Earlier that month, Barbara Swan and Dora MacOverton, two African-American students from St. Augustine's College, expressed a desire to join the church. The session discussed the matter on 12 May 1963. The elders indicated that the young women should first discuss the matter with the pastor and then the session would deliberate further about the matter during its next monthly meeting.[42] The following month, when the elders revisited the issue, a motion passed that instructed Albert Edwards to contact the president of St. Augustine's College to determine if the women were enrolled in summer school and to report back to the session. If they were not enrolled in summer school, his instructions were to try and determine if they were expected to return in the fall. The vote on the motion was split. Micou F. Browne made the motion, and it is noteworthy that John R. Powell "requested that his negative vote on the motion be recorded."[43] The motion, and the session's desire to know more about the young women, may indicate their potential willingness to accept them into the church's membership, perhaps prompt-

---

[38]McPherson, *History of First Presbyterian Church*, 65.
[39]Ibid.
[40]Minutes of the Session, 14 May 1963.
[41]Ibid., 19 May 1963.
[42]Ibid.
[43]Ibid., 16 June 1963.

ing Powell's desire to go on record in opposition. Or, the matter could be seen from the opposite perspective. The session may have been leaning in the direction of opposing membership for the women and Powell wanted his name on record to the contrary. The final reference to Swan and MacOverton came in July as Edwards reported back to the session that neither of the young women was enrolled for summer school at St. Augustine's College. The fall semester was not mentioned in the record.[44]

An important milestone as the church moved in the direction of integration is seen in the following statement from the minutes of the session, 19 May 1963: "It was moved and seconded that Negroes be served at the Wednesday luncheons should they appear. The motion passed."[45] This was the first clear signal that First Presbyterian Church, under Edwards's leadership, was gradually moving toward a willingness to integrate.

By 1965, other hints reveal that the church was still struggling with the issue of civil rights. That year, the General Assembly of the Presbyterian Church in the United States endorsed civil disobedience as a legitimate means of promoting civil rights. On 17 October, the First Presbyterian Session raised a motion that the elders "go on record as opposing civil disobedience," in response to the General Assembly action.[46] A substitute motion was made for a committee to be appointed that would compose a statement of opposition to the General Assembly action, which would be discussed in the session the following month. The substitute motion passed. It is noteworthy that Albert Edwards "asked that his opposition to this motion be recorded in the minutes."[47] Nothing further appeared in the minutes until December, when the session passed a motion to request that the Granville Presbytery "overture" the General Assembly "to reconsider its action in approving the report on 'The Civil Rights Movement in Light of Christian Teaching,' and to amend such report to emphasize the necessity of maintaining the democratic processes of law and order and to correct the impression that the Presbyterian

---

[44]Ibid., 28 July 1963.
[45]Ibid., 19 May 1963.
[46]Ibid., 17 October 1965.
[47]Ibid.

Church, U. S., encourages or condones lawlessness."[48] Both Albert Edwards and associate pastor William McCorkle requested that their opposition to the motion be recorded in the minutes, a clue that Edwards was more progressive on the civil rights issue than the session.[49]

The action by the session was most likely caused by two events in 1965, which both occurred at Montreat. In April of that year, the General Assembly met in Montreat and openly supported civil disobedience to procure civil rights. Four months later, Martin Luther King Jr. was invited by the General Assembly to speak at a Christian Action conference in Montreat. The invitation to King suggested a General Assembly endorsement of his message and was opposed by many Southern Presbyterian churches.[50]

By 1970, there is evidence that the church's attitude as a whole to issues of race had shifted. In April of that year, the choir from Stillman College, a traditionally African-American school supported by the Presbyterian Church in the United States at the time, performed a concert at First Presbyterian Church. Members of the choir were received warmly by the church. Earlier in the year, as the session had made plans for the choir's visit, Albert Edwards and William McCorkle had both been of the opinion that the choir members would be able to lodge in homes of church members—an option that would have been less likely a decade before.

---

[48]Ibid., 19 December 1965.

[49]Ibid.

[50]Joel L. Avis, *Religion and Race: Southern Presbyterians, 1946–1983* (Tuscaloosa, AL: University of Alabama Press, 1994) 114–15. Avis provides a very good account of the events surrounding the 1965 meeting of the General Assembly, which was moved from the intended location of Second Presbyterian Church in Memphis, Tennessee, to Montreat, North Carolina, because the session of the Memphis church earlier had passed a non-integration policy in 1957 and had even turned away African Americans at their front door who sought to worship there. The General Assembly attempted to pressure the Memphis church, which refused to back down from its segregation stance. Once the decision to move the 1965 General Assembly was made, the Memphis church backed down and changed its policy, but not without serious internal conflict (see Avis, *Religion and Race*, 101–103).

On the one hand, it is possible to see this gradual shift as evidence that throughout the 1960s the church as a whole made slow progress toward acceptance of civil rights and integration.[51] On the other, a more helpful designation for First Presbyterian's stance in matters of race during that period might be that of cautiously progressive. While the General Assembly of the Presbyterian Church encouraged openness to civil rights and integration as far back as the mid-1950s, it took time for most of the Southern Presbyterian churches to arrive at the same position. Joel L. Avis has argued that "some progress toward desegregating Presbyterian facilities and institutions was made in the 1960s but it was limited at best."[52] Eventually, like many other Southern churches, First Presbyterian Church accepted desegregation, largely due to the steady, patient leadership of Albert Edwards.

Television Ministry and Property Acquisitions. The church began to establish a media presence as far back as 1956, when WUNC television broadcast the Sunday services for several weeks, the first time the church's worship services had ever been broadcast on television.[53] From 1961 to 1974, the church services were broadcast over the air by the radio station WPTF.[54]

In 1974, the church began to explore the possibility of broadcasting the Sunday worship service on local television. WRAL offered to broadcast the services for free, furnish the necessary equipment (which was valued at $225,000 [$1.06 million]) provided that the church would pay $32,500 [$153,000] annually for two years and cover any other incidental expenses.[55] The church raised the money easily, and the broadcasts began in fall 1974, continuing for many years. Eventually, the broadcasts became self-sustaining as viewers began to contribute to their support. The WRAL viewing audience covered much of eastern North Carolina, mak-

---

[51]Minutes of the Session, 15 February 1970.

[52]Avis, *Religion and Race*, 100.

[53]McPherson, *History of First Presbyterian Church*, 61.

[54]Ibid., 65. The church discussed broadcasting the Sunday service on the radio back in 1940 but decided against it because doing so would force a time limit on the music and preaching. See Minutes of the Session, 11 November 1940 and 7 April 1941.

[55]Minutes of the Session, 7 July 1974.

ing the worship service on Sunday morning accessible to thousands of viewers.[56]

During Edwards's pastorate the expanded media presence by the church helped foster an increase in membership numbers. That made it necessary for the church to expand its facilities. As early as 1966, the church became interested in an adjacent building occupied by the North Carolina Association of Educators.[57] Although it took eleven years for the property to become available to the church and for the church to decide to purchase it, by 1977, there were serious negotiations occurring. In the meantime, property located at 116 Salisbury Street, called the "Layfield property," became available to the church for the purchase price of $100,000 [$669,000] in 1968. The property was renovated, named "Memorial Hall," and used for Sunday school space.[58]

In early January 1978, the NCAE building was available for purchase, and the church made an offer of $365,000 [$1.3 million] for its purchase. The NCAE rejected the offer and countered with a price of $450,000 [$1.61 million]. In May 1978, the church and the NCAE reached an agreement on a purchase price of $375,000 [$1.34 million].[59]

Almost immediately, discussions ensued concerning the means for raising the necessary funds for the building. In a joint meeting between the diaconate and the session, Dave Permar was selected to chair the steering committee tasked with raising the money.[60] The church hired an architect to draw plans for the building's renovation, and there were discussions about what to name the building. Within a short time, the building was debt-free. It was occupied in May 1980.[61] Originally, a proposal was made to name the building the "Al Edwards Building," but

---

[56]McPherson, *History of First Presbyterian Church*, 65; Minutes of the Session, 20 October 1974, 26 January 1975, and 23 November 1975.

[57]Minutes of the Session, 17 July 1966.

[58]McPherson, *History of First Presbyterian Church*, 74.

[59]Minutes of the Session, 23 October 1977, 8 January 1978, 26 February 1978, and 4 May 1978.

[60]Ibid., 5 June 1979.

[61]McPherson, *History of First Presbyterian Church*, 66; Minutes of the Session, 11 May 1980.

that proposal was rejected.[62] A few months later, the session selected the name "Cairn Hall."[63] Shortly before the building's renovation was complete, a Cairn monument, in the best of Scottish tradition, was erected in front, containing stones from various places brought by the church's members and their families. Some of the stones came from Raleigh, some came from Edwards's hometown in Scotland, others came from the Holy Land, and others from Egypt and other areas of Africa. Ultimately, the names of both the building and the monument, which use the old Scottish tradition, served indirectly as a testament to Edwards's ministry at the church, which was moving into its twenty-first year as the building neared completion.[64]

Additional Noteworthy Events. One of the most interesting references in the sessional records is found in the entry from 22 December 1963: "James Wright moved that the loose offering at the Christmas Day Service go to the family of the late Lee Harvey Oswald. The motion was seconded and passed."[65] The following month, a report appeared in the record indicating that "$210.37 was sent to the Dallas Police Department in behalf of the family of the late Lee Harvey Oswald."[66]

Why would the session choose to send the offering taken at the church's Christmas Day worship service to the family of the alleged assassin of President John F. Kennedy? There is no evidence of a connection between anyone in the church and the Oswald family. There is, however, a connection between a resident of Raleigh and Oswald, although it has nothing to do with First Presbyterian Church. It has been established that on the night before Oswald was killed by Jack Ruby, there is a record from the Dallas Police Department of a phone call attempt (whether successful or not is a matter of speculation) between Oswald and a man named John David Hurt in Raleigh. Hurt and his wife lived in an apartment at 201 Hillsboro Street. He worked as an insurance investigator, but was disabled by the time of the Kennedy assassination.

---

[62]Minutes of the Session, 26 August 1979.
[63]Ibid., 28 October 1979.
[64]McPherson, *History of First Presbyterian Church*, 66.
[65]Minutes of the Session, 22 December 1963.
[66]Ibid., 19 January 1964.

Years later, when investigators and journalists interviewed him about the phone record, he steadfastly denied that he knew Oswald or that a conversation between the two men ever took place. If that was the case, how did his phone number appear on a record of a call between Oswald and Hurt on the night before Oswald was killed? The matter has become fodder for JFK conspiracy buffs because during World War II, John Hurt served as a special agent of U. S. Army Counterintelligence. For the conspiracy theorists, this phone call may serve as a clue that Oswald and his "handler" were attempting to communicate the night after the JFK assassination.[67]

Given that the Oswald phone call to Raleigh had nothing to do with First Presbyterian Church, the central question concerning the Christmas Day offering remains. Why would the church choose to send it to the Oswald family? The answer is that it was a simple act of compassion on the part of the church. Marina Oswald had two children at the time, a two-year-old and an infant. She was an immigrant from Russia and spoke very little English. A naturally shy person, she was thrust onto the national scene because of the events that took place on 22 November 1963 involving her husband. Much of the nation felt compassion for Mrs. Oswald and the children that Christmas season, which explains why exactly one month to the day after the Kennedy assassination, the session decided to send the Christmas offering to Oswald's widow.[68]

---

[67]The assassination of John F. Kennedy is one of the most popular government conspiracy topics of the last half century. As one might imagine, research into this topic can quickly move from fact to speculation. The information in his section came from Randolph Benson, "JFK, Oswald and the Raleigh Connection," *Indy Week* (Durham NC), 14 November 2012, http://www.indyweek.com/indyweek/jfk-oswald-and-the-raleigh-connection/Content?oid=3192079. This article seems to give a thorough explanation of the issues related to the phone record between Oswald and Hurt. It is not certain whether Oswald initiated the call or whether it was initiated by Hurt, but there does seem to be a consensus that the two men did not communicate that evening.

[68]See *News and Observer*, 24 December 1963, 7 and 27 December 1963, 3. Information about Marina Oswald and her children can be found in many places although she has attempted to avoid the limelight as much as possible. A television station in Dallas, Texas, obtained an interview with her in 2013. See Eric

Another important event occurring during Edwards's pastorate happened on 21 January 1966 when the church celebrated its sesquicentennial anniversary in a gathering in the state capitol building, where the church was constituted in 1816. During the celebration, the cornerstone from the present church was removed and opened to display the contents. Albert Edwards's message for the event was titled "The Cornerstone that Isn't the Corner." Subsequently, the contents of the cornerstone box were returned, and the cornerstone was placed back in its original location; however, a second box containing contemporary materials was also included. During the celebration in the capitol building, representatives from Ernest Myatt, Westminster (formerly North Vanguard), Milner Memorial (formerly First Vanguard), West Raleigh, and White Memorial Presbyterian churches were present and recognized all churches that were birthed from First Presbyterian. The keynote speaker for the evening was Samuel J. Patterson, moderator of the General Assembly, who delivered a message for the occasion titled "The Witness of the Church."[69]

On the national denominational level, significant changes took place among American Presbyterianism during the Albert Edwards pastorate at First Presbyterian. As early as 1954, there was an attempt at reunification between Southern Presbyterians (Presbyterian Church in the United States) and their Northern counterparts (United Presbyterian Church of the United States of America). The merger attempt failed, but talks of reunification continued for years afterward. In 1973, some of the conservative churches left the Presbyterian Church in the United States and formed the National Presbyterian Church over charges of liberalism. In 1974, National Presbyterian Church would change its name to the Presbyterian Church in America (PCA).[70] Its first General Assembly met in Augusta, Georgia, and on 7 December 1973, adopted a document called

---

Aasen, "Whatever Happened To Marina Oswald?" *KERA News* (Dallas, TX), 20 November 2013, http://keranews.org/post/whatever-happened-marina-oswald.

[69]McPherson, *History of First Presbyterian Church*, 72–73.

[70]"A Brief History of the Presbyterian Church in America," accessed 12 October 2015, http://www.pcanet.org/history/.

A Message to all Churches of Jesus Christ Throughout the World From the General Assembly of the National Presbyterian Church. The document decried liberal tendencies in the PCUS, such as "a diluted theology, a gospel tending towards humanism, an unbiblical view of marriage and divorce, the ordination of women, financing of abortion on socio-economic grounds and numerous other non-Biblical positions."[71] The withdrawal of the most conservative voices from the PCUS made the possibility of reunification between the PCUS and the UPCUSA more realistic. That reunification finally occurred on 10 June 1983.[72]

Representatives from First Presbyterian Church seem to have had mixed feelings about the reunification effort. On 13 February 1983, Dan Roebuck, one of the church's deacons, made a motion that the diaconate go on record as opposed to the merger. When the vote on his motion was registered, the motion failed to pass the diaconate.[73] At the meeting of the session on 27 February 1983, the elders heard a report from the recent meeting of the presbytery, which had voted on the issue of the reunification. The presbytery "by a substantial margin" voted to approve the action, but the elders representing First Presbyterian Church (Henry Smith, Paul Jordan, Bill Williams, and John Moore) were opposed.[74] Within a few months, however, the church had accepted the reunification without any further mention of opposition from either the deacons or the elders.[75] The Presbyterian merger did mandate that the church include women on both the diaconate and session, a requirement that most of the church was ready to accept. On 11 November 1984, the congregation elected Sue Hayes as the church's first female deacon. A few

---

[71]General Assembly of the National Presbyterian Church, *A Message to all Churches of Jesus Christ Throughout the World From the General Assembly of the National Presbyterian Church, 7 December 1973*, accessed 30 September 2015, http://www.pcahistory.org/documents/message.pdf.

[72]*Dictionary of Christianity in America*, ed. Daniel G. Reid et al. (Downers Grove, IL: InterVarsity Press, 1990) s.v. "Presbyterian Church (U. S. A.)."

[73]Minutes of the Diaconate, 13 February 1983.

[74]Minutes of the Session, 27 February 1983.

[75]Ibid., 24 July 1983, 28 August 1983, and 25 March 1984.

weeks later, Mrs. Faye McGinnis was chosen to be the first female elder, filling a vacancy within the session class of 1986.[76]

On 28 July 1985, Albert Edwards announced to the session that he expected to retire the following year on 30 June.[77] With "great reluctance" the congregation acceded to his wishes.[78] His ministry at First Presbyterian Church had lasted for more than twenty-eight years. During that time, Raleigh grew from a population of 93,000 to 219,000. The membership of First Presbyterian kept pace with the city population, more than doubling during that era.[79] New leadership would take the church into its third century.

---

[76]Minutes of the Meeting of the Congregation of First Presbyterian Church, 11 November 1984; Minutes of the Session, 9 December 1984. Two other women, Mary Bates Sherwood and Mrs. Dot Smith, became elders in the "Class of 1987."

[77]Minutes of the Session, 28 July 1985.

[78]McPherson, *History of First Presbyterian Church*, 67.

[79]Ibid., 68.

10

Facing a New Century

The Context

In a speech at the Brandenburg Gate in West Berlin on 12 June 1987, President Ronald Reagan uttered the now famous words, "Mr. Gorbachev, tear down this wall!" Although the wall separating East and West Berlin stood for another two years, and its destruction came at the hands of the East German people rather than the Soviet Union, these words still capture the mood of the United States in the late 1980s as the Cold War came to an end. Since the end of World War II, the United States and the Soviet Union had been opponents in a global effort to promote competing ideologies of capitalism and communism, respectively. The competition had been dangerous, and at least once (the Cuban Missile Crisis in 1962) the two nations could have engaged in full-scale nuclear war. The fall of the Soviet Union in 1991 ushered in a new era in American history, one free from concerns about a competing superpower.

Despite the Iran-Contra Scandal that engulfed the Reagan White House during his second term, Ronald Reagan remained one of the most popular presidents in American history. His popularity helped his vice president George H. W. Bush to be elected to the presidency in 1988. Bush is widely regarded today as a "moderate" Republican, having signed into law a number of important pieces of legislation, including the Americans with Disabilities Act (1990), a re-authorization of the Clean Air Act (1990), and the Immigration Act of 1990—a measure that increased legal immigration into the United States. Bush also led a multinational coalition supported by the United Nations to attack Iraqi military forces in 1991, which had invaded the smaller neighboring country of Kuwait, an important American ally in the region. The Gulf War ended shortly through a cease-fire negotiated with Saddam Hussein.

More controversially, at home, Bush appointed Clarence Thomas to succeed Thurgood Marshall on the United States Supreme Court in 1991. While Thomas was widely regarded as conservative in his judicial philosophy, it was his confirmation hearing before the Senate Judiciary Committee that captured the nation's attention for several days. Anita Hill, a former legal associate with Thomas, claimed that he had sexually harassed her in the workplace. The salacious nature of her testimony and the charges that she brought against him made his confirmation hearing one of the most controversial in history. The Senate nevertheless confirmed Thomas by a vote of fifty-two to forty-eight in 1991.

By 1992, the political winds in the nation were blowing from a different direction. The Republicans had held the White House for twelve years. Bill Clinton, Democratic governor of Arkansas, was elected president that year largely by capturing the attention of younger voters. He became the first president from the "Baby Boomer" generation. His campaign theme song "Don't Stop Thinking about Tomorrow" by Fleetwood Mac conveyed the optimism of his campaign. Clinton presided over a long period of economic growth, one of the longest of the twentieth century. His administration, however, was tainted by scandal—most notably, the Monica Lewinsky scandal. In his grand jury testimony at the height of the scandal, Clinton committed perjury when asked about his adulterous relationship with Lewinsky. The House of Representatives passed two articles of impeachment against him in 1998: (1) lying under oath and (2) obstruction of justice. The Senate, however, refused to find him guilty and he remained in office for his full term.

Fresh on the heels of the Clinton-Lewinsky scandal, the presidential election of 2000 became one of the most acrimonious in American history. Clinton's vice president, Al Gore, was the Democratic candidate while George W. Bush, son of Clinton's predecessor, was the Republican nominee. Early on election night, the major news networks projected that Gore would be the winner when Florida was called in his favor. But the race was so close in Florida, that within an hour it was taken out of the Gore column and returned to "toss-up" status. It took several weeks of vote counting, political wrangling, and eventually a ruling from the United States Supreme Court in the case *Bush v. Gore* to declare George W. Bush the ultimate victor in the bitter race.

On 11 September 2001, barely nine months after George Bush assumed the presidency, the nation suffered the worst terrorist attack in American history. Terrorists that morning hijacked four passenger jets that had departed for the West Coast from Boston, Newark, and Washington, D.C. Two of the planes were deliberately flown into the twin towers of the World Trade Center, causing their collapse. One plane was crashed into the Pentagon. The passengers of the fourth plane attacked the hijackers, leading to the crash of the plane in a rural Pennsylvania field. More than three thousand Americans died on that day.

America went to war against Al Qaeda in Afghanistan in 2002 in retaliation for the 9/11 attacks. Intelligence reports determined that the mastermind was Osama Bin Laden, a Saudi national. Bin Laden had been bitterly opposed to the American presence in the Middle East—particularly America's support for Israel. Bin Laden built the Al Qaeda terrorist network and resided with his terrorist training camps at the time in Afghanistan. The following year, American forces also launched an attack on Iraq, based largely on claims that Saddam Hussein had weapons of mass destruction and might potentially use them against American troops still stationed in the region since the first Gulf War. That two-front war drained American financial resources, caused thousands of American causalities and untold numbers of Afghan and Iraqi civilian deaths, and sparked a bitter debate in American society that remains to the present. Hussein was captured by American forces in 2003, tried by the new Iraqi government, and executed in 2006. In 2011, Osama Bin Laden would be killed in a raid led by U.S. Navy SEALs on his hideout in Pakistan. Currently, the majority of American troops have left Iraq while the war in Afghanistan continues.

Just four years after the 9/11 attacks, one of the worst natural disasters in American history occurred on 29 August 2005. Hurricane Katrina, a powerful category-three storm, came ashore near the area of New Orleans, Louisiana, bringing with it a huge storm surge that devastated much of the Gulf Coast from Florida to Louisiana. The storm killed more than 1,800 people and caused more than $100 billion in property loss, with the majority of the damage suffered by the city of New Orleans.

The presidential election of 2008 was historic. George W. Bush had completed his two terms as president, and his vice president, Dick Cheney, was not running, making that election the first open election since 1952. Barack Obama won the Democratic primary and became his party's nominee, overcoming a hotly contested primary challenge from Hillary Clinton, wife of former president Bill Clinton. The Republican nominee was longtime Arizona senator John McCain. Obama's election made him the first African American ever elected to the presidency. He assumed the presidency during the worst economic slowdown since the Great Depression, making his first term challenging when coupled with the two-front war still being waged in Iraq and Afghanistan.

City of Raleigh

The decade of the 1990s marked a significant milestone for the city of Raleigh. In 1992, the city celebrated its bicentennial. To commemorate the celebration, the city commissioned artist David Benson, who produced a giant acorn sculpture, located at Moore Square, in keeping with the city's nickname the "City of Oaks." The copper and steel acorn is ten feet tall and weighs 1,250 lbs. It is dedicated to the late John Watkins, who dreamed up the idea and spearheaded the effort to enlist local businesses to pay for the expense of its creation. The giant acorn has become a part of Raleigh tradition since the bicentennial—it has been dropped from a crane at midnight for Raleigh's "First Night" celebrations on New Year's Eve ever since.[1]

Natural disaster struck Raleigh, as well as other parts of eastern North Carolina, when, in the early morning hours of 6 September 1996, Hurricane Fran blew ashore from along the Atlantic coast as a category-three storm. After coming ashore, the storm blew inland along the I-40 corridor, leaving a wake of destruction. The storm was responsible for

[1]See "Raleigh Drops Giant Acorn with Lift from Southern Crane," *Construction Equipment Guide*, 4 February 2011, http://www.constructionequipmentguide.com/Raleigh-Drops-Giant-Acorn-With-Lift-From-Southern-Crane/15690/#. John Watkins was an active member at First Presbyterian Church until his death. His wife, Alice, remains active in the church.

thirty-seven deaths and more than $2.2 billion in property damage.[2] Three years later, on 16 September 1999, Hurricane Floyd swept through the state, again causing tremendous devastation. In North Carolina alone, Floyd was responsible for thirty-five deaths, 7,000 destroyed homes, and more than $3 billion in damages.[3]

An important advancement for the city of Raleigh occurred in 1997 when the Hartford Whalers of the National Hockey League moved the team to Raleigh and became the Carolina Hurricanes. The move prompted the city to construct the Raleigh Entertainment and Sports Arena (later renamed the RBC Center) now called the PNC Arena, which serves as the home arena for the Hurricanes, as well as the home basketball arena for the North Carolina State Wolfpack. The venue also serves host to numerous concerts and other entertainment events each year. Skeptics wondered whether professional hockey would be popular enough in Raleigh for the city to support the team. They were proven wrong in 2006 when the Carolina Hurricanes won the coveted Stanley Cup. The National Hockey League recognized Raleigh's love of the sport by awarding the 2011 NHL All-Star Game to the city, which brought an estimated $11.4 million in revenue from outside visitors. The city also received national acclaim for its preparation and hospitality.[4]

During the first decade of the new millennium, the city of Raleigh made efforts to revitalize its downtown district. Plans included a new convention center and hotel, the opening of Fayetteville Street to traffic once again (it had been closed since 1977), and a commuter rail system. By the end of the decade, some progress had been made, but some of the

---

[2]See "Hurricane Fran, September 1996," accessed 11 December 2015, http://www4.ncsu.edu/~nwsfo/storage/cases/19960906/.

[3]See "Hurricane Floyd, September 1999," accessed 11 December 2015, http://www4.ncsu.edu/~nwsfo/storage/cases/19990915/.

[4]Greater Raleigh Convention and Visitors Bureau, "NHL All-Star Weekend Generates $11.4 Million in Direct Visitor Spending and $49 Million in Media Value," 7 March 2011, http://hurricanes.nhl.com/club/news.htm?id=555295; Katie Carrera, "2011 NHL All-Star Game: Alex Ovechkin Scores the First Goal, but His and Mike Green's Team Staal Falls to Team Lidstrom, 11–10," *Washington Post*, 31 January 2011, http://www.washingtonpost.com/wp-dyn/content/article/2011/01/30/AR2011013003534.html.

work had to be cancelled or delayed due to the economic recession beginning in 2008.[5]

First Presbyterian Church of Raleigh

After a search that lasted two years, Dr. Edwin W. Stock became the pastor to shepherd First Presbyterian Church into the twenty-first century. Stock was born on 23 September 1937 in New Orleans, Louisiana, to Edwin Witte and Thelma Marie Grady Ferron Stock. He received his BA in 1959 from Southwestern at Memphis College (now Rhodes College). He completed his MDiv degree at Union Theological Seminary of Virginia (now Union Presbyterian Seminary) in 1962. The following year, Stock earned an STM from Yale Divinity School. In 1979, he earned a DMin from Louisville Presbyterian Theological Seminary.[6]

Stock had considerable ministerial experience before arriving in Raleigh. He was ordained by the New Orleans Presbytery at Canal Street Presbyterian Church, his home congregation, on 24 June 1962. That same summer, he served as a summer assistant at Canal Street Presbyterian Church in New Orleans. From 1963 to 1965, he served as pastor of the Carolyn Park Presbyterian Church in Arabi, Louisiana, and the Creedmoor Presbyterian Church in Toca, Louisiana. He worked on the staff of his alma mater, Southwestern at Memphis, as director of church relations from 1965 to 1966 and then as the first director of the Briggs Student Center and associate in admissions from 1966 to 1967. In 1967, he became the senior pastor of the Buntyn Presbyterian Church in Memphis, a position he occupied until 1976. From 1976 to 1979, he was the senior pastor of the Second Presbyterian Church in Lexington, Kentucky. He then became the senior pastor of the First Presbyterian

---

[5]Tim Nelson, "Economy Stalls Downtown Revitalization," *ABC 11 Eyewitness News* (Raleigh, NC), 13 February 2009, http://abc11.com/archive/6657254/.

[6]Edwin W. Stock, "Biographical Sketch and Recollections" (unpublished manuscript, n.d.) 2. This document was presented by Stock to the author.

Church in Wichita Falls, Texas, from 1979 to 1988, the position he occupied before moving to Raleigh.[7]

While he was working on his MDiv degree in Richmond, Stock met Martha Dale Johnston, a graduate student across the street at the Presbyterian School of Christian Education. Originally from Mississippi, Martha had earned a BM degree from the University of Mississippi before coming to Richmond. The couple met, both earned their graduate degrees (he in divinity, she in Christian education), and were married on 17 August 1962 at the First Presbyterian Church in Okolona, Mississippi. They had two children, Edwin and Sarah. They were married for fifty years before Martha died after a long struggle with complications from Parkinson's disease and Lewy body dementia. Her ashes are inurned in the columbarium, located in the Hyde Memorial Garden of the First Presbyterian Church of Raleigh. On 31 August 2013, Stock married Anne Munch Thomas, a high school classmate from Alcee Fortier High School in New Orleans, where they both attended, and who had also lost her longtime spouse, Charles Thomas. Ed and Anne now divide their time between Anne's home in Poulsbo, Washington, and Ed's home at Glenaire, a Presbyterian retirement community in Cary, North Carolina.[8]

An important aspect of Ed Stock's ministerial work throughout his career was his advocacy for civil rights. That was on full display back in the turbulent decade of the 1960s in Memphis. A year after he became the senior pastor of the Buntyn Presbyterian Church in Memphis, Stock found himself in one of the most stressful periods of his life. The tension in the city began on 1 February 1968 when Echol Cole and Robert Walker, two of the city's sanitation workers, were crushed to death by a malfunctioning garbage truck. Within less than two weeks, frustration with the city's neglect and abuse of its black employees motivated more than 1,300 black men from the Memphis Department of Public Works to go on strike. They demanded recognition of their union, better wages, and better safety standards. Henry Loeb, the newly elected mayor, only intensified matters by his refusal to remove faulty equipment from service

[7]Ibid.

[8]Ibid., 1.

or pay higher wages.[9] Later that spring, Martin Luther King Jr. visited the city to lead a protest march on behalf of the striking workers, but it was quickly halted when violence toward the marchers began to erupt. Loeb instituted martial law and called in several thousand National Guard troops. After much consideration, King returned to the city on 3 April and delivered the last speech of his life, the famous "I've Been to the Mountaintop" speech. He was assassinated the following day as he stood on the balcony of the Lorraine Motel.[10]

The day after King's assassination, Stock attended a memorial service with other Memphis ministers at St. Mary's Episcopal Cathedral in downtown Memphis. Following the service, he joined 178 other clergy who marched in procession from the cathedral to the mayor's office to present a joint resolution from both the white and black ministerial associations, calling for the mayor to resolve the strike. A week later, with several of his church members, Stock joined thousands of black and white marchers downtown in a protest march with the streets lined with National Guard troops for protection. Later, after the settlement of the strike, the chamber of commerce hosted a gathering of more than 1,000 civic leaders in the city, which was divided into smaller working groups designed to discuss how racial discrimination could be resolved in the city. From that meeting, Buntyn and Balmoral Presbyterian churches joined in a project to support a summer program in a lower-income area of the city. This project involved more than 150 people.[11]

Reflecting on that time, Stock would later recall that it was his "hardest ministry in a congregation."[12] Along with the stress from the

---

[9]"Memphis Sanitation Workers Strike (1968)," accessed 16 December 2015, http://kingencyclopedia.stanford.edu/encyclopedia/encyclopedia/enc_memphis_sanitation_workers_strike_1968/.

[10]Ibid.

[11]Stock, "Biographical Sketch," 15–16.

[12]Ibid., 15; Edwin W. Stock, e-mail message to author, 15 December 2015. Stock gives further explanation: "Prior to King's assassination, but after the first King march was broken up by the Black Panthers, approx. 20 congregations through the senior pastor were invited to come to City Hall. The purpose was to have town hall meetings in sanctuaries from mid-city out to the suburbs

pastorate and the civil unrest in the city, Stock's daughter Sarah was born with osteogenesis imperfecta (OI) in 1969. Eventually, due to overwork and stress, he suffered a health crisis and had to be hospitalized for sever-

---

with representatives speaking on behalf of the 2,000 sanitation workers and Town Council reps and to get a conversation going with citizens. When I arrived at City Hall, I rode up in the elevator with Will Campbell, who was the head of the Tennessee Council of Human Relations. There were several city council members present who supported the town hall meeting concept. On the way up, Will Campbell in a very positive tone assumed that I was a "Yes" participant. I indicated that I was all for the concept, but had to get session permission for Buntyn Presbyterian Church to participate. I indicated to those present, I would call a special meeting of the Session on the upcoming Sunday, in early afternoon. (The Sunday before Palm Sunday/Passion Sunday.) When I returned I contacted a wise sage on the session that had rotated off the session, but who was a touch-stone whose opinion I respected. He was John Welford, who had owned a car dealership, had served on the PCUS Major Mission Campaign to raise $40 million. He advised me to make sure that every person on the session voiced an opinion before any action or vote. His wise advice was that when everyone's opinion was given a chance to be heard, that person felt he/she was contributing and also had a stake in the outcome. After a thorough discussion, when the vote was taken, there was a better chance that even those who had voted against the proposal, would not work against it and undermine the action taken. We had a long four-hour discussion by 28 elders, in three classes. There were 3 or 4 female elders then. It seemed the concern raised by those who were against Buntyn being a host congregation for the town-hall meeting, were concerned that members of the Black Panthers would infiltrate and make a shambles of the sanctuary. (They had trashed downtown Memphis, after breaking up the King march which was supporting the Sanitation workers). Finally, it came time to vote. It was by secret ballot. The proposal to host the town hall meeting won by four votes. I then named a committee to work with organizers of this town hall meeting, selecting three whom I was confident had voted for, and three whom I likewise thought would have voted in the negative. It was agreed that we would all work together to make this a success. One elder who had voiced concern about the trashing of the sanctuary, who was the church's insurance underwriter, got everyone's attention. He said when we go to the congregation with the announcement that we are hosting a town hall meeting, we need the strong support of everyone. He moved that we approve the hosting by acclamation. The next vote without a secret ballot was unanimous. I notified by a telephone call the action of the session to a contact person. None of this hard work came to fruition. Dr. King was assassinated during that week."

al weeks. The result of this experience was a changed lifestyle and a different approach toward his faith, family, and career.[13]

When Stock arrived in Raleigh in June 1988, he was a seasoned minister with a wealth of experience from several previous pastorates, the perfect qualifications for taking the helm of the First Presbyterian Church following the long, successful pastorate of Al Edwards. Stock's first day on the job was 20 June 1988. He would recall that his first week was very busy as the associate pastor at the time, Rev. Richard Brand, traveled the city with him, introducing him to various members of the congregation and making visits to the hospitals. He also spent much of the week preparing for his first sermon preached the following Sunday titled, "Lost in the Crowd," taken from the story of Zacchaeus in Luke 19. Stock's official installation worship service by the New Hope Presbytery occurred on 21 August 1988.[14]

175th Anniversary. During 1991, First Presbyterian Church celebrated its 175th anniversary. Planning began the previous year when the 175th anniversary committee was selected by the session. Edward Finley became the committee's chair with the remainder of the committee including Ted Chappell, Betty Jordan, William P. McPherson, Calvin Parks, Harold Ramsey, and Olive Worth.[15] By April 1990, the committee had met several times, and significant plans were underway for the year-long celebration. Finley made a request to the session that the anniversary committee be allowed to raise approximately $50,000 outside of the budget for the celebration, one-half of which would be contributed to three benevolent causes: (1) Peace College; (2) Union Theological Seminary; and (3) Dr. and Mrs. Ronald Stringer, a medical mission couple serving in Zaire. The session passed the motion.[16]

The year-long anniversary celebration began with a comprehensive history of the church compiled by William P. McPherson. A church banquet was held on 19 January 1991 at the Mission Valley Hotel, which kicked off a weekend of celebratory events. A special communion service

---

[13]Stock, "Biographical Sketch," 15.
[14]Ibid., 2.
[15]Minutes of the Session, 28 January 1990.
[16]Ibid., 29 April 1990.

with preaching by Albert Edwards occurred the following day. Then, on Monday, a special commemorative event was held in the Senate chamber of the old capitol building and was attended by former governors Jim Holshouser and Jim Hunt, both Presbyterians. Former governor Bob Scott was scheduled to appear but was unable to attend.[17] Other events were held throughout the year with guest speakers and preachers, including Herbert D. Valentine, moderator of the General Assembly; Price Gwynn, a layman and elder from Sugar Creek Presbyterian Church in Charlotte; Patrick Miller, professor of Old Testament at Princeton Theological Seminary and son of Patrick D. Miller, former pastor of the church; and Richard Sommers, pastor of River Road Presbyterian Church in Richmond and son of Maurice O. Sommers, former pastor of the church.[18] The year's events were closed with another communion service, in which Albert Edwards preached, on 19 January 1992.[19]

White Gate Farm. In September 1981, Mrs. Elizabeth Anderson donated 90.5 acres of land valued at $750,000 to the church in order that a Presbyterian retirement community might be constructed on the property.[20] The project, encouraged by Dr. Al Edwards and supported by members primarily at First and White Memorial Presbyterian Churches in Raleigh, sought the interest of the Presbyterian Homes, Inc., an organization based in Jamestown, North Carolina. A little more than two years later, the congregation voted to transfer the property to Presbyterian Homes, Inc. for that purpose.[21] Following a careful land use study of the property called "White Gate Farm," it was determined that the property was not suitable for such a development, and the property was returned to the church. The church then returned the property to the original donor.[22]

---

[17]Stock, "Biographical Sketch," 14; Minutes of the Session, 27 January 1991.

[18]Stock, "Biographical Sketch," 14.

[19]Minutes of the Session, 15 December 1991.

[20]Ibid., 20 September 1981.

[21]Minutes of the Meeting of the Congregation of First Presbyterian Church, 20 November 1983.

[22]Minutes of the Session, 24 April 1988.

The vision for a Presbyterian retirement community located in the area of the Research Triangle did not die, however. In 1987, a thirty-acre parcel of land located in Cary became available from an owner interested in the land's being developed in just such a way, and by January 1989, the plans were underway. "Challenge to Care" was the name of the capital campaign, which had the goal of raising $3 million. First Presbyterian Church heartily endorsed the plan and contributed $1.7 million toward the goal, which included more than $390,000 that the church had previously raised for the White Gate Farm endeavor.[23] In December 1988, the land was purchased for $1.2 million, a certificate of need was issued by the State of North Carolina, and the building project began. Through the influence of Albert Edwards, the new development took the name "Glenaire," a name that calls to mind the Scottish landscape. The community opened to the public in 1993.[24]

The Korean-Bolivian-First Presbyterian Mission. During Ed Stock's tenure as pastor, the church developed a very successful mission endeavor that connected three continents and cultures. In 1996, the church received a request from the Suhnam Presbyterian Church in Kwang-ju, Korea, to begin a mission partnership. The effort began with a membership exchange for the purpose of building a sense of Christian community across cultural boundaries. The exchange was the brainchild of Dr. Young Ro Ahn, pastor of the Suhnam church, who contacted Ed Stock through Dr. Youngil Cho, an elder at the Duraleigh Korean Presbyterian Church in Raleigh. Subsequently, from 1996 to 2000, fifty members of the Suhnam Presbyterian Church made visits to Raleigh, and thirty members from First Presbyterian Church made visits to the Suhnam church.[25]

Following the exchanges between the two congregations, First Presbyterian Church became interested in joining with their fellow Korean

---

[23]"Glenaire's History" (unpublished document, n.d) n.p. This one-page document is now included in the archives of the First Presbyterian Church, Raleigh, North Carolina. See also Minutes of the Session, 19 March 1989.

[24]"Glenaire History," n.p.

[25]Bill Miller, "The Korean-Bolivian-FPC Mission" (unpublished manuscript, n.d.) 1. This document is located in the archives of First Presbyterian Church, Raleigh, North Carolina.

Christians to support Rev. Ik Bai Moon, a Korean Presbyterian missionary working in Santa Cruz, Bolivia. Moon had already established twenty-five Presbyterian churches in Bolivia, and the Suhnam church had supported him since 1992. The Suhnam partnership with Moon helped to build the Eden School in Santa Cruz, Bolivia, in 1992, which provided a facility with a capacity for 650 K-12 students..[26]

The Session of First Presbyterian Church approved this joint effort on 20 December 2000. David Kesterson, the moderator of the committee to evaluate the relationship between First Presbyterian Church and Suhnam Presbyterian Church, presented to the elders his committee's report, which contained a four-part motion: (1) to "maintain and nurture" the relationship that already existed between First Presbyterian and the Suhman Church; (2) to refocus the cultural exchange efforts "to create joint mission efforts with the Suhnam Church in Bolivia;" (3) that members from First Presbyterian Church be provided the opportunity to support financially the Bolivian mission established by Rev. Ik Bai Moon in several possible ways, including scholarships for the Eden School or contributions to the creation of a health clinic or any other ministry need; (4) that First Presbyterian Church participate in a "leadership role" in both the synod and General Assembly efforts to bolster the Presbyterian mission effort in Bolivia. The elders passed the motion unanimously.[27]

Three successive trips to Bolivia between 2000 and 2002 allowed the First Presbyterian congregation to gain firsthand information about the mission work there. Dr. Garrett Briggs, Mrs. Betty Jordan, and Dr. William Miller visited the Eden School in June 2000 to gauge the work being done to educate the Bolivian students there. According to one account, "It was clear Rev. Moon's ministry was first-rate and helped the poorest of the poor.... Eden was truly an oasis of Christian-oriented solid education in the midst of a very poor neighborhood."[28] The following year, Gerry Rogers, a Raleigh banker, member of FPC, and elder, visited the Eden School and determined that the financial affairs of the school were handled well and that it would use donations from First Presbyteri-

---

[26]Ibid.

[27]Minutes of the Session, 20 December 2000.

[28]"The Korean-Bolivian-FPC Mission," 3.

an Church prudently. Then in 2002, John Hester, William Miller, and Charles and Margaret Peacock visited the mission to determine its feasibility for hosting a medical clinic. Their conclusion was that a health clinic could be developed over time with additional visits.[29]

Over the last fifteen years, First Presbyterian Church has been continuously involved in the Bolivian mission in numerous ways. A scholarship program initiated by Garrett Briggs in 2000 continues to provide students with a quality education. In order to continue receiving a scholarship, the students must maintain a B+ average in their studies. During the fifteen-year period from 2000 to 2015, 174 members of First Presbyterian Church have provided more than 1,800 full scholarships for poor Bolivian students to be educated at Eden School.[30]

Between 2002 and 2009, Briggs became aware of an orphanage run by a Dutch couple named Dick and Theresa Altena and located near the Eden School. The school enrolled approximately thirty children from the orphanage, and Briggs began a food program to provide breakfast to these children at school each day. The meal program continued until the political situation in Bolivia forced the Dutch couple to close the orphanage.[31]

First Presbyterian Church began yearly medical missions to Bolivia in 2005, and to date, there have been a total of nine trips. Approximately $6,500 per year is designated in the First Presbyterian budget to provide for the medical clinic they helped establish at the Eden School. Today, the clinic is able to provide ongoing dental, medical, and vision care. A surgical facility is in the process of being built.[32]

Theological Restlessness. From a careful reading of the sessional records during Ed Stock's tenure as pastor, beginning in the late 1980s, several members of First Presbyterian Church began to express concerns over certain theological matters, particularly the national denomination and its influence in the local churches. First Presbyterian was not alone in this concern. Other mainline denominational churches were encoun-

---

[29]Ibid., 4.

[30]Ibid.

[31]Ibid.

[32]Ibid.

tering similar issues within their congregations. The 1980s represented the pinnacle of power for the Religious Right in America. Large, conservative non-denominational mega-churches dominated the religious landscape as well as the religious media. Mainline denominations were declining as they were being forced to surrender their place of prominence to the power of Evangelicalism. The religious climate in America was in a state of "restructuring" by the end of the twentieth century.[33]

The merger in 1983 between Northern and Southern Presbyterians (discussed in the previous chapter) created an uneasy tension within some Southern local congregations that took many years to resolve. The United Presbyterian Church, U.S.A., located predominantly in the North, tended to be more progressive on social and theological issues whereas the Presbyterian Church U.S. in the South was more traditional. Although the merger has proven to be positive for national Presbyterianism, the fusion of the two bodies has not been without conflict in local synods, presbyteries, and churches.[34]

Sessional records from First Presbyterian record a few concerns from members about the direction of the national Presbyterian body beginning in 1989. In August of that year, the Vanguard Class wrote a letter to the session expressing "considerable concern…by class members regarding the recent news reports of proposed restriction of the use of sacred and traditional hymns of The Presbyterian Church." The letter continued that the class's concern moved beyond just the matter of hymns to issues of theology: "Will activist pressure groups be able to influence decisions concerning the basic beliefs expressed in our Holy Bible and the creeds and confessions of The Presbyterian Church? Will we be asked to deny that God, our creator, is the *Father* of us all? Will we be

---

[33]See Robert Wuthnow, *The Restructuring of American Religion: Society and Faith Since World War II* (Princeton: Princeton University Press, 1988) for a detailed analysis of the change in American religion since the middle of the twentieth century.

[34]Randall Balmer and John R. Fitzmier, *The Presbyterians* (Westport, CT: Greenwood Press, 1993) 109–10.

asked to deny that Jesus Christ, our Lord and Savior, is the *Son* of God? [emphasis original.]"[35]

In that same month, Charles A. Harper, Jr. wrote a letter to Dr. James Andrews, stated_clerk of the General Assembly, expressing similar concerns over politically correct language, particularly that the Presbyterian Committee on Congregational Song wanted to remove the hymns "Onward Christian Soldiers," "Faith of our Fathers," and "God Rest Ye Merry Gentlemen" from the hymnal. "It is no wonder that Presbyterian churches and the denomination as a whole are going backwards," Harper wrote. Expressing his opposition to gender-inclusive language, he declared, "The devil must be happy when he hears that female chauvinists are asking that 'Father, Son, and brother' be removed from our religion. They seem to want to pray: *Our mother who art in heaven* [emphasis original]."[36]

The following year, Allen Barwick wrote a letter to the clerk of the session and to the chair of the Christian education committee, complaining about liberalism in the fall 1989 Bible Discovery Sunday school curriculum. Included with his letter was a theological critique that he coauthored with former member Ben Harward titled "A Critique and Alternative View of the Fall 1989 Adult Sunday School Bible Discovery Quarterly." In the preface to the document, the authors stated that it was being presented "out of Christian love and conviction that the literature used by the Presbyterian Church USA has become in recent years slanted more and more toward the general attitude that the scriptures are fallible containing errors and diverse theologies." They continued, "The contrasting view taken here is based on the belief that the scriptures are in-

---

[35]The Vanguard Bible Class to the session, 14 August 1989, Minutes of the Session, 27 August 1989. The Bettie Penick Class added their affirmation to the Vanguard Class in a letter to the session the following month. See the Bettie Penick Bible Class to Session of First Presbyterian Church, 16 September 1989, Minutes of the Session, 24 September 1989.

[36]Charles A. Harper Jr. to Dr. James Andrews, 4 August 1989, Minutes of the Session, 27 August 1989. For context on controversial issues surrounding hymn selection, see Mary Louise Bringle, "Debating Hymns," *The Christian Century*, 1 May 2013, https://www.christiancentury.org/article/2013-04/debating-hymns.

fallible and provide a unifying thread from Genesis to Revelations [*sic*]—that thread being Christ."[37] A subcommittee of the Christian education committee, composed of Barton J. Barham (chair), Steve Austin, Faye McGinnis, and Anne Vickers, provided a response "in general terms from the standpoint of curriculum design, theology and Church doctrine."[38] They concluded that although the Bible Discovery curriculum is "not perfect and infallible, it does appear to be consistent with the Reformed tradition and Presbyterian doctrine and does not present false scripture nor obscure their truths."[39] Continuing, they agreed that no Sunday school curriculum would provide complete satisfaction to "the wide range of interpretative positions present within our denomination," but nevertheless, a "tolerance of a variety of interpretations within a framework of basic beliefs can be a strength and asset for our Church as we learn and grow in faith."[40]

The following month, Elaine Funderburk spoke before the session, conveying her concerns over some recent denominational actions, specifically three things: (1) A proposed statement of faith, which utilized gender-inclusive language such as "Mother God" and refers to God "in the feminine gender"; (2) the denomination's position on abortion; and (3) the denomination's position on homosexuality.[41] In a very well-crafted, written response to Funderburk, Ed Stock explained that the statement utilized feminine terminology, not to describe God as female, but instead to describe the "characteristics of God's actions toward us acting like a

---

[37]Ben Harward and Allen Barwick, "A Critique and Alternative View of the Fall 1989 Adult Sunday school Bible Discovery Quarterly" (unpublished manuscript, n.d.) 1. This document is contained in Minutes of the Session, 27 May 1990.

[38]"Christian Education Committee Report on 'Allen Barwick Letter'" (unpublished manuscript, April 1990) 1. It is contained in Minutes of the Session, 27 May 1990.

[39]"Christian Education Committee Report," 2.

[40]Ibid.

[41]Minutes of the Session, 24 June 1990. A copy of "A Brief Statement of Faith," eventually published by the Presbyterian Church (U. S. A.) in 1991, can be found at "A Brief Statement of Faith," accessed 24 December 2015, http://www.creeds.net/reformed/brief.htm.

father and a mother to deal with our predicament."[42] He did not speak to the issue of abortion raised by Funderburk, but he did address the denomination's stance on homosexuality by indicating that the official stance on the issue since 1978 had been that homosexuals should not be ordained and should be encouraged to live celibate lifestyles: "While rejecting the lifestyle of a practicing homosexual or lesbian, the Presbyterian Church has always maintained the dignity and worth of these individuals. They are loved by God even in their sinfulness because of what God did to take the initiative to rescue us from the bondage of sin."[43]

Other indicators of displeasure with the denomination appeared in November 1990. In the monthly meeting of the session, the clerk read a letter to the session from Henry H. Smith, an inactive elder and a member and inactive elder of the church. In his letter, Smith "expressed his concerns that we blindly vote to send substantial money to our Presbytery, Synod, and General Assembly." He proposed that the payments for 1991 to the three entities be decreased rather than increased as was proposed. The session voted to refer his letter to the missions committee.[44] In that same meeting, Edward S. Finley Jr. and David Kesterson, the church's representatives to the N.C. State University Campus Christian Ministry, shared concerns about the campus minister "and his beliefs on certain provocative issues such as Gay and Lesbian Rights." The session encouraged Finley and Kesterson to share with the campus minister the denomination's stance on the issue.[45]

The denominational report titled "Keeping the Body and Soul Together: Sexuality, Spirituality and Social Justice," issued by a special task force on human sexuality in 1991 within the Presbyterian Church (U. S. A.), also generated some discussion among the membership of First

---

[42]Edwin W. Stock, "Theological and Biblical Reflections on Issues Related to the Presbyterian Church (U. S. A.)" (unpublished manuscript, n.d.) 2. It is contained in Minutes of the Session, 26 August 1990.

[43]Stock, "Theological and Biblical Reflections," 4.

[44]Minutes of the Session, 18 November 1990.

[45]Ibid.

Presbyterian Church.[46] The report recommended, among other things, that approval be given for same-gender sexual relations as well as sexual relations between heterosexuals outside of marriage. The report brought down a firestorm of opposition from all over the country, and delegates to the General Assembly meeting in Baltimore in June 1991 overwhelmingly rejected the proposal. Instead, the General Assembly affirmed the traditional role of sexuality within the confines of heterosexual marriage.[47]

The FPC Session first grappled with the issue as it was presented in the report from the commissioners who attended the New Hope Presbytery meeting in February 1991. The presbytery expressed its disapproval of the task force report. The session then affirmed the presbytery's resolution of opposition.[48] In April, the session voted that the report was "inconsistent with scriptural teaching and Reformed confessional documents," and authorized making a copy of the report available to the congregation.[49] Following the General Assembly's rejection of the report in June 1991, there was no further discussion in the sessional records of FPC.

On 4–7 November 1993, approximately 2,000 feminist theologians and supporters from the mainline Protestant denominations met in Minneapolis for a three-day conference. The conference, titled "Re-Imagining: A Global Theological Conference by Women: For Men and Women" was an "effort to understand God in terms of women's spiritual and bodily experience."[50] Although the conference was ecumenical in nature, its strongest support came from the Presbyterian Church (U.S.A.), which contributed $66,000 toward its expense from the de-

---

[46]Peter Steinfels, "Sex Report Fails at Church Meeting," *New York Times*, 9 June 1991, http://www.nytimes.com/1991/06/09/us/sex-report-fails-at-church-meeting.html.

[47]Balmer and Fitzmier, *Presbyterians*, 110.

[48]Minutes of the Session, 24 February 1991.

[49]Ibid., 28 April 1991.

[50]Peter Steinfels, "Cries of Heresy After Feminists Meet," *New York Times*, 14 May 1994, http://www.nytimes.com/1994/05/14/us/cries-of-heresy-after-feminists-meet.html.

nomination's mission funds.[51] Numerous activities from the conference were reported in the media, such as the concluding ceremony on Sunday morning, 7 November, in which attendees shared milk and honey in a communion-like ceremony and prayed a prayer that included phrases such as "Our maker Sophia, we are women in your image; with the hot blood of our wombs we give form to new life." Other phrases included were "With nectar between our thighs we invite a lover," and "with our warm body fluids we remind the world of its pleasures and sensations."[52] Presbyterians all over America were outraged. Threats to withhold funding came into the headquarters of the General Assembly in Louisville, and when the annual meeting occurred in June 1994, the conference was condemned by denominational leaders. Mary Ann Lundy, one of the denomination's top female officials and supporter of the "Re-Imagining" conference, was forced to resign her position.[53]

On 24 April 1994, the FPC Session expressed its disapproval to the conference and its proceedings and recommended that funding for the General Assembly be held in escrow.[54] The session's denominational relations committee chair, Faye McGinnis, reported to the session the General Assembly's condemnation of the conference and indicated that in her view "our system works."[55] The following month, the session voted to rescind action on withholding General Assembly funding.[56]

The opposition from FPC to the "Re-Imagining" conference should not give the reader the impression that the church was opposed to equality for women in leadership positions or women in ministry. On the

---

[51]Timothy C. Morgan, "Re-Imagining Labeled 'Reckless,'" *Christianity Today*, 18 July 1994, http://www.christianitytoday.com/ct/1994/july18/4t8049.html.

[52]Steinfels, "Cries of Heresy," n.p.

[53]Morgan, "Re-Imagining Labeled 'Reckless,'" n.p.

[54]Minutes of the Session, 24 April 1994.

[55]Ibid., 26 June 1994.

[56]Minutes of the Session, 24 July 1994. The "Re-Imagining" conference continued to meet for the next ten years although on a much smaller scale and with little support from mainline denominations. See "Re-Imagining (Christian feminist conference)," accessed 26 December 2015, http://www.it1me.com/learn?s=Re-Imagining_(Christian_feminist_conference).

contrary, five years before the "Re-Imagining" conference, First Presbyterian Church called its first female associate pastor, Rev. Donna Harder.[57] During the pastorate of Albert Edwards, as seen in the last chapter, the church ordained women to both the session and diaconate. And, numerous female ministry candidates have been supported by the congregation over the last several decades.

Capital Campaign. In December 1989, the session approved an extensive long-range plan for the church, which was designed to prepare both the congregation and the facilities for the needs of the twenty-first century. The plan had five major points: (1) worship, evangelism and missions; (2) congregational nurture and unity; (3) Christian education; (4) facilities and property; (5) stewardship and finances.[58] The report set the stage for launching a multimillion-dollar capital funds campaign over the next decade and a half, which resulted in major property and facility improvement.

The "facilities and property" point within the long-range plan occupied a great amount of attention during the 1990s. This included the objectives of procuring available property adjoining the church's parking lot, establishing a maintenance program for existing facilities, locating additional parking options for weekday and Sunday parking, and, more specifically, renovating Cairn Hall and constructing a new education building. The plan was ambitious, to say the least![59] The "stewardship and finance" portion of the long-range plan provided the means for the extensive building and renovation that took place over the next decade.[60]

Within a few years, organizational plans were beginning to take shape. In January 1993, the diaconate and session met in a joint meeting to hear reports about possible renovations of existing buildings.[61] By early

---

[57]Minutes of the Session, 30 October 1988. The congregational vote to call Harder was 234 in favor and 137 opposed, almost a two-thirds majority but a sign that some in the congregation may have had reservations about calling a woman to the associate pastor role.

[58]"Long Range Plan" (unpublished document, n.d.). This document is contained in Minutes of the Session, 17 December 1989.

[59]"Long Range Plan," 10.

[60]Ibid., 12.

[61]Minutes of the Session, 10 January 1993.

discussed in chapter 3. In 1843, Mrs. Frances Pollock Devereux gave the property for the church to construct a manse for the pastor. The old 1843 manse was demolished in the mid-1930s when the church built a new one, but the Devereux property on the corner of Hargett and Dawson Streets was leased throughout the rest of the twentieth century and eventually became a parking lot that generated income for the church. In 1998, a developer seeking to purchase the property approached the church, but the church refused. The developer agreed, however, to lease the property in a one-hundred-year lease and construct a four-story building, which housed forty-eight condominiums, in exchange for a $1-million fee. In 100 years, the church would become owners of both the land and the condominiums, a great deal for the church. This provided additional assets for the capital campaign.[71]

The construction portion of the capital campaign unfolded in several stages. In stage one, the Green building and Cairn Hall were both demolished, and a new building named the "Stock Building," containing more than 39,000 square feet, was constructed in its place. The Stock Building provided office space as well as space for an expanded outreach ministry. The first and second floors provided Christian education space, and the second floor contains the Albert G. Edwards Family Life Center, complete with locker rooms and showers. The building also provided space for a daycare center.[72] Construction of Hyde Memorial Garden was the second stage of the capital campaign. Nancy Ann Wright, a granddaughter of the Hyde family, provided a major gift for this portion of the campaign. The garden also houses the church's columbarium and provides a peaceful place for prayer and meditation on the church's property. Parking and landscaping constituted the third stage of the capital campaign. The parking lot was attractively landscaped and reconfigured, providing more parking spaces along with handicapped spaces. A wrought-iron gate allowed entrance from Morgan Street, and a parking lot attendant office was provided for the other entrance from Hargett Street. The final stage of the campaign provided for payment on the debt

[71]Stock, "Biographical Sketch," 9; Minutes of the Session, 6 May, 10 May, 27 May, and 27 December 1998.

[72]Stock, "Biographical Sketch," 8.

accrued from the purchase of the Green property.[73]

Another aspect of the capital campaign designated $400,000 for benevolence causes. Peace College and Union Theological Seminary received $100,000 each. The other $200,000 was designated for the PCUSA's Major Mission Bicentennial Fund Campaign of 1999. New Hope Presbytery was to receive 50 percent and the Synod of North Carolina and General Assembly were to receive 25 percent each. The church made the payments to Peace College and Union Seminary with the intention to provide the other $200,000 to the PCUSA at a later date. The capital campaign, however, ended up lasting longer than originally intended due to the opportunity to purchase the Green property. When the church was finally in the position of being able to fulfill its commitment to the PCUSA Bicentennial Fund Campaign, the fund campaign had ended. Therefore, the church gave the full $200,000 to New Hope Presbytery and designated it for new church development. From this effort came a new Presbyterian congregation in Raleigh—Cornerstone Presbyterian Church. Its founding pastor was Dr. James Eller, who was the former associate pastor at FPC.[74]

Retirement of Edwin Stock. In July 2002, after fourteen and a half years as senior pastor of First Presbyterian Church, Edwin Stock announced his intention to retire from active parish ministry.[75] His retirement date was 31 December 2002. The session included in its minutes on 20 November 2002 a beautiful resolution of appreciation for his years of service and leadership at the church, emphasizing his faithful preaching, pastoral presence, financial support, administrative leadership, service to the larger denomination, and his "Making 'my right and your left' a joyful phrase that will forever bring us a smile.'"[76] The church was on the threshold of its third century, and a new pastor was about to take the helm of leadership.

---

[73]Ibid., 9.

[74]Ibid., 6.

[75]Minutes of the Session, 28 August 2002.

[76]"Resolution of Appreciation," (unpublished document, 20 November 2002) n.p. It is contained in Minutes of the Session, 20 November 2002. Stock worked with Union Theological Seminary in Richmond in its Development Office from 2003 to 2008. He continues to remain active in his retirement.

Conclusion

Serving Christ for Two Centuries

Dr. Edward A. McLeod, Jr.

At a congregational meeting on 20 June 2004, Edward Finley, the moderator of the pastor nominating committee, placed before the congregation the name of Dr. Edward A. "Ed" McLeod to become the church's next senior pastor. McLeod brought to the church a wealth of experience in previous ministry opportunities. A 1980 graduate of the College of William and Mary with a BA in government, he earned his DMin degree from Union Theological Seminary in Richmond, Virginia. In 1983, he married his wife, Jenny, and two years later became the associate pastor of the Eastminster Presbyterian Church in Columbia, South Carolina, where he served until 1989. That year, he became the senior pastor at First Presbyterian Church in Greer, South Carolina, where he served for six years. In 1995, he accepted a call to the First Presbyterian Church in Sumter, South Carolina, where he remained until his call to Raleigh.

McLeod's inaugural sermon at First Presbyterian Church was titled "What Have I Gotten Myself Into?" The text he selected for the sermon was from Genesis 12:1-9 and Matthew 14:22-33. Likening himself to the Apostle Peter, whom Jesus challenged to "step out of the boat" and walk on the water in Matthew 14, McLeod said,

> My friends, I cannot walk on water.... But believe me when I tell you that in coming to this new place, in coming here to live among you and serve beside you, I have stepped out of the boat. In all honesty, it would have been very easy for me to stay in a place that was very safe and very secure, but I am here today because I am confident that God wanted me to take a step forward and to trust that this is where God intends for me to be.[1]

---

[1]Ed McLeod, "What Have I Gotten Myself Into?"(sermon, First Presbyterian Church, Raleigh, NC, 8 August 2004) 4–5.

Quoting a phrase given to him by a classmate from seminary, McLeod encouraged the congregation, "The will of God won't lead you where the grace of God can't keep you."[2] Concluding the sermon, McLeod issued this challenge to the church:

> I will again and again and again challenge and invite you to do the faithful thing. I will invite you to jump off the high dive rather than climb down the ladder. I will invite you to step out onto the water rather than cling to a sinking ship. I will invite you to look forward to God's promise, rather than looking over your shoulder to the slavery of your past. I will ask you to believe that the will of God won't lead you where the grace of God can't keep you, so that when, like me, you ask yourself "what have I gotten myself into," your answer will be, "I have gotten myself into the hands of God."[3]

One year later, on McLeod's first anniversary as the church's pastor, he revisited that initial sermon and then creatively called attention to a tangible need in the church. He referenced the capital campaign begun during the pastorate of Ed Stock, which had given the church the Stock Building, housing the child development center, the outreach center and church school classes for children and adults. That building comprised phase I of much-needed facility improvements. McLeod then drew the attention of the church to a needed phase II. He indicated that the session would soon be considering a second building campaign that would provide work on the sanctuary and the educational building. In his challenge, he said, "Where this involves a leap of faith, of course, is that these will not be inexpensive projects."[4] His final word to the church that day returned to the idea of a leap of faith: "God never challenges us to leaps of faith when it's a good time for us. God challenges us to leaps of faith when the time is right. And from where I'm standing…and have been standing for a year now…the time is right."[5]

An important step toward the next building program occurred in August 2005. The capital campaign still had a balance of $1,004,000 and

---

[2]Ibid., 5.

[3]Ibid., 6.

[4]Ed McLeod, "Same Old Sermon" (sermon, First Presbyterian Church, Raleigh, NC, 7 August 2005) 6.

[5]Ibid., 8.

continued to be maintained separately on the books. At this meeting, the session gave approval to close out the capital campaign and transfer all the pledges to the "Visions for Tomorrow Campaign," to pay down the debt in order that the second phase of the building project could commence.[6] By April 2006, the debt had been reduced to $660,000. Darcy Dye, speaking for the Visions for Tomorrow committee, reported plans for a "Thanks a Million" luncheon after the 7 May worship service to celebrate the church's effort in paying down the debt to below $1 million.[7]

At the meeting of the session on 23 August 2006, Ed Finley, capital campaign subcommittee moderator, reported that some preliminary steps had been taken in order to prepare for the second capital campaign.[8] By March 2007, the Visions for Tomorrow committee reported that the debt had declined to $256,784. Jim Nichols and Ken Gwynn presented to the session an outline of the work that the building committee had been doing over the previous several months related to the sanctuary, kitchen, and the old educational building. Numerous architects were considered, and the process of selecting an architect for the work was progressing.[9]

As the Visions for Tomorrow committee worked diligently during 2007 to encourage the church to retire the debt, the building committee was actively involved in planning for the next phase of building improvement. In November 2007, the building committee presented to the session a summary of its work since 2005. Architects were present as the session brainstormed ideas for what needed to be done and reviewed old photographs of the church. In an effort to "use the old to build the new," the elders heard of four possible financial levels that the project could take, ranging from $7.75 million to $11.25 million.[10]

In February 2008, the Visions for Tomorrow committee reported to the session that the debt for phase I of the capital campaign had been

---

[6]Minutes of the Session, 25 August 2005.
[7]Ibid., 26 April 2006.
[8]Ibid., 23 August 2006.
[9]Ibid., 28 March 2007.
[10]Ibid., 28 November 2007.

paid in full. McLeod commended the members of the committee "for their faithfulness and diligence in encouraging a remarkable expression of stewardship by the First Presbyterian Church family."[11] At that same meeting, the building committee reported that the church had hired a consultant to provide guidance to the congregation for the next phase and acknowledged that if the decision were made to proceed with the building effort, it would "demand sacrificial gifts from our congregation."[12]

A major step occurred in April 2008 at a called meeting of the session. Bob Kukla, a consultant from Church Financial Campaign Service, who had been retained to work with the capital funds committee, presented his report titled "Readiness Study Major Funds Campaign for First Presbyterian Church, Raleigh, North Carolina." The detailed report gauged the ability and readiness of the congregation to embark on another multimillion-dollar capital campaign. Following the presentation of the report, Ken Gwynn, co-moderator of the building committee, moved that the session approve three motions: (1) that the capital funds committee be given authorization to begin solicitation of potential major donors to allow for the undertaking of the project, projected to cost $11.5 million; (2) that the building committee be authorized to hire Frank Harmon as architect for the project; and (3) that Frank Harmon be asked to design pictures, schematics, etc., to aid in the solicitation process for funds. All three motions passed unanimously.[13]

"Our Hope for Years to Come" became the theme for the new capital campaign by the middle of 2009.[14] It was divided into several stages. The first stage was designated for major gifts, seeking to raise money from twelve to fourteen families with gifts ranging from $100,000 to $1 million each. Stage two hoped to raise money from fifty families with gifts ranging from $50,000 to $100,000 each. Given the reality of the economic situation in the nation at the time, the new capital campaign seemed particularly ambitious. The minutes acknowledge that reality in a

[11]Ibid., 27 February 2008.

[12]Ibid.

[13]Ibid., 2 April 2008.

[14]Ibid., 24 June 2009.

comment made by Ed McLeod: "this is not the *best* time but it is *our* time."[15]

Authorization for the building committee to enlist the architect to draw plans for renovation of the sanctuary, demolish the old educational building, and replace it with a new structure came from the session in early 2010.[16] By the end of 2010, the session heard a report from the building committee that revealed plans for the new educational building to have more than 24,000 square feet of space, three stories, space for a modern library, and improved lighting. The sanctuary renovation would include a new energy system, wireless technology, and new security and lighting. Additionally, the choir would have improved facilities, and a space was planned to house the church's historical archives.[17]

The building effort began and continued through 2011. At a congregational meeting in April 2010, the church unanimously approved a motion authorizing the church to borrow up to $10 million to finance the building and renovations needed to the church property, including renovating the sanctuary and constructing a new educational building.[18] Several months later, Jim Nichols of the building committee presented an overview of the project to the session in August 2011, indicating that the cost of the construction was estimated to be $8,447,000.[19] As the building effort progressed into 2012, the capital campaign committee proposed to the session that the new educational building should be named in memory of Walter Edge, whose estate provided $2.27 million toward the building project (approximately 25 percent of the entire cost of the capital campaign). The session approved the proposal, allowing the capital campaign committee to approach Edge's heirs for permission.[20]

---

[15]Ibid. (emphasis in the original).

[16]Ibid., 24 February 2010.

[17]Ibid., 17 November 2010.

[18]Minutes of the Meeting of the Congregation of First Presbyterian Church, 10 April 2011 (contained in the sessional record book covering the year 2011).

[19]Minutes of the Session, 24 August 2011.

[20]Ibid., 25 April 2012.

The building and renovation work reached completion in late summer 2012. The church held its first worship service in the newly refurbished sanctuary on 9 September.[21] A dedication ceremony occurred a few weeks later on 30 September. Dr. Brian Blount, the president of Union Theological Seminary in Richmond, Virginia, was the guest preacher that day, a fitting choice given the long relationship between the church and the seminary. The choice of Blount also called to mind the dedication of the new sanctuary in 1906, when Dr. Walter W. Moore, the seminary president, was invited to preach.[22] Blount's sermon that day from Mark 5 was titled "Rise." He focused on the stories in the text of the woman healed from touching the hem of Jesus' garment and the raising of Jairus's daughter. Challenging the congregation while celebrating and commending them for completing the building program, Blount said,

> I suspect that redoing and expanding this building required faith from you. As a church, you had to rise to this moment. You knew there was a chance this project could falter. Your capital campaign might fail to raise the required pledges. The economy might go bad, and people might not be able to fulfill their pledges. But the prospect of the project's dying did not deter you from doing what you wanted to do. Enacting the vision you wanted to enact. Making possible the ministry you wanted to make possible. Take that kind of believing, that kind of rising, into every aspect of your ministry, and you cannot only change this block; you can also change this world.[23]

Celebrating 200 Years

In the preface to this book, I referenced the "cloud of witnesses" in Hebrews 12:1 and drew a parallel between the biblical allusion and the thousands of faithful witnesses through two centuries of service at First Presbyterian Church. For 200 years, this church has provided a faithful witness in the heart of Raleigh, North Carolina. Its commitment to serving Christ has also extended beyond Raleigh to other parts of the world. As noted in chapter 2, the earliest surviving records of the session date to

---

[21]Dr. Ed. McLeod to author, e-mail correspondence, 14 January 2016.

[22]See ch. 6 above.

[23]Brian K. Blount, *Invasion of the Dead: Preaching Resurrection* (Louisville: Westminster John Knox Press, 2014) 116–17.

1831. The very first entry into that record reflects a willingness on the part of the earliest members to connect their church with the larger world:

> Rev. John Witherspoon, agent of the Board of Missions of the General Assembly of the Presbyterian Church visiting this congregation in the prosecution of his agency was requested by the Session to spend a few weeks in laboring among us.... Having visited a number of the families of the congregation and the members of the church, thirty four subscribed to the fifty cent plan [and] were obtained and the church formed into a missionary society auxiliary to the Board of Missions of the General Assembly under the direction of the church Session.[24]

In 1875, the Ladies Foreign Missionary Society was formed, bringing significant energy to the cause of missions within the congregation. The organization (and others that were later spawned from it within the church) provided an opportunity for women to take leadership roles in the church and kept the church educated about the efforts of Presbyterian missionaries around the world. The early meetings of the Ladies Foreign Missionary Society focused on Presbyterian missions in select foreign countries. The women discussed the missionaries' work, corresponded with them, and provided tangible support to them as well.

By the early twentieth century, the men of the church, particularly in the Vanguard Sunday school class, developed a heart for missions. The Vanguard Class, organized in 1904, was more than just a Sunday school class. It provided members with the opportunity to participate in organizing new Presbyterian churches in Raleigh, as well as other mission efforts in Wake County. The class also focused on missions in other parts of the world, particularly in China, where its support for Edward and Gay Currie, missionaries to China, extended from 1920 to 1952. More recently, the Korean/First Presbyterian Cultural exchanges leading to a major mission effort in Bolivia, as well as mission trips to Haiti, show that the foreign missionary spirit within First Presbyterian Church of Raleigh still remains vibrant.

Since the nineteenth century, the church has also been a leader in local missions, particularly in the area of social ministry. Beginning in

---

[24]Minutes of the Session, 20 January 1831.

1879, the women of the church organized the Ladies Home Missionary Society as a complement to their work with foreign missions. The spirit of local mission work is best exemplified by the work of Lisette Friedlan Bunch, who organized the Four Square Sunday school class in 1920 and served as its teacher for the next forty-seven years. In addition, she organized and energized the Cary Street Mission, an outreach opportunity to the needy of the city. Throughout the twentieth century, the church has been involved in other social ministry efforts, such as providing a place for Narcotics/Alcoholics Anonymous groups to meet, establishing a parish nurse program and a prison ministry, developing a child daycare program, helping to organize the Shepherd's Center, and numerous other efforts to ease the lives of hurting people in Raleigh. The church's effort to build Glenaire Retirement Community is also a part of its local social ministry outreach.

As the church closes out 200 years of Christian service and mission "from the heart of the city to the ends of the earth," it is helpful to reflect upon its importance to the city of Raleigh. Born in the old statehouse and then located for all of its history directly across the street from Capitol Square, this church has been not only a good neighbor but also a positive presence in the city. It has extended hospitality when needed to the state government, hosting the North Carolina Supreme Court when fire destroyed the old statehouse, as well as hosting the North Carolina Constitutional Convention. Governors have worshipped in its pews. In fact, in 1985, the church hosted newly-elected governor James G. Martin, himself a Presbyterian and a concert musician, for a special service of music that he had composed.[25]

The church has also been hospitable to the community, beginning with permission for the church bell to be used as the fire alarm for the young city of Raleigh and continuing through the years as a welcoming place for troops passing through the city during both World Wars. Its outreach to Peace College (now William Peace University) students and other college and university students in the area further shows its willingness to be a warm and welcoming place to all in need of ministry and friendship. There have also been countless community meetings, con-

[25]*News and Observer* (Raleigh, NC), 7 January 1985, C-1.

certs, and other social gatherings held in its facilities over the years, all for the good of the Raleigh community.

What explains the longevity of this congregation? While numerous answers might be given, the best answer is summarized in that wonderful hymn by Isaac Watts, a phrase from which became the theme of the second capital campaign: "O God our help in ages past, our hope for years to come." The First Presbyterian Church is a strong community of faith. For two centuries, the members sought to understand and live out their faith, to hear the voice of God and to respond to God's leadership as they understood it. That commitment, beyond anything else, has been their strength. And, that will be the church's "hope for years to come." As this 200 year-old congregation enters its third century, its "cloud of witnesses" from the past serves to inspire and challenge the present and future generations to persevere in its call to "serve Christ from the heart of the city to the ends of the earth."

Appendix 1

God, the Giver of Victory and Peace: A Thanksgiving Sermon[1]

Correspondence[2]

Raleigh, 23 September 1862

Rev. and Dear Sir:

It is desired by a large portion of your audience, who heard your very able, eloquent and instructive sermon on the late "Thanksgiving day," Sept. 18th—that the discourse should be printed in pamphlet form. We think that the very original and forcible manner in which you presented the issue involved in our present struggle, would not only prove instructive to the reading public generally, but that, if sent to our soldiers in camp, *as a tract*, it would prove very acceptable to them, and would tend to keep constantly before their minds the great truth—*that to God along belongs the glory!* 'Tis He, who in fact fights our battles; and to Him should our thanks and praises be ascribed. You will confer a favor on us, and very many others of those who heard you, if you will furnish us with a copy of your discourse, on the occasion alluded to.

Most respectfully,

L. E. Heartt,

R. H. Battle,

H. A. Badham,

C. Dewey,

---

[1]Delivered by Rev. Joseph M. Atkinson at First Presbyterian Church Raleigh, North Carolina, on 18 September 1862. The following comes from a digitized reproduction of Atkinson's sermon published and distributed as a tract for the Confederate Army. The digitized copy of the tract can be found at http://babel.hathitrust.org/cgi/pt?id=dul1.ark:/13960/t2t44hr74;view=1up;seq=3 .

[2]The following correspondence, dated 23 September 1862 and 1 October 1862, respectively, is included with and precedes the actual sermon text in the tract published for the Confederate Army.

Wm. Peace,
J. Brown,
T. McGee,
K. Rayner,
H. D. Turner,
F. L. Roberts,
R. E. Maddox.

Raleigh, 1 October 1862.
Messr. L. E. Heartt, H. A. Badham, William Peace and others.
Gentlemen:

The discourse which you have thought proper to ask for, was originally prepared without the remotest thought of publication.

But since in your judgement, its more extensive circulation might be of service at this time, and especially to our soldiers, I do not feel at liberty to withhold it.

Accept my thanks for the very kind terms in which the request was conveyed, and believe me to remain,

With high regard,
Your friend and brother.
Joseph M. Atkinson

God the Giver of Victory and Peace[3]

"Weeping may endure for a night, but joy cometh in the morning."[4] What a perfect picture of the providence of God and the experience of man! Alternation of good and evil, pain and pleasure, light and darkness, joy and weeping is the law of this lower world. In Heaven where "transport and security combine," all is fixed, stable, everlasting; the experience of good is absolute, unmingled, unbounded. There shall be no succession, save of ever-growing felicities; no change, save of a continual rise from glory to glory.

---

[3]The text of Atkinson's sermon begins here.
[4]Psalm 30:5

On all those wide extended plains,
Shines one eternal day;
There God the Son forever reigns,
And scatters night away.

On earth, whether our state be one of joy or sorrow, we need to be reminded of this glorious prospect—in the one case to sober, in the other to cheer us. The mind takes the colour of the passing time, and thinks it will ever be as now it is, and fancies it will always feel as now it feels. But we should know from the varied dispensations of God in the past, from what others and ourselves have undergone, and from the repeated testimonies of the inspired Word, how false this estimate of things!

This is signally illustrated in the recent history of our country. God had good reason to send sorrow; but when sorrow has done its appointed work—when, by the sadness of the countenance the heart has been made better, we may expect the darkened cloud to withdraw and a glorious burst of sunlight to appear, like that which even now "Flames in the forehead of the morning sky," flashes its gladdening rays from east to west, and calls our whole Confederacy to thanksgiving and praise.

It is in happiest accordance with the spontaneous impulse of a Christian people that the honored Chief Magistrate of these States, banded in a common brotherhood of love, on interest, of suffering and of mercies, has called us to grateful ascription and religious rejoicing.

On a memorable occasion, in the personal history of our Lord, when the envious Pharisees rebuked the jubilant rejoicings of the disciples, He said, "[I]f these should hold their peace, the stones would immediately cry out."[5] We might well look for a stern and audible rebuke from brute insensate things, if we should withhold our thankful tribute on this day to the God of our salvation. The Lord hath done great things for us, whereof we are glad.[6] Bless the Lord, O, our souls, and forget not all His benefits.[7]

[5]Luke 19:40.
[6]Psalm 126:3.
[7]Cf. Psalm 103:1-2.

At no distant day in the past, a dark cloud of uncertainty, of disaster, of wrath, overhung our whole Confederacy and discharged its collected fury on our devoted land. A series of unexpected and appalling reverses, beginning with the ill-fated battle of Somerset, followed in rapid succession by the capture of Roanoke Island, the loss of Newbern, Nashville, and of various intermediate points, and culminating in the surrender of New Orleans, the commercial emporium of the South, the evacuation of Norfolk and the blowing up of the Merrimac, had caused all faces to gather blackness. Then the boldest was filled with apprehension. The most sanguine were tempted to despair. The head of every patriot was bowed in profoundest grief. Shall we not be permitted to hope that the heart of every Christian was bowed in humility, confession and supplication? We felt that vain was the help of man, and we cast ourselves on the fatherhood of God.[8] When brought to the lowest point of public depression and of conscious dependence, our deliverance was at hand. God poured the spirit of dauntless heroism into the hearts of a whole people—soldiers, legislators, leaders, alike. The generous resolution was taken to defend the Capitol of the Confederacy to the last extremity. From that moment our prospects began to brighten. Then came the successful repulse of the enemy at Drury's Bluff, flushed with anticipated triumph and glorying in imagined invincibility. Again our coveted and hated capital was beleaguered by the numerous and best appointed army of modern times, led by their most trusted and skillful generals. But day after day that mighty host was baffled and beaten back, like the surges of the sea raging against Gibraltar. Their strongest entrenchments were stormed. Their most costly munitions were captured or destroyed by the valor of our troops, animated, sustained and guided by the Lord of Hosts. The defence of Richmond was a prodigy, not only of human heroism but of Divine might. From that day to this, our march has been an unbroken series of splendid successes, under the invisible presence of the pillar and the cloud. Shall we not henceforward ascribe all glory to the Lord of Hosts, while mindful of our inextinguishable debt of gratitude to those noble patriots and martyrs whom He employed for our defence?

---

[8]Cf. Psalm 60:11; 108:12

When the eyes of the prophet's servant were opened, he beheld the mountain filled with chariots of fire and horses of fire.[9] In the first great battle of Cortes against the Mexicans the enthusiastic invaders imagined that they saw St. James, the patron St. of Spain, leading their fiery forces on to victory.[10] If our eyes could have been unsealed during those seven day's memorable battles before Richmond, we should doubtless have seen a more awful and a more glorious spectacle. We should have seen an angel, terrible as that which smote the host of Sennacherib, hurling back the multitudinous cohorts of our self-confident invaders, filling their ranks with confusion, dismay and death.[11] Weeping may endure for a night, but joy cometh in the morning.[12]

Never in the history of mankind has the wonder-working providence of God been more strikingly manifest than in the successive phases of this contest. We wholly misapprehend the real significance of this revolution if we fail to discern His hand and His counsel in all that has been done, or, with high providence, permitted to be done. For the present, not joyful but grievous, it has doubtless been a divine agency for the spiritual education of our people in the highest lesson of religious wisdom, akin to that painful economy by which Jehovah led His ancient people through the perils of the pathless wilderness to the possession of the promised land. In the successive periods and phases of its progress, it has disappointed all probable anticipations; putting to shame the confident predictions of the wise and vindicating the superior sagacity of humble piety. Its principal agents were themselves even unconscious, beforehand, of the important part which they were designed to bear in the execution of the decrees of infinite wisdom. So far as it may be permitted to man to interpret it, the great purpose of God would appear to have been to exalt His own glorious sovereignty in debasing the pride of material power and illustrating the supremacy of moral forces. In this point of

---

[9]Cf. 2 Kings 6:17.

[10]"The same inspiring but imaginary vision, only in a form still more glorious, was again vouchsafed during the expulsion from Mexico.—*Prescott's Conquest of Mexico*, vol. ii. p. 341." (Atkinson's note).

[11]Cf. 2 Kings 19:35-36.

[12]Psalm 30:5.

view, its progress has been to us singularly instructive and cheering. Not only does it stand aloof from all vulgar revolutions, but from that which we have been taught to regard with almost superstitious veneration as the most wonderful and noble in the annals of our race; that by which, under the divine favor, we achieved our independence of the British crown and became the freest and most powerful people in the New World. The course of Providential development in our first Revolution was essentially unlike what we have thus far witnessed in this. Compared with the former, the hand of God is more bare, more open, more visible, in that which is now in process of consummation. The personal history of one man is the record of that revolution. The portion of the life of Washington comprehended within the period, contains and exhausts the Revolution itself. He was not only the type and hero of the Revolution, but what was silently transacted in his thoughtful mind and conceived in his patriotic heart, and executed by his own individual prowess, constituted the sum of the Revolution. Thus far at least there is no one man of whom this can be said. There is no one man to whom the glory of these splendid achievements can be so eminently ascribed. It is this circumstance which especially distinguishes it from our first Revolution. In consequence of his undisputed ascendancy Washington received among us, it is to be feared the glory which is due to God only, and other eminent patriots and statesmen of that day, Henry, Hamilton, Jefferson, Madison and Marshall, were unduly exalted and relied on. The illustrious men of that generation constitute a grand Pantheon, each having his own proper altar and his own particular worshippers. It should indeed be to us a matter of grateful acknowledgement that God has raised up for us in this our time of need, able and godly leaders, like Lee, Jackson, Hill and others, whose character would confer honor on any cause, as their public services would shed lustre on any age. But, perhaps, it is well for us that there is no one name with which the transcendent glory of this period of our country's history is too exclusively connected. Thus the apparent sphere of the Divine operation is enlarged, and our dependence on His favor, though not more immediate and absolute, is more conscious and visible.

In perfect consistency with this view, it may be affirmed as a uniform method of Divine Providence, springing, perhaps, from profound causes hidden in the nature of things and in the nature of man, that in all great Revolutionary movements, religious or political, the tendencies of the times should embody themselves in some one heroic individual whom all men are content to take as the type and representative of the whole period. Thus Luther stands forth confessed as the representative of the German reformation, Calvin of the reformation in France, Zwingle of the Swiss, and Knox of the Scottish reformation. Passing now to the domain of civil Revolution, we recognize at once Napoleon, with his brilliant endowments, his indefatigable power of bodily endurance, his inexhaustible fertility of resource, his insatiable thirst of military glory and supreme indifference to human life as the incarnate genius of the great Revolution in France, near the close of the last and the opening of the present century. At the mention of the American Revolution every eye turns at once to the majestic image of Washington, with his unsullied patriotism, his consummate prudence, his immeasurable self-control, as the model of all natural and all civil virtues. When we come to our own day, may we not hope that Jackson, the Christian hero, the man of piety and prayer, with a fervency of spirit, like David's in the sanctuary, and a martial ardour like David's in the field, has been graciously given us as the interpreter and impersonation of the Christian element and the Christian consciousness of this grand conflict?

We cannot but regard it as a singular mercy of God, that the men for the most part who are the chief agents of Providence in conducting this Revolution, should be in personal piety, in such perfect correspondence with its religious character; and that the recognition of God in His incommunicable glory as Supreme Disposer of all events, should be so universal among our Rulers and people. So long as we shall deeply feel our dependence on God alone, and put our trust in Him, He will favor us, and our progress will be irresistible as the march of time. Faith is the principle of endeavor and endurance. It prompts energy and produces patience. In its relation to God, it waits and is dependent. They that believe shall not make haste. It says to the subject soul, stand still and see the salvation of God. In its relation to man, it is daring and defiant; seemingly desperate, imprudent, wild and reckless. But when apparently most adventurous, it is in fact most guarded and most prudent; for it is animated by a sublime enthusiasm which links the feebleness of the creature with the almightiness of God. The great virtue, therefore, which the crisis demands, and, we trust, has called forth, is faith in God—the perennial source of patience, courage and hope.

We are prone to rebel against the dispensations of the Most High and murmur as did Israel of old. But how is faith in the Divine Providence vindicated even in time! How often within the limited sphere of our own personal concerns, have we seen that our own plans would have been our ruin, and that the events which appeared most disastrous when they occurred, were blessings in disguise. It is the sovereign prerogative of God to bring good out of evil. Thus the awful catastrophe of our apostacy as a race is made the occasion of the eternal salvation of His elect, and of affording therein the most amazing illustration of His glorious attributes, to all intelligent creatures, throughout never-ending ages. And doubtless, each inferior but to us perhaps, scarcely less mysterious evil, as the rupture of what once seemed to us the golden chain that bound together in firm concord this bright sisterhood of States, and in place of amity and peace, gave us the alarms and atrocities of war, will yet find means even out of this visible chaos, to cause a brighter and a more beautiful creation to emerge.

In that magnificent plea of Milton for the liberty of unlicensed printing, the glorious image of his beloved country rises up before him in poetic vision, and he exclaims,

> Methinks I see in my mind a noble and puissant nation, rousing herself like a strong man after sleep and shaking her invincible locks; Methinks, I see her as an eagle mewing her mighty youth and kindling her undazzled eyes at the full midday beam; purging and unscaling her long abused sight at the fountain itself of heavenly radiance.

This picture and prophecy we would transfer to our own dear Southern land. Now, she is involved in the heat and dust and blood of the battle: Hereafter, she shall repose in victory and triumph and peace. Now she sits as a widow, forsaken of the nations: Hereafter she shall arise, radiant as a queen, resplendent as the day, crowned with immortal honour, in favor with God and man. Now, she is oppressed, but not overwhelmed; enveloped in flames, but not consumed; in peril, but not appalled; putting her trust under the shadowing wings of the Almighty. Weeping may endure for a night, but joy cometh in the morning.[13]

She is now toilfully learning those precious lessons which she shall teach hereafter to oppressed and struggling nations; and to the proud and heartless Tyrants, who in other lands and in future days, may seek to degrade the noble and enslave the free. She is now making her herself a name which shall be gratefully and admiringly murmured wherever freedom has a friend or the God of Providence a worshipper! The only proper view of this Revolution, is that which regards it as the child of Providence, who "maketh the wrath of man to praise Him and the remainder thereof He restrains."[14] The ends contemplated by men and the actions permitted, not approved by God, are in many cases, very unlike His ultimate designs. And we may say to our Northern oppressors, as Joseph to his cruel brethren, "As for you, ye thought evil against us, but God meant it unto good."[15] All that was affirmed, and more than was imagined of the ulterior aims of those who inaugurated this atrocious war, has been already done or plainly indicated already.

Were we able to interpret aright the painful dispensations of the Almighty, we might find that our frightful series of reverses during the winter and spring, were as truly merciful in their intent as our recent splendid successes. It was a humiliating but needful part of our education as a people. It was a bitter medicine, but we hope it wrought a lasting cure. It taught us our prostrate dependence on Him who, sitting on the circle of the Heavens, hath appointed to the nations of the earth the bounds of their habitation and rules with absolute sway over the councils of Cabinets and the event of battles. It was the indispensable condition of the exercise of virtues, without which no character is complete, whether of an individual or a whole people—virtues less obtrusive and less glaring than heroic prowess on the field of bloody strife, but not less magnanimous, less essential or less rare—the virtues of self-control, of patience, of fortitude and hope. It has served to exhibit a striking characteristic of our people, previously unknown, it may be, to themselves. I

[13]Ibid.

[14]Cf. Psalm 76:10.

[15]Cf. Genesis 50:20.

mean their marvelous recuperative energy. In a week after a defeat or disaster, they have seemed as resolute, as hopeful, and as eager as ever. In the presence of terrible calamity, under the pressure of heavy affliction they exclaim,

> All is not lost; the unconquerable will
> And resolution never to submit or yield,
> And what is more, not to be overcome.

Another quality conspicuously evinced in the progress of this contest has been the singular unselfishness of the great body of our troops, many of them belonging to the best families of our Southern country, born in affluence, nurtured in ease and honour; yet entering the ranks and serving with "proud submission"—with "dignified obedience" under men in every way inferior to themselves, but invested by lawful authority for a temporary purpose with the right and the place of command. The true history of this war will show that nobler instances of knightly courtesy, of generous valour and of chivalrous emprise, have not been found among the best and bravest of our officers, than among the men subject to their authority.

I have spoken thus far of the gallantry of our soldiers and the patriotism of our people, but assuredly not with the design of giving the supreme glory to them. They have been but instruments in the hand of a higher power; channels through which the Divine goodness has streamed forth upon us. For the singular preservation of the precious lives of our leaders and troops exposed beyond all former precedent; for the signal victories vouchsafed to our arms over an arrogant and exulting foe; for the patriotic unity which has animated all classes and both sexes; for the spirit of moderation, of firmness and of humanity which has marked the policy and conduct of our rulers, our fervent thanks are due to that benign Providence who alone bestowed and inspired it all. The glorious deliverances which we have so often experienced heretofore, so far from exhausting the Divine bounty, may under an economy of grace, be turned into an argument for still greater mercies hereafter. When the stripling David armed only with a sling and pebbles from the brook, went forth to meet the giant of Gath, the thought of ancient deliverances kindled his courage. And David said, "Moreover, the Lord that delivered me out of the paw of the lion and out of the paw of the bear, He will deliver me out of the hand of this Philistine."[16]

There ought to be not the spirit of carnal rejoicing and self-complacent boasting among us now, but great solemnity of heart and great tenderness of walk. We should humble ourselves even in the hour of victory, before the eternal Majesty of Heaven and earth, whose right hand and holy arm hath gotten Him the victory.[17] If, by ingratitude and unbelief, we provoke Him to depart from us, our failure and ruin will not be more deserved than dreadful. The brilliant successes with which His favour has crowned our arms and gladdened our hearts, will be like a single star or a small cluster of stars in a firmament of gloom—a bright chapter in a volume written within and without in characters of mourning, lamentation and woe. This contest is not ended. Infuriated by defeat, our enemies are more rancorous and implacable than ever. They are summoning new levies of hundreds of thousands, to effect, if possible, the subjugation of our people, and will resort to every device which cruelty, sharpened by malice and mortification, can suggest to effect their purpose. In these circumstances we look to that God who delivered David and Israel, and while we celebrate His past goodness, hopefully invoke His future favour. Some trust in chariots and some in horses, but we will remember the name of the Lord our God.[18] Not unto us, not unto us, but unto thy name, give glory for thy mercy and for thy truth's sake.[19] Weeping may endure for a night, but joy cometh in the morning.[20] Abiding in such a posture of spirit as this, may we not hope that what He hath so auspiciously begun He will carry on to a glorious consummation?[21] A conflict waged in self-defence for all that man holds dear, and consecrated by the martyr-blood of the best men in these Confederate States—by the solemn voice of all our religious convocations, of all

[16]1 Samuel 17:37
[17]Cf. Psalm 98:1.
[18]Psalm 20:7.
[19]Psalm 115:1.
[20]Psalm 30:5.
[21]Cf. Philippians 1:6.

Christian churches and above all by the visible favour of Almighty Power, cannot but terminate happily. We should learn, therefore, to exercise a cheerful trust in God and cherish perfect unity among ourselves.

And amid all the excitements of war, let us not cease to feel that a people's spiritual interests are their supreme interests; especially in a time of political convulsion, when so many moral and social bonds are relaxed or broken. He, therefore, who at this crisis does most for his own soul and the souls of others, does most for his country; and he who by his conduct or teaching lowers the standard of Gospel piety, is an enemy not only to religion but to liberty. There are times when extraordinary energies should be put forth by the servants of the Most High. Whenever men are profoundly agitated by a political convulsion or by a war, such as that which is now raging throughout our extensive borders, vice of all kinds abounds. Satan and his agents are active and vigilant. At such a time the people of God should evince a corresponding energy. Never were Christians called to more diligence, self-denial, courage, benevolence and industry than at this solemn juncture; and it is, at such a time as this, that God and all good men are most fruitfully active. In a contest like this every man must serve his country according to his several ability and in his appointed sphere. Every man must find the place and the duty suited to him, and to which he is suited. None can be more important than practical and prayerful labor for the religious welfare of our heroic soldiers; directly seeking their salvation by preaching to them—by writing and distributing Tracts and Hymns and Bibles—by praying for them—and by tender sympathy with them in the trials and temptations to which they must be inevitably exposed. If God should breathe over these Confederate States the spirit of devotion, of humility, of dependence and of faith, it would be better than any victory in the field, however brilliant—for it would be at once proof of His favour and a pledge of our prosperity.

Instructed by the calamities of war, we shall estimate more highly the blessings of peace. We hardly ever value as we ought uninterrupted prosperity, or estimate as we should any good while it is ours. The evils of this trying period will not be lost to us, if they shall impress upon us all an adequate sense of the preciousness of peace and bring the policy of our Rulers and the temper of our people into perfect harmony with the spirit of the Gospel, peace on earth, good will to men.[22] Such have been the gallantry and patriotism of our troops in the field, and such the charity and courage of our women in anticipating and ministering to their wants, that we may pursue our chosen policy of peace with all nations without the imputation of effeminacy or cowardice. After the lapse of a few years, we trust that we shall look back upon these trying times as on a troubled dream, and in the secure enjoyment of peace repeat, with even more solemn and tender emphasis than on this day of thanksgiving and praise. Weeping may endure for a night, but joy cometh in the morning.[23]

The martyred dead have taken possession of this Southern soil for the Southern people. It was theirs originally, by the gift of God, and they have bought it anew by their blood. This land will be endeared to us and to our posterity, because it is the earthly resting-place of our immortal dead. It was the boast of the ancient Greek, as his eye wandered over his beautiful and beloved land, that every hill bore the tomb of a hero or the temple of a god. But more noble dust mingled not with the soil of Attica than that which reposes in the bosom of our own dear native land. It surely lends attraction to Heaven, viewed with reference to our present constitution, to think that there we shall behold and converse with the best and lovliest we have known on earth. If Socrates could talk of transports of joy at the prospect of seeing Palamedes, Ajax, and other heroes of antiquity in a future world—how should the Christian feel when he looks forward to an everlasting abode, not a transient meeting with the saints of all ages—with Christ Himself, the Author and Finisher of our faith.[24] If he hoped for felicity in comparing his experience with theirs—how shall we rejoice in reviewing dispensations of providence now impenetrably dark, or imperfectly understood, but then shining in the light of Heaven. The *past* and *future* meet in the memory of the dead. The sweetest and brightest link in the chain that stretches back over the past, binds us to the dead; and that chain stretches forward to eternity and attaches itself to the Throne of the living God. Thus death joins on to life; and all that is sacred in memory connects itself with all that is inspir-

[22]Cf. Luke 2:14.
[23]Psalm 30:5.
[24]Cf. Hebrews 12:2.

ing in hope. Weeping may endure for a night, but joy cometh in the morning.[25]

[25]Psalm 30:5.

Appendix 2

Casting Our Burden on the Lord[1]

There is no class of men who excite a deeper interest in every loyal son of the South than our gallant soldiers, who have exposed themselves to the manifold hazards of the battlefield and of the camp, in defence of our honor, our liberties and our lives. There are none who in seclusion and sickness—in the lonely hours of confinement and sorrow—in wounds and in weariness more need the consolations and hopes of the Gospel of peace.

I would lead such directly to the Savior. I would point them to the Lamb of God that taketh away the sin of the world.[2] I would commend them to Him who though he was rich, yet for our sakes became poor, that we through His poverty might be made rich—who though he was the Lord of glory, yet became a man of sorrows—who hath borne our griefs and carried our sicknesses, and who invites us to cast our burden upon Him and says that He will sustain us—that he will never suffer the righteous to be moved.[3]

If we wish to know the worth of true faith, and experience all its consolations, we should not content ourselves with barren tributes to the power of God, but at the time that we feel the burthen pressing upon us, confide in Him. We should receive every affliction as a challenge to try His faithfulness, as an invitation to trust His love; and the more cheerless our prospect on earth believe that the brighter is our inheritance in Heaven.

---

[1]The following is a reproduction of a digitized tract written by Joseph M. Atkinson, and originating possibly from one of his sermons preached at First Presbyterian Church of Raleigh. The digitized copy can be found at http://babel.hathitrust.org/cgi/pt?id=dul1.ark:/13960/t5m911z1p;view=1up;seq=2.

[2]Cf. John 1:29.

[3]Cf. 2 Corinthians 8:9; 1 Corinthians 2:8; Isaiah 53:3-4; Psalm 55:22.

True godliness, does not require us to deny that we are afflicted when God has laid His heavy hand upon us; nor does it require us to be insensible to pain. When we become Christians, we do not cease to be men. The feelings of natural affection are not quenched but purified and regulated by faith. We are therefore, at liberty, like David, to number our afflictions; not that we may murmur against our Sovereign Judge or sink into despair, but that we may be reminded like David, of the only sure consolation, and directed like him to the only true Refuge.

Among the first things, for the afflicted to consider is, *the disposition of mind which is connected with Divine relief.* It is not enough that we hear a burden; we must cast our burden upon the Lord. The temper befitting the burdened soul is *humble, meek, submissive* and *confiding.* God ever looks to the man that is humble and contrite, and that trembles at His word.[4] The mere fact that we are miserable does not entitle us to the promised blessing; nor will suffering alone, constitute any claim to the provisions of God's goodness. This is a common error into which superficial readers of the promises are prone to fall and therefore, it is one against which it is especially important to guard. When we read in the Bible, that God's compassions fail not—that he does not willingly afflict the sons of men—that he delighteth not in the death of the sinner[5]—we may be insensibly led to suppose that the circumstance that we are subjects of compassion—children of sorrow and withal wretched offenders—of itself—gives us some sort of claim to His blessing. But such an impression, will prove most delusive. The fact that we are miserable, only proves that we are guilty. It is far from being an evidence that hereafter we shall be happy. If misery alone were the object and measure of the Divine benevolence, then would the lost spirits in Hell be the principal recipients of the Almighty's bounty; for of all His creatures, they are the most completely miserable. It is evident then, that something more is necessary to share in God's promises, than simply to be miserable; that something must be done as well as endured; that we must not only have a burden, but cast it upon the Lord. There is not a word of comfort for those who are conscious of misery and are trying to bear it in their own

---

[4]Cf. Isaiah 66:2

[5]Cf. Ezekiel 33:11.

strength—who are too proud or too unbelieving to cast their burden on the Lord—who trust in an arm of flesh rather than in the mighty God of Jacob—who betake themselves to the polluting cup of sensual pleasure to assuage their sorrows by stupefying their souls, or turn to a false philosophy for consolation rather than to God their Maker, who giveth songs in the night.[6] But, they who put their trust in the Lord for deliverance in humble submission to His Sovereign will, and in fervent gratitude for His gracious help, shall be sustained.

For we are *forbidden to assign any limit to the promised deliverance or to specify any channel through which the blessing is to flow.* All that is required is, that we shall cast our burden on the Lord. The miserable man is to be conceived of as bending under a heavy load, but what that burden—from whom derived—of what composed—is wholly immaterial. It may be the recent loss of a large estate—the treachery of a trusted friend—the death of a beloved child, whose expanding beauties filled your heart with natural gladness, and whose opening virtues warranted the hope of future excellence—a child that you had been fondly rearing up to be an ornament and a pillar in the house of God—perhaps such an one has been snatched away suddenly, when your hopes were highest and your love warmest, and perhaps the paleness of the heart's agony, is still upon your brow and the tears of parental sorrow still bedew your cheek—O! I cannot say to such, weep no more—I cannot say that you have not been bitterly tried and that you have not bitter trials now: but this I can say, cast thy burden upon the Lord and He shall sustain thee. He will never suffer the righteous to be moved.[7]

It may be that you mourn what you imagine to be the darkening prospects of the community in which your lot has fallen, or the more extensive aboundings of iniquity in the land, the horrible desecrations of God's holy Sabbaths, the prevailing ignorance of Divine truth, the apparent apathy of good men, the increase of drunkness , profaneness, dishonesty and debauchery—whatever be the source of your trouble or the nature of your burden, you are invited to cast it on the Lord.

---

[6]Cf. Job 35:10.
[7]Cf. Psalm 55:22.

But perhaps sorrows of a more personal kind are yours. The heart knoweth his own bitterness.[8] Every man shall bear his own burden.[9] Perhaps you are drooping under some strong temptation, and are to some extent acquainted with the deceitfulness and desperate wickedness of your own heart; and are afraid that you will be left to yourself, and fall into some scandalous sin. Be not high-minded but fear, watch and pray that ye enter not into temptation.[10] Therefore, we ought to give the more earnest heed to the things which we have heard lest at any time we should let them slip.[11]

Take heed brethren, lest there be in any of you an evil heart of unbelief, in departing from the living God. But exhort one another daily, while it is called to-day lest any of you be hardened through the deceitfulness of sin.[12] Let us therefore, fear lest a promise being left us of entering into His rest, any of you should seem to come short of it.[13] These passages, in strict accordance with the uniform tenor of the word of God, show that we must diligently use the means of grace if we would escape the damnation *of Hell and attain the inheritance* of the Saints in light.[14] While it is the height of presumption, to look for Salvation while destitute of the fruits of the Spirit, yet we need not be alarmed by the slavish dread of eternal death, while giving all diligence to make our calling and election sure, and putting our trust in the living God who giveth us richly all things to enjoy.[15]

Accordingly the deliverance, which we are taught to expect with most confidence, and to desire, with most earnestness, is not deliverance from any temporal evil, but from the intolerable burden of sin. Ask with reference to this object and ye shall receive. Seek and ye shall find. Knock and it shall be opened unto you. For every one that asketh receiveth and

---

[8]Proverbs 14:10.
[9]Galatians 6:5.
[10]Cf. Matthew 26:41.
[11]Hebrews 2:1
[12]Hebrews 3:12-13.
[13]Hebrews 4:1.
[14]Cf. Colossians 1:12-13.
[15]Cf. 2 Peter 1:10; 1 Timothy 6:17.

he that seeketh findeth and to him that knocketh it shall be opened.[16] For this gracious assurance, we have no less authority than that of Christ Himself. If then our burden of sin be not taken off, it is because we will not. This is the solution of the mystery which the Master Himself gives: "Ye will not come unto me that ye might have life."[17] This is the condemnation that light is come into the world, and men loved darkness rather than light because their deeds were evil.[18] Our sin, which ought to drive us to Christ, is the very thing that keeps us from Him. Thus He testifies of Himself: "I came not to call the righteous, but sinners to repentance. The whole need not a Physician but they that are sick."[19] No one who has passed through this bitter struggle, will be disposed to glory over another who may be even now involved in it. The strong man armed, will not leave his house without a furious contest.[20] Satan will not surrender the victim of his wiles and the partner of his woes, without a desperate effort to retain him; and bitter is the pang and horrible the agony endured by the penitent when he exclaims,

> Oh! That my load of sin were gone.
> Oh! That I could at last submit,
> At Jesus feet to lay me down;
> To lay my soul at Jesus feet.

But *there is, in the Gospel, encouragement for those most deeply dejected and a hope full of immortality for the most despondent. Let us therefore consider the certainty of Divine relief.* We by no means affirm that the burden whatever it may be, shall be taken away, but that the soul shall be strengthened to bear it. The needful succor shall be administered and it shall be adapted to the burden. If the thing complained of be sin, it has been atoned for and it shall be remitted. For him hath God exalted to be a Prince and a Savior, to give repentance unto Israel and remission of

---

[16]Cf. Luke 11:9-10.
[17]Cf. John 5:40.
[18]John 3:19.
[19]Cf. Luke 5:31-32.
[20]Cf. Matthew 12:29.

sins, and the blood of Jesus Christ, His Son, cleanseth us from all sin. But what if the burden be necessary either for our good or for His glory? What if it be sent to humble us—to bend our proud necks to His yoke? What if it be an indispensable part of our spiritual discipline? What if it be needed to make us meet for the inheritance of the Saints in light?[21] What though He remove it not, yet shall He give us grace to bear it. Affliction is not always an evidence of the Divine displeasure, for whom the Lord loveth He chasteneth and scourgeth every son whom He receiveth. If ye then be without chastisement whereof all are partakers, then are ye bastards and not sons.[22] There was once a servant of God who had been distinguished by extraordinary marks of favor, and by revelations of peculiar glory. He had been caught up to the third Heavens whether in the body he knew not, and whether out of the body he knew not, but there he was admitted to visions of God, and he beheld things that ought not to be spoken or that human tongue was incompetent to express. And yet after all this, God sent a messenger of Satan to buffet him. What is the explanation of this seeming mystery? Why did the favored Apostle find this apparent inconsistency in the Divine dealings toward him? We have the answer in his own words, "Lest I should be exalted above measure by the abundance of the revelations." These opposite experiences of the same man at different times, were not merely consistent but related and dependent. It was *because* he had been so exalted that he must be depressed; because he had been so highly favored that he must be so deeply afflicted. And when he besought the Lord thrice that it might depart from him, did it depart? Was the burden removed—the thorn extracted—Satan's messenger dismissed? No! The appropriate answer is my grace is sufficient for thee, for my strength is made perfect in weakness.[23]

The instance which we have just contemplated, of a servant of God, in some respects highly exalted, in others unusually afflicted, is by no means an exception or departure from the common course of His providential dispensations. Doubtless when afflicted, not less than when exalted, the Apostle accomplished the will of his Divine Master.

---

[21]Cf. Colossians 1:12.
[22]Cf. Hebrews 12:6, 8.
[23]Cf. 2 Corinthians 12:1-10.

We may therefore gather from his experience and example that it is possible to glorify God in suffering. This is perhaps the most difficult service which man can render to God, and it is one which our mortal condition often makes it our duty to yield. It is comparatively easy to perform many *active duties*, because they are such as *reputation*, *interest* and *natural affection* dictate. Nothing is plainer than that we are bound to provide for the support and comfort of those dependent upon us; for the man that fails to do this is said to have denied the faith and to be worse than an infidel.[24] We are likewise required to honor our father and mother, and he who can treat with ingratitude those from whom he has derived his earthly being, is justly regarded as a monster and a miscreant. The Christian religion also renders the obligation of speaking the truth to our neighbor and of the strictest honesty in our pecuniary transactions imperative and universal. But we find men scrupulous in the performance of these duties, from no higher or better principles than the world acknowledges, and although they are necessary to the character of a Christian, they do not alone constitute it, though no one who neglects them can be a Christian, yet all who observe them are not Christians. These ought ye to have done and not left the others undone. Give unto Caesar the things which are Caesar's and unto God the things which are God's.[25] But it is the peculiar privilege of the people of God to bear what He sends upon them with religious resignation—to suffer joyfully the spoiling of their goods for His name's sake; and nothing but His grace can enable them to do it. When the people of God are cut off from active service—when by some painful dispensation affecting their *health*, their *fortune* or their *families,* they are so disabled as no longer to be capable of performing those duties which habit had rendered familiar and the blessing of God delightful, they are too apt to conclude that they can be useful no more. But they may as truly glorify God when stretched upon a bed of sickness as when employed in active duty; and there is perhaps no more pleasing spectacle which God beholds on earth than that of a good man patiently resigned to His will when it appoints the loss of all things and humbly trusting in His mercy, when all His waves and His billows are going over

[24]Cf. 1 Timothy 5:8.
[25]Cf. Matthew 23:23; 22:21.

him.[26] They that trust in the Lord shall be as Mount Zion, which cannot be removed, but abideth forever. As the mountains are round about Jerusalem, so the Lord is round about His people from henceforth even forever.[27]

[26]Cf. Psalm 42:7.
[27]Psalm 125:1-2.

Index

abolitionism, 22, 41, 42, 70, 73
abortion, 247
"Acres of Diamonds" (Conwell), 172-73
Act of Toleration, 8
Action Corporation, 209
Adams, John, 17, 18
Adopting Act of 1729, 8
Aerotron, 209
Afghanistan, 232, 233
Ahn, Young Ro, 241
Al Edwards Building, 224. *see also* Cairn Hall
Al Qaeda, 232
Albert G. Edwards Family Life Center, 253
Alcorn State University, 135n.4. *see also* Oakland College
Alexander, Archibald, 77
Alexander, Dorcas J., 33
Alexander, Joseph, 16
Alexander, Mary, 33
Alfred Moment Sunday School Class, 150, 156, 203-204. *see also* Moment, Alfred Harrison
Allen, George, 143
Altena, Dick, 243
Altena, Theresa, 243
Ambassador Theatre, 200, 218, 219
American Dream, 132, 158
American Federation of Labor, 133
American Red Cross, 170
American Revolution, 9, 15, 18, 44, 65, 91
American Society for the Promotion of Temperance, 57
American Temperance Union, 57
Americans with Disabilities Act, 230
Anderson, Elizabeth, 240
Andrews, Helen, 220
Andrews, Jedediah, 7n.7
anti-Catholic sentiment, 42, 78, 80, 197-99, 199n.79
Anti-Saloon League, 158
anxious bench, 20
Appomattox, 92
Apthorpe, George H., 49
Arminianism, 4-5, 19
Arminius, Jacob, 4
Arthur, Chester A., 133
Asbury, Francis, 31
Astor, John J., 101
Athey Products, 209
Atkinson, Jane P., 110n.32, 117n.60
Atkinson, John M. P., 74, 76
Atkinson, Joseph Mayo, 73-76, 77-82, 84n.47, 87-92, 98-99, 102, 104-105, 105-106, 106n.18, 107, 109, 110n.34, 115, 117, 117n.60
Atkinson, Sally P., 110n.32
Atkinson, Thomas, 74
atomic bomb, 181
Austin, Steve, 246
Azuza Street, 158
Baby Boomer generation, 231
Baghdad-on-the-Neuse, 209
Balch, Hezekiah James, 16
Balch, Hezekiah, 16
Bank of North Carolina, 83
Baptists: organization of in Wake County, 30; organization of in Raleigh, 31; membership totals in antebellum Raleigh, 43-44
Barham, Barton J., 246
Barwick, Allen, 245-46
Battle of Koppel, 2
Battle, Amos J., 68
Bauer, Adolphus Gustavus, 139, 141-43
Bauer, Rachel Blythe, 142-43
Baumann, Albrecht, 86, 127, 127n.100, 128, 146n.47
Baumann, Mary Penick, 86
Bay of Pigs invasion, 206
Beckwith, Byron De La, 218
Beecher, Lyman, 52, 52n.43, 57
Bell, Alexander Graham, 101
Benson, David, 233
Bethel church (Raleigh, NC), 31
Bettie Penick Bible Class, 163, 191, 200, 245n.35. *see also* Penick, Bettie
Bible Discovery curriculum, 245-46
biblical criticism, 71-72, 77-80, 159
Bin Laden, Osama, 232
Birch, Mary, 33
Birch, Sarah, 33
Black Panthers, 237n.12, 238n.12
Bloom, E., 175

Blount, Brian, 260
blue laws. *see* theocracy
Bonaparte, Napoleon, 17
Boushall, John, 169
Bowne, Bordon P., 72n.3
Boylan, William, 20
Brand, Richard, 239
Brandenburg Gate, 230
Briggs, Charles A., 72n.3
Briggs, Garrett, 242, 243
Brodie, Charlotte, 21
Broom, Jesse, 33
"Brother, Can You Spare a Dime?" (Harburg and Gorney), 180
Brown v. Board of Education, 202-203, 218
Brown, Charles Lynnwood, 192
Brown, Jesse, 63-64
Brown, John, 70, 73
Brown, Samuel, 24
Browne, Micou F., 220
Brueggemann, Walter, 184
Bruner, T. K., 139, 139n.22
Bryan, William Jennings, 133, 159
Buffalo Vanguard Church, 173. *see also* St. Barnabas Presbyterian Church (Raleigh, NC)
Buie, Archibald, 14n.23
Bunch, Mrs. B. R., 175
Bunch, Lisette Friedlan, 186, 186n.20, 262
Burned-over District, 20, 42n.10
Burwell, John Bott, 85, 98-99, 104, 105, 118, 136
Burwell, Robert, 85, 86, 127, 146n.47, 152
Bush v. Gore, 231
Bush, George H. W., 230-31
Bush, George W., 231-33
Busy Bee Band, 144, 150, 163
Cairn Hall, 225, 250, 253
Cairn monument, 225
Caldwell, Joseph, 32
Calvin, John, 2-4, 6, 80
Calvinism, 4-5, 77, 80
Cameron Village, 183
Camp David Accords, 208
Camp Holmes, 92, 95
Camp Polk, 165, 170
Campbell, James, 12-15
Campbell, Thomas, 42
Campbell, Will, 238n.12
Campbellites, 42; organization of in Raleigh, 31; membership totals in antebellum Raleigh, 43-44. *see also* Christian Church: membership totals in antebellum Raleigh
Capa, Margaret, 33
capital campaign, 241, 250-54, 256-60, 263. *see also* "Challenge to Care." *see also* "Step of Faith-Building for the Future, A." *see also* "Visions for Tomorrow." *see also* "Our Hope for Years to Come"
Capital City Telephone Company. *see* Southern Bell Telephone Company
state capitol, 31, 32, 37, 54-55, 63, 147, 209, 218, 227, 240, 262
Cardinal Latin High School, 218
Carington, Mayo, 44
Carnegie, Andrew, 101, 173
Carolina Hurricanes, 234
Carter Center, 208
Carter, Jimmy, 208
Cary Street Mission, 186, 262
Cassell, Charles E., 143
Casting Our Burden on the Lord (Atkinson), 75, 88-89
Catherine of Aragon, 5
Cave, W. E., 147-48
Centennial School, 55n.51
"Challenge to Care," 241
Chamberlain, Jeremiah, 135n.4
Chambers, Maxwell, 53-54
Chappell, Ted, 239
Chautauqua circuit, 162
Chavis, John, 44-47
Cherokee, 39. *see also* Native Americans
Chickasaw, 39. *see also* Native Americans
Cho, Youngil, 241
Choctaw, 39. *see also* Native Americans
Christian Church: membership totals in antebellum Raleigh, 43-44
Christian socialism, 132
Christianity and the Social Crisis (Rauschenbusch), 132
Christianizing the Social Order (Rauschenbusch), 132
Christmas Day offering, 225, 226
church anniversary celebration, 189, 189n.34, 227, 239-40,
church construction/renovation, 33-37, 66-69, 97, 136, 139-41, 143-144, 144n.42, 145, 145-46, 146n.47, 147, 174, 175-76, 176n.76, 177, 185, 199-200, 200n.83, 201, 224-25, 250, 252-53, 256-60
church discipline, 56, 57-61, 61n.70, 62

Index

Church Financial Campaign Service, 258
church membership totals, 62, 69, 96-97, 103, 105, 107, 120, 130, 138, 144, 145, 147, 160, 211
Church of Jesus Christ of Latter Day Saints, 42
City Cemetery (Raleigh, NC), 21, 85n.49
City Missionary, 186
City of Oaks, 233
civil disobedience, 221-222
Civil Rights Act of 1964, 207
"Civil Rights Movement in Light of Christian Teaching, The" (PCUS), 221
civil rights movement, 202, 207, 217-23, 236-37, 237n.12, 238n.12
Civil War, 42, 75, 84-85, 86-91, 91n.76, 92-94, 97, 107, 111, 119, 126, 127, 154, 161
Clark, Gilbert, 14n.23
Clark, Mark W., 198
Clark, William F., 66
Clarke, William Newton, 194n.62
Clean Air Act (1990), 230
Cleveland, Grover, 161
Clinton, Bill, 231, 233
Clinton, Hillary, 233
Clinton-Lewinsky scandal, 231
"cloud of witnesses," 260
Cold War, 182, 230
Cole, Echol, 236
College of New Jersey, 10, 44, 74. *see also* Princeton University
Colony Theatre, *see* Rialto
Commercial National Bank, 172
Committee on Program for Soldiers and Sailors, 190
communism, 197-98
Compromise of 1850, 70
Compromise of 1877, 100
Comte, Auguste, 78-79
congregational polity: definition of, 1
Congressional Reconstruction Acts, 92
Connecticut Society for the Reformation of Morals, 57
Connor, Bull, 217-18
Conwell, Russell, 172-73
Cooke, Lucy Ann, 63
Cooke, William Dewey, 63, 64
Copeland, John A. Jr., 73
CORE, 218
Cornbury, Lord, 7
Cornerstone Presbyterian Church (Raleigh, NC), 254
"Cornerstone that Isn't the Corner, The" (Edwards), 227
Corning Glass, 209
Cranmer, Thomas, 80
Crawford, J. H., 143
Creek, 39. *see also* Native Americans
Crestfield, James, 96
Creswell, James, 16
Crinkley, Andrew, 170
"Cross of Gold" (Bryan), 133
Crow, Edmund Burwell, 152-53, 171-73, 174. *see also* Vanguard Class
Crow, Nannie Burwell, 153, 174
Crow, Mrs. William, 121
Crow, W. H., 103, 114
Crown Zellerback, 209
Cuban Missile Crisis, 230
Cunningham, Jane, 92, 92n.80
Currie Sundays, 169
Currie, Archibald, 109
Currie, Edward Smith, 167-68, 168n.39, 169, 170, 261
Currie, Gay Vaughan Wilson, 168, 169, 261
Dahlberg, Edwin T., 219n.36
Dallas Police Department, 225
"Danger of an Unconverted Ministry, The" (Tennent), 9-10
Daniel, Chesley, 21, 22
Daniel, Eugene, 36, 134-36, 138, 139, 147
Daniel, Susannah Witherspoon, 135
Daniels, Addie, 146n.47
Daniels, Josephus, 170
Darrow, Clarence, 159
Darwin, Charles, 71, 77, 101
Davidson College, 38, 52-54, 134, 155, 161, 166, 167, 168, 183, 197
Davidson, James A., 174
Davie Street Presbyterian Church (Raleigh, NC), 96, 96n.92
Davis, Samuel, 7n.7
Day/Age Theory, 79, 79n.26
deacon: definition of. *see* diaconate
Declaration of Independence, 17, 34
Deere, John, 40
Democratic Party, 133, 161, 162, 207, 231, 233
Democratic-Republican Party, 18
desegregation. *see* integration
Detargny, Martin, 21

Devereux, Frances Pollock, 65-69, 185, 201, 253
Devereux, John, 65-66
Devereux property, 66-69, 146, 185, 200, 200n.83, 201, 252-53
Devereux, Thomas Pollock, 66
Dewey, Charles, 63-64
diaconate: definition of, 1
Dinwiddie, James, 86, 153-54, 155
Directory of Public Worship, The, 6
discrimination, 236-37
divine election, 81. *see also* Synod of Dort
divine providence, 81-82
Dobbin, John, 15
Documentary Hypothesis, 71-72
Dodge, William A. III, 209
"Don't Stop Thinking About Tomorrow" (Fleetwood Mac), 231
Dorothea Dix Hospital, 142
Doughton, Virginia, 94n.86
Downey, Samuel Smith, 45
Downey, W. W., 128n.104
Dred Scott v. Sanford, 70
Drunkard, The (Smith), 182
Duke, James B., 101
Duncan, Mrs. L. P., 151
Dunn, R. W., 188
Duraleigh Korean Presbyterian Church (Raleigh, NC), 241
Duraw Manufacturing, 209
Durfey, Carey K., 153
Dye, Darcy, 257
Early Birds, 212
East Vanguard Chapel (Raleigh, NC), 173. *see also* East Vanguard Church (Raleigh, NC). *see also* First Vanguard Church (Raleigh, NC). *see also* Milner Presbyterian Church (Raleigh, NC)
East Vanguard Church (Raleigh, NC), 173, 227. *see also* Milner Presbyterian Church (Raleigh, NC)
Eastern Airlines, 182
ecumenical movement, 158-59
Eden School, 242-43
Edenton Street Methodist Church (Raleigh, NC), 185, 200
Edge, Walter, 259
Edinburgh Conference, 158
Edward VI (King), 5
Edwards, Albert George, 210-12, 213, 219-220, 221, 222, 223, 224-25, 227, 229, 239, 240, 241, 250
Edwards, Jonathan, 20, 65, 67
Edwards, Margaret Early, 211
Eighteenth Amendment, 158
Eisenhower, Dwight D., 182
elder: definition of, 1
Elizabeth I, (Queen), 5, 6
Eller, James, 254
Emonds, Jane, 33, 33n.48
Emonds, Thomas, 32, 33
England, John, 56n.53
Enlightenment, 78
Enloe, William G., 218-19, 219n.34, 220
episcopal polity: definition of, 1
Episcopalians: membership totals in antebellum Raleigh, 43-44
Ernest Myatt Presbyterian Church (Raleigh, NC), 174, 227
Evarts, Jeremiah, 57
Evers, Medgar, 218
Exide, 209
"Faith of our Fathers" (Faber), 245
Farel, William, 3
Federal Council of Churches, 195-96. *see also* National Council of Churches
Federal Theatre Project, 182
Federalist Party, 18
Female Classical Institute, 60
feminism, 248-50
Fergerson, L. M., 170
Finley, Edward S. Jr., 247
Finley, Edward, 239, 255, 257
Finney, Charles Grandison, 19-20, 52, 52n.43, 67-68
First Baptist Church (Raleigh, NC), 68, 185, 200
First Blast of the Trumpet against the Monstrous Regiment of Women, The (Knox), 6
Great Awakening (First), 1, 9-11, 16, 20, 67
First Night celebration, 233
First Presbyterian Church (New York, NY), 194n.62
First Presbyterian Church, Colored (Raleigh, NC), 96, 96n.92. *see also* Davie Street Presbyterian Church (Raleigh, NC)
First Vanguard Church (Raleigh, NC), 186, 227. East Vanguard Chapel (Raleigh, NC). *see also* East Vanguard Church (Raleigh, NC). *see also* Milner Presbyterian Church (Raleigh, NC)
Flora McDonald College, 213, 213n.16
Ford, Henry, 157

Form of Presbyterial Church Government, The, 6
Fort Sumter, 86
Fort, David I., 153
Fosdick, Harry Emerson, 194, 194n.62
Fountain, George, 216
Four-Square Class, 186n.20, 262
Freedman's Bureau, 85, 94, 94n.86, 96n.92
French Revolution, 17
"frozen chosen," 1
Fundamentalism, 159, 194n.62, 197
Funderburk, Elaine, 246-47
Gales, Joseph, 20, 22-23, 37
Gap Theory, 79, 79n.26
Garfield, James, 133
Garrison, William Lloyd, 42
General Motors Corporation, 185, 185n.15
General Tract Agency, 88
Geneva Bible, 6
Gibson, Thomas, 14n.23
Gilded Age, 101, 133, 134
Gilded Age, The, 101
Gino's Restaurant, 218
Ginter Park Presbyterian Church (Richmond, VA), 169n.42
Glenaire Retirement Community, 236, 241, 262. *see also* White Gate Farm
Glendinning, William, 31
Glenn, Robert Brodnax, 154, 161-62
"God Rest Ye Merry Gentlemen," 245
God, the Giver of Victory and Peace (Atkinson), 75, 88, 89-92
Goldwater, Barry, 206
Goodwise, Rebecca, 33
Gore, Al, 231
"Gospel of Wealth" (Carnegie), 173
Gould, Ezra P., 72n.3
Government House, 55, 55n.51. *see also* governor's mansion
governor's mansion, 55, 55n.51, 83, 141, 209-210
Governor's Palace, 55n.51. *see also* governor's mansion
Graham, W. H., 170
Graham, William, 23
Great Depression, 180, 185n15, 186, 189, 210
Great Society, 206-207
Greater Houston Ministerial Association, 199
Green property, 252, 253, 254
Griffin Free School, 66
Grimké, Angelina, 41
Grimké, Sarah, 41
Gulf War, 230, 232
Gwynn, Ken, 257, 258
Gwynn, Price, 240
Halifax Court, 186
Hall, Sugar, 95
Hall, William T., 118
Hampden, John, 7, 7n.7, 8
Hardaway, B. R., 104
Hardee, John W., 146n.47
Harder, Donna, 250, 250n.57
Harding, B. R., 120
Harding, Fred F., 185
Harding, Nehemiah H., 48, 49
Harper, Charles A. Jr., 245
Harper, F. M., 177
Harpers Ferry, 70, 73
Harrison Construction Company, 177
Harrison, Robert, 33
Hartford Whalers, 234
Harward, Ben, 245-46
Hayes, Rutherford B., 133
Hayes, Sue, 228
Haywood, Elizabeth, 33
Haywood, John, 20
Haywood, Sherwood, 47
health and wealth gospel, 172-73
Heartt, Leo D., 103, 104, 120
Helper, Hinton Rowan, 73
Hemphill, J. Edwin, 164, 171
Henderson, Archibald, 46
Henderson, John L., 46
Henderson, Leonard, 46
Henry VIII (King), 5
Hermann, Grover M., 217
Hester, John, 243
High Y, 185n.14
Hill, Anita, 230
Hill, D. H., 143
Hill, Daniel Harvey, 53
Hill, Thomas, 84-85
Hinton, Elizabeth, 33
Hinton, John, 33
Hinton, Priestly, 46
Hipp, Edward, 214
Hiroshima, 181
Hitler, Adolf, 180
Hodge, Charles, 77
Hodges, Luther, 209
Hoey, Clyde R., 199
Holden, William W., 85n.49

Holding, H. G., 160
Holmes, Nancy, 33, 33n.50
Holshouser, Jim, 240
Homestead Act, 101
homosexuality, 247-48
Hope, Eliza L., 110n.32
Hostess Houses, 169
Hudson, Karl, 173
Hudson, W. J., 170
Hughes, Nelson B., 57-59
Humphrey, Hubert, 207
Hunt, Jim, 240
Hunt, Thomas P., 37n.65, 48, 49
Hunt, Wright, 92, 95n.89
Hurricane Floyd, 234
Hurricane Fran, 233
Hurricane Katrina, 232
Hurt, John David, 225-26, 226n.67
Hussein, Saddam, 230, 232
Hussey, Obed, 40
Hyde Memorial Garden, 236, 253
"I Have a Dream" (King), 218
"I've Been to the Mountaintop" (King), 237
IBM, 209
Immigration Act of 1990, 230
immigration, 41, 132, 197, 230
Impending Crisis of the South, The: How to Meet It (Helper), 73
"In God We Trust," 182
Inco Electro Energy, 209
Indian Removal Act
Industrial Revolution, 157
Institutes of the Christian Religion (Calvin), 3, 4
integration, 194, 202-203, 218, 219, 219n.34, 219n.36, 220-21, 222-23
Interdenominational Ministerial Alliance, 219
International Conference on Theological Education, 167
Inter-state Telephone and Telegraph. *see* Southern Bell Telephone Company
Iran-Contra scandal, 208, 230
Iranian revolution, 208
Iraq, 232, 233
irresistible grace. *see* Synod of Dort
Jackson, Andrew, 39
Jackson, Thomas "Stonewall," 91
Jacksonian Democracy, 39
Jacobs, William P., 195
Jamieson, James, 55
Jefferson, Thomas, 18, 91
Jeffersonian Democracy, 39
Jenkins, W. F., 151
Jim Crow, 100, 202
Johns, Hannah, 110n.32
Johnson, Lyndon B., 206-207
Jones, Atlas, 22
Jones, Calvin, 35
Jones, Whitney, 251-52
Jones, William, 25
Jordan, Betty, 239, 242
Jordan, George C., 145
Jordan, Paul, 228
Joseph, 92, 95
Junior Presbyterians, 145
Kate C. Sprunt Memorial Library, 201. *see also* Sprunt, Kate C
"Keeping the Body and Soul Together: Sexuality, Spirituality and Social Justice" (PCUSA), 247-48
Kennedy, James, 110n.32
Kennedy, John F., 206, 225-26, 226n.67; assignation of, 206, 225-26, 226n.67
Kennedy, Robert F., 207
Kennison, J. S., 188n.32
Kesterson, David, 242, 247
Kettering, Charles, 185n.15
Kilpatrick, Hugh Judson, 92, 93-94
King, Martin Luther Jr., 207, 217-18, 222, 237, 237n.12, 238n.12; assignation of, 207, 237, 237n.12, 238n.12
Kingsley, M. H., 110n.32
Kingsley, T. A., 110n.32
Kirkland, Helen, 122-23
Kirkland, Mrs. S., 97
Knights of Labor, 132
Knox, John, 5-6, 80
Korean War, 182
Ku Klux Klan. *see* Beckwith, Byron De La
Kukla, Bob, 258
labor strikes, 133
labor unions, 132-33
Lacy, Mrs. Benjamin Rice, 151. *see also* Lacy, Mary Burwell
Lacy, Benjamin Rice Jr., 166-67, 170
Lacy, Benjamin Rice, 166
Lacy, Drury, 38, 47, 51-54, 56, 58, 62, 65, 69, 73, 85, 118, 121, 166
Lacy, Emma Elizabeth White, 167
Lacy, Mary Burwell, 151, 166
Lacy, Mary Rice, 54, 85, 121
Lacy, Thomas A., 170
Lacy, Williana Wilkinson, 54

Ladies Aid Society, 144, 145
Ladies Foreign Missionary Society, 121-22, 122n.82, 123-25, 126, 144, 261
Ladies Home Missionary Society, 125, 125n.93, 126-27, 127n.98, 144, 262
Ladies Society for Christian Work, 150, 151, 163, 167n.35; Home Mission Department, 150-51; Foreign Mission Department, 150, 151; Local Department, 151. *see also* Women's Society for Christian Work
laissez-faire, 101
Lam, Mawkins, 95, 95n.88
Lancaster, Joseph, 28
Lane, Lunsford, 47
Larger Catechism, The, 6
Layfield property, 224
League of Nations, 165
Lectures on Revivals of Religion (Finney), 20
Lee, Robert E., 91, 92
Lemay, Thomas J., 82
"Letter from a Birmingham Jail" (King), 217
Lewinsky, Monica, 231
Lewis, A. M., 94
Lewis, Julius, 143
liberalism. *see* Modernism
Liberator, The, 42
Liberty Hall Academy, 23, 45. *see also* Washington and Lee University
limited atonement. *see* Synod of Dort
Litchford, Sallie, 97
literalism, 78, 159
Litho Industries, 209
Loeb, Henry, 236-37
Log College, 9
Lorraine Motel, 237
Lost Cause narrative, 91n.76
"Lost in the Crowd" (Stock), 239
Louisiana Purchase, 18
Loyalists, 15
Lundy, Mary Ann, 249
Luther, Martin, 80
Lyceum Bureau, 162
MacOverton, Dora, 220-21
Madison, James, 91
Makemie, Francis, 7-8
Mallinckrodt, 209
Mangum, Willie Person, 46
Manifest Destiny, 39
Manly, Charles, 46
Marshall, John, 91
Marshall, Peter, 211
Marshall, Thurgood, 230
Martin, James G., 262
Mary (Guise) (Queen), 6
Mary (Tudor) (Queen), 5, 6
Massachusetts Society for the Suppression of Intemperance, 57
McAden, Hugh, 12, 16
McAlister, Alexander, 14n.23
McCadden, Hugh. *see* McAden, Hugh.
McCain, John, 233
McCarthy, Eugene, 207
McCorkle, William, 222
McCormick, Cyrus, 40
McGinnis, Faye, 228, 246, 249
McGreachy, R. W., 170
McGready, Aaron F., 22
McGready, James, 19
McGurkin, E. B., 196-97
McIlwain, William B. Jr., 163-64
McIntire, Carl, 197-98
McKay, Archibald, 14, 14n.23
McKinley, William, 157
McLean, Angus, 209
McLeod, Edward A., 255-56, 258, 259
McLeod, Jenny, 255
McLeod, John, 15
McNeill, Franklin, 162n.16
McNeill, Hector, 14n.23
McNeill, Neill, 14n.23
McNeill, Roger, 14
McNish, George, 7n.7
McPheeters, Elizabeth McDowell, 24
McPheeters, Fannie, 146n.47
McPheeters, H. M., 104, 136
McPheeters, Lavinia Moore, 24
McPheeters, Lavinia, 24
McPheeters, Margaret Ann McDaniel, 27, 33
McPheeters, William, 23-25, 27, 28, 29-30, 31, 32, 32n.47, 33, 34, 35n.57, 37, 38, 45, 47, 48-49, 50, 51, 53, 55, 62, 69, 146, 146n.47, 205
McPherson, Anguish, 14n.23
McPherson, William P., 239
McVea (Miss), 117
Mebane, William N., 83
Memorial Auditorium, 55n.51
Memorial Hall, 141
Men's Association for Christian Work in Wake County, 163
Message to all Churches of Jesus Christ Throughout the World, A, 228

Metcalf, Luella Corell, 191
Methodists: organization of in Wake County, 30; organization of in Raleigh, 31; membership totals in antebellum Raleigh, 43-44
Milburnie Church (Raleigh, NC), 97-98
Milburnie Paper Mill, 97
Miller, Belle, 183-84
Miller, Lila Bonner, 183
Miller, Mary, 183-84
Miller, Patrick Dwight, 183-84, 184n.13, 185, 185n.14, 186-89, 240
Miller, Patrick Jr., 183, 240
Miller, William, 242, 243
Milner Presbyterian Church (Raleigh, NC), 173, 186, 227. *see also* East Vanguard Chapel (Raleigh, NC). *see also* East Vanguard Church (Raleigh, NC). *see also* First Vanguard Church (Raleigh, NC).
Milner, Henry H., 173, 186
Minerva, The, 20
Minister's Annuity Fund, 186-88
Mission Chapel, 120, 138-39. *see also* Mission School
Mission School, 120. *see also* Mission Chapel
Mission Valley Hotel, 239
Mitchell, Hinkley G., 72n.3
Modernism, 72, 72n3, 77
Moffet, (Mrs.). *see* Moffit, Mrs. E. E.
Moffit, Mrs. E. E., 145
Moment, Alfred Harrison, 148-49, 149n.67, 150, 150n.71, 152, 153, 155-56, 160, 172, 203-204. *see also* Alfred Moment Sunday School Class
Moment, Julia Wilson, 149
Moment, Magdalena Wurst, 149
Monie, Mrs. J. M., 110n.32
Monie, J. M., 110, 110n.32, 135, 177-78
Monroe Doctrine, 18
Monroe, James, 18
Montreat, 222, 222n.50
Moon, Ik Bai, 242
Moore, Emily Ann L., 126
Moore, J. M., 143
Moore, John, 228
Moore, Walter W., 146
Moore, Walter, 260
Morgan, John Pierpont, 101
Morse, Samuel, 40
Mott, Lucretia, 41
Mount Holyoke College, 41
Munn, McAlpin, 15
Mussolini, Benito, 180
"my right and your left," 254
NAACP, 218
Nagasaki, 181
Narcotics/Alcoholics Anonymous, 262
Narrative of a New and Unusual American Imprisonment of Two Presbyterian Ministers and Prosecution of Mr. Francis Makemie, The (Hampden), 8
Narrative of a Surprising Work of God (Edwards), 20
Nat Turner Rebellion, 45-46, 47n.26
National Council of Churches, 219n.36
National Presbyterian Church, 227. *see also* Presbyterian Church in America
National Trades Union, 40
Native Americans, 39, 39n.1, 71, 100, 123, 124, 125
NCAE building, 224. *see also* Cairn Hall
Nelson, Murray, 174
Nettleton, Asahel, 52, 68
Neuse Manufacturing Company, 97
New Deal, 158, 180, 182
New Haven Theology, 76-77
New Lebanon Conference, 52
new measures, 20, 52
New School Presbyterianism, 71.
New Side Presbyterianism, 9-11, 12, 19-20, 67, 70-71
New York Institution for the Instruction of the Deaf and Dumb, 63
NHL All-Star Game, 234
Nichols, Jim, 257, 259
Nichols, John, 166
Nineteenth Amendment, 158
Nixon, Richard, 207
North Carolina Advisory Committee on Education, 202-203
North Carolina Agricultural and Mechanical College, 163. *see also* North Carolina State University
North Carolina Bible Society, 37
North Carolina Constitutional Convention, 55-56, 63, 147, 262
North Carolina Hospital for the Insane. *see* Dorothea Dix Hospital
North Carolina Institution for the Instruction of the Deaf and Dumb, 37, 62-63, 116
North Carolina School for the Deaf, 141

North Carolina State University, 163, 174, 218; Campus Christian Ministry, 247
North Carolina Supreme Court, 37, 46, 55, 63, 126, 147, 216-17, 262
North Carolina Symphony, 218
North Carolina Temperance Society, 57
North Vanguard Chapel (Raleigh, NC), 174, 192, 227. *see also* Westminster Presbyterian Church (Raleigh, NC)
"Not Why, but How" (Sprunt), 201
Nye, Susan D., 33
O'Neal, Mrs. Alan S., 201
O'Neal, Alan S., 201
Oakland College, 134, 135n.4. *see also* Alcorn State University
Oakwood Cemetery (Raleigh, NC), 143, 155
Obama, Barack, 233
Oberlin College, 20, 41
Old School Presbyterianism, 67, 71, 77.
Old Side Presbyterianism, 9-11, 12, 19, 67, 70-71, 77
Olds, Fred A., 160
"Onward Christian Soldiers" (Sullivan), 245
organ, 127, 127n.100
Origin of the Species (Darwin), 71, 77, 101
original sin, 77
Osborne, Michael, 37n.65, 50, 50n.36
Oswald, Lee Harvey, 225-26, 226n.67
Oswald, Marina, 226, 226n.68
"Our Hope for Years to Come," 263
Pace, E. R., 170
Painter, G. W., 122
Panama Canal, 208
Panic of 1873, 102
Panic of 1893, 140
Parade of Progress, 185, 185n.15
Park Avenue Baptist Church (New York, NY), 194n.62
Parks, Calvin, 239
Parks, Rosa, 202
pastor's indicator, 128
Patriots, 15
Patterson, John, 14n.23
Patterson, Samuel J., 227
Pattillo, Henry, 16
Peace College, 213, 213n.16, 214-17, 239, 254, 262. *see also* Peace Institute. *see also* William Peace University
Peace Institute, 54, 83-84, 84n.47, 85-86, 94, 94n.86, 96n.92, 119, 127, 153-55, 163, 166, 170. *see also* Peace College. *see also* William Peace University
Peace of Koppel. *see* Battle of Koppel
Peace, William, 32, 33, 35, 47, 82-84, 84n.47, 85, 85n.49
Peacock, Charles, 243
Peacock, Margaret, 243
Peale, Norman Vincent, 172
Pearl Harbor, 181, 190
Pearsall, Thomas, 202
Pearson, Charles, 143
Pearson, Richmond, 161
Peet, Harvey Prindle, 63
Penick, Bettie, 163. *see also* Pilathea Class for Young Women. *see also* Bettie Penick Bible Class
Pentecostalism, 158
perseverance of the saints. *see* Synod of Dort
Petersilia, Karl, 60-61
Petersilia, Lucy, 60
pews: sale of, 35-36; annual tax, 35-36, 50
Pilathea Class for Young Women, 163. *see also* Bettie Penick Bible Class. *see also* Penick, Bettie
Plessy v. Ferguson, 100
PNC Arena, 234
Polk, Frances Ann Devereux, 66
Polk, Leonidas, 66
Pollock, Thomas, 65
Populism, 133
Populist Party, 133
positivism, 78-79
Potter, Henry, 33, 35
Potter, Sylvia, 33
Powell, John R., 220-21
predestination, 4, 77
Prempert, L., 110n.32
Presbyterian Church (USA), 247-48, 249, 254; Major Mission Bicentennial Fund Campaign, 254
Presbyterian Church in America, 227
Presbyterian Church (US), 71, 87, 167, 186, 193, 195, 196n.66, 221-22, 222n.50, 223, 227-28, 238n.12, 244; Major Mission Fund Campaign, 238n.12
Presbyterian Church, Colored (Raleigh, NC), 96, 96n.92. *see also* Davie Street Presbyterian Church (Raleigh, NC)
Presbyterian Committee on Congregational Song, 245
Presbyterian Fund, 186
Presbyterian Homes, Inc., 240

Presbyterian Junior College, 213
presbyterian polity: definition of, 1
Presbyterians: first General Assembly in the United States, 11, 16; organization of in Wake County, 30; organization of in Raleigh, 31; membership totals in antebellum Raleigh, 43-44; Northern, 70-71, 193n.61, 196, 227, 244; Southern, 70-71, 151, 193n.61, 194-96, 223, 227, 244
Presbytery of Granville: opposition to North Carolina Advisory Committee on Education, 203; approval of civil rights movement, 221-22
Presbytery of Hanover, 16
Presbytery of Orange, 16, 36
Presbytery of Philadelphia, 7, 7n.7
presbytery: definition of, 1
Price, Mrs. H. B., 151
Primrose, Mrs. J. D., 110n.32
Primrose, John, 47, 105
Primrose, Mrs. William Stuart, 151
Primrose, William Stuart, 104, 143, 162-63
Princeton Theological Seminary, 10, 50, 74, 76, 77, 149, 183, 197
Princeton Theology, 76, 77
Princeton University, 10, 44, 45, 74. *see also* College of New Jersey
Progressive Era, 134
Prohibition, 57, 158, 162
Protestantism. *see* Reformation
Pryor Street Presbyterian Church (Atlanta, GA), 171
Pullen Memorial Baptist Church (Raleigh, NC), 174
Pullen, Richard Stanhope, 95
Pupil Assignment Act, 202-203
Puritans, 5, 6, 57
Quakers, 42
Rabeteau, Susannah, 33, 33n.48
radio ministry, 223, 223n.54
Rainey, Godfrey, 95
Raleigh Academy, 21-23, 25-30, 32, 34, 37, 83; Lancasterian method, 28-29
Raleigh Chapter of the Fellowship of Southern Churchmen, 219
Raleigh Citizens Association, 218
Raleigh Council of Church Women, 219
Raleigh Entertainment and Sports Arena, 234. *see also* RBC Center. *see also* PNC Arena
Raleigh Garden Club, 183
Raleigh Little Theatre, 182
Raleigh Ministerial Association, 184, 185n.14, 219
Raleigh Municipal Airport, 182
Raleigh Register, 20
Raleigh: surrender of, 92-94; race riot, 134
Raleigh-Durham Airport, 182-83
Ramsey, Harold, 239
rationalism, 77, 78, 79
Rauschenbusch, Walter, 132
RBC Center, 234. *see also* Raleigh Entertainment and Sports Arena. *see also* PNC Arena
Reade, Edwin Godwin, 114, 125, 126, 146n.47
Reade, Mary Parmele, 125-26, 146n.47
Reagan, Ronald, 208, 230
Reconstruction, 85, 86, 92, 94, 94n.86, 95-99, 100, 111, 117, 126, 127
Redding, T. H., 170
Reformation: in Continental Europe, 2-5; in England, 5-6; in Scotland, 5-6
Reformed theology. *see* Calvinism
Re-Imagining Conference, 248-49, 249n.56
Religious Right, 244
Remonstrance, 4
Rencher, Abraham, 46
Republican Party, 133, 207, 231, 233
Research Triangle Park, 209
reunification, 193, 193n.61, 195-96, 227-28, 244
Rex Hospital Fund, 83
Rex, John, 83
Rialto, 192. *see also* Colony Theatre
Rickenbacker, Eddie, 182
"Rise" (Moore), 260
Riverside Church (New York, NY), 194n.62
Roaring Twenties, 158
robber barons, 101
Roberts, Guy A., 177
Robinson, William, 12
Rockefeller, John D., 101, 194n.62
Roebuck, Dan, 228
Rogers, Gerry, 242
Rogers, W. H. Jr., 170
Roman Catholics: membership totals in antebellum Raleigh, 43-44
Roosevelt, Franklin Delano, 158, 180, 198
Ross, William G. 217
Rotary Club (Raleigh, NC), 152
rotation system for deacons and elders, 204
Rounseville, Benjamin, 33

Royster, James D., 46
Ruby, Jack, 225
Ruth, Mary, 33, 33n.48
S&W Cafeteria, 218
Sabbath observance, 184-85, 192-93
SALT II, 208
Sanford, Terry, 218
sanitation workers' strike, 236-37, 237n.12, 238n.12
Saunders, S., 33
Saunders, Sarah, 33
Scales, Alfred M., 83
Scarlette, C. C., 187
Schuller, Robert, 172
Scopes Monkey Trial, 159
Scott, Bob, 240
Scott, Mrs. Charles H., 117n.60
Scott, Charles H., 110, 110n.32, 111
Scott, Mrs. J. W., 151
Scott, Mary A., 110n.32
Scott, Thomas G., 46
Seawell, Malcom B., 214
Seawell, Richard B., 97
Great Awakening (Second), 1, 18-20, 52, 57, 61, 67, 76
Second Presbyterian Church (Memphis, TN), 222n.50
Second Presbyterian Church (Philadelphia, PA) 11
Second Presbyterian Church (Raleigh, NC), 105-107, 107n.22, 108-110, 110n.32, 110n.34, 111-17, 135-36
Second Presbyterian, Colored (Statesville, NC), 95n.90
segregation, 94-95, 100, 222n.50
Seminole, 39. *see also* Native Americans
Senior Volunteer Association, 46
September 11th, 232
Session House, 37
session: definition of, 1
Seventeenth Amendment, 158
Seymour, William J., 158
Shaw Institute, 94n.86. *see also* Shaw University
Shaw University, 94n.86, 140, 218. *see also* Shaw Institute
Shaw, Dushee, 14n.23
Shaw, Pricilla, 33, 33n.49
Shaw, William, 32, 33, 36
Shepherd's Center, 262
Sherman, William Tecumseh, 92, 93
Sherwood, F. W., 170
Sherwood, Fleming, 170
Shorter Catechism, The, 6, 14
Simpkins, Floyd E., 165-66
Simpkins, W. A., 165-66
Singer, Isaac, 40
Sioux, 123, 124. *see also* Native Americans
Sir Walter Hotel, 218
Sixteenth Amendment, 158
Sixteenth Street Baptist Church (Birmingham, AL), 218
slavery, 22, 41, 42, 45, 47, 47n.26, 70-71, 73, 90, 92, 95
Sloan, Samuel, 141
Smith, Ann P., 110n.32
Smith, E. C., 146n.47
Smith, Henry H., 247
Smith, Henry Preserved, 72n.3
Smith, Henry, 228
Smith, Hudson, 175
Smith, J. Henry, 109, 110
Smith, John, 32, 33
Smith, Joseph, 42
Smith, L. M., 219, 219n.37
Smith, Mrs. M. O., 146n.47
Smith, Malcom, 14n.23
Smith, W. R., 175
Smith, W. W., 146n.47
Smith, William Nathan Harrell, 106n18, 146n.47
Smith, Willis, 199
Smyth, J. Jones, 74
Snow, R. A., 192
Social Darwinism, 101, 132, 173
Social Gospel, 132
Sommers Maurice Omar, 189-90, 191, 192, 196, 240
Sommers, Richard, 240
Southern Bell Telephone Company, 159
Southern Bell. *see* Southern Bell Telephone Company
Southern Railway, 161
Spanish influenza epidemic, 178, 178n.85
Spanish-American War, 133
Spencer, Herbert, 101
Spring Branch Presbyterian Church, 83, 83n.44
Sprunt, James S., 197, 200-201, 201n.88, 202, 204-205
Sprunt, Kate C., 201. *see also* Kate C. Sprunt Memorial Library
Sprunt, Melvina Hobson, 202

St. Andrews Presbyterian Church (Wilmington, NC), 141
St. Andrews Presbyterian College, 213-17
St. Augustine's College, 218, 220-21
St. Barnabas Presbyterian Church (Raleigh, NC), 173
St. Mary's Episcopal Cathedral (Memphis, TN), 237
St. Mary's School, 85
Stalin, Joseph, 180
Stamps, E. R., 104, 120
Stamps, Elizabeth, 191
Stanley Cup, 234
Stanton, Elizabeth Cady, 41
Stell, Lawrence I., 188n.32
"Step of Faith-Building for the Future, A," 252
Stigbie, Thisbe, 33
Stillman College choir, 222
Stock Building, 253, 256
stock market crash, 158, 180
Stock, Anne Munch Thomas, 236
Stock, Edwin W., 235-37, 237n.12, 238, 238n.12, 239, 241, 243, 246-47, 251, 252, 254, 254n.76, 256
Stock, Edwin, 236
Stock, Martha Dale Johnston, 236
Stock, Sarah, 236, 238
Stockton, Henry, 177
Stowe, Harriet Beecher, 70
Stringer, Mrs. Ronald, 239
Stringer, Ronald, 239
Stronach, Alexander B., 37, 127n.100
Subscription Controversy, 8
Suhnam Presbyterian Church (Kwang-ju, Korea), 241-42
Swan, Barbara, 220-21
Synod of Dort, 4-5
Synod of New York and Philadelphia, 11, 16
Synod of New York, 10
Synod of North Carolina, 87, 186, 187, 188, 196n.66, 213, 213n.16, 214-16
Synod of Philadelphia, 7n.7, 8, 10
synod: definition of, 1-2
Taj Mahodges, 209
Taylor, A. D., 110, 110n.32
Taylor, H. D., 170
Taylor, Nathaniel William, 76-77
Taylor, Nathaniel, 7n.7
Taylor, Sallie L., 110n.32
television ministry, 223-24
temperance movement, 22, 57, 158
Temple University, 172
Tennent, Gilbert, 9-10
Tennent, Will Sr., 9
Tennessee Council on Human Relations, 238n.12
"Thanks a Million" luncheon, 257
theocracy, 3
Theology for the Social Gospel, A (Rauschenbusch), 132
Theory of the Leisure Class (Veblen), 132
Third Raleigh Conference on Faith and Human Relations, 219, 219n.36
Thirteenth Amendment, 94
Thomas, Clarence, 230
Thompson, A. A., 139, 146
Thompson, Cy Jr., 170
Thompson, H. A., 170
Thompson, John, 12
Thornton, Mrs. James I., 215. *see also* Thornton, Myra Williams
Thornton, Myra Williams, 215
total depravity. *see* Synod of Dort
Towles, James M. Jr., 110n.32
Towles, James M., 63-64, 110, 110n.32, 115
Towles, M. Alice, 110n.32
Towles, Mary Ann., 110n.32, 135
Towles, Mary C., 110n.32
Towles, Robert H., 110n.32
Towles, Sallie B., 110n.32
Treaty of Guadalupe Hidalgo, 40
Treaty of Versailles, 165
True Path, The: or the Young Man Invited to the Saviour (Atkinson), 75-76, 77-82
Truman, Harry S., 198, 199
Tucker, Harry, 170
Tucker, Ruffin, 94
TULIP. *see* Synod of Dort
Tupper, Henry Martin, 94n.86
Turner, Jesse, 34, 35
Turner, William Leftwich, 22-23, 31-32, 34
Twain, Mark, 101
Tweed, William "Boss," 133
Twentieth Amendment, 158
U. S. Army Counterintelligence, 26
Umstead, William, 202
Uncle Tom's Cabin (Stowe), 70
unconditional election. *see* Synod of Dort. *see also* divine election
"under God," 182
union services, 185

Union Presbyterian Seminary (Richmond, VA), 235. *see also* Union Theological Seminary (Richmond, VA)
Union Theological Seminary (Richmond, VA), 52, 72n.3, 119, 146, 161, 163, 166, 167, 168, 183, 189, 197, 211, 235, 254, 254n.76, 255, 260. *see also* Union Presbyterian Seminary (Richmond, VA)
United Nations, 230
United Presbyterian Church of the United States of America, 227-28, 244
University of North Carolina at Chapel Hill, 21, 22, 32, 66, 82, 111, 119
Upchurch, Everett, 170
Valentine, Herbert D., 240
Valentine, J. P., 110n.32
Valentine, Martha, 110n.32
Vance, Charlie, 113
Vance, David, 113
Vance, Harriett Espy, 113, 113n.43, 114, 115
Vance, Mira Margaret Baird, 112-13
Vance, Thomas, 113
Vance, Zebbie, 113
Vance, Zebulon Baird, 111-13, 113n.43, 114-15, 115n.49, 134n.2
Vanderbilt, Cornelius, 101
Vanguard Class, 152-53, 169, 170-74, 175, 204, 244, 245n.35, 261. *see also* Crow, Edmund Burwell
Vass, L. C., 118, 119
Vatican, 198, 199
Vaughan, Clement Read, 102-103, 110n.34, 114, 117-18
Veblen, Thorstein, 132
via media, 5
Vickers, Anne, 246
Vietnam War, 207, 208
"Visions for Tomorrow," 257-58
Wake Superior Court, 215-16
Walderon, E. H., 170
Walker, Robert, 236
Wallace, George, 207
Walsh (Lieutenant), 93, 93n.85, 94
War of 1812, 18, 83
War on Poverty, 207
Waring, George W., 140
Warner, Charles Dudley, 101
Washington and Lee University, 23, 45, 161. *see also* Liberty Hall Academy
Washington, George, 17, 91
Watergate scandal, 207, 208
Waters, Vincent C., 218
Watkins, Alice, 233n.1
Watkins, John Sims, 118-20, 121, 128-31, 134, 146, 147
Watkins, John, 233n.1
Watts, Isaac, 263
Wedding, Rebecca, 59-60
Wednesday lunch, 212
Welford, John, 238n.12
Wellhausen, Julius, 71-72
Wesleyan College, 41
West Raleigh Presbyterian Church (Raleigh, NC), 174, 214, 227
Western North Carolina Hospital for the Insane, 141
Western Union Telegraph Company, 161
Westminster Assembly of Divines, 6
Westminster Confession of Faith, The, 6, 8, 9, 19, 20, 77, 144
Westminster League, 145
Westminster Presbyterian Church (Atlanta, GA), 211
Westminster Presbyterian Church (Raleigh, NC), 174, 227. *see also* North Vanguard Chapel (Raleigh, NC)
Wetherall, Mary E., 110n.32
Wharton, Mrs. Cyrus P., 193. *see also* Wharton, Sarah Duncan
Wharton, Cyrus P., 138, 143, 193
Wharton, Sarah Duncan, 193
"What Have I Gotten Myself Into?" (McLeod), 255
Whitaker plantation, 30
White Gate Farm, 240-41
White Memorial Presbyterian Church (Raleigh, NC), 191-92, 214, 227
white supremacism, 162
White, H. M., 161-62
White, Lorens, 170
White, Susie Lorentz, 161
White, William McClanahan White, 160, 160n.10, 161, 163-64, 167, 168, 172, 173, 174, 175, 177, 179, 183, 192
Whitefield, George, 13
Whitelaw, John, 110n.32
Whiting, Chester G., 145
Whiting, L. W., 120
Whiting, Seymour W., 104, 120, 136
Whiting, Seymour, 170n.47
Whitney Jones and Associates, 252
Wildes, Rachel, 121
Willett Stained Glass Company, 200

William Peace University, 54, 152, 262. *see also* Peace Institute. *see also* Peace College
Williams, Bill, 228
Williams, Jane, 95, 95n.90
Williams, William John, 95, 95n.90
Wilson, Alexander, 74
Wilson, Edith Bolling, 170-71, 171n.50
Wilson, John, 7n.7
Wilson, Woodrow, 164, 165, 166, 170
Windows on the Word, 201n.88
Witherspoon, John Knox, 34, 48, 261
Witherspoon, John, 34, 44, 45
"Witness of the Church, The" (Patterson), 227
Womack, J. A., 109
Womble, Jordan, 73
Womble, Louis D. Jr., 153
Women's Auxiliary, 191
Women's Rights Convention, 41
women's rights movement, 41-42, 158
Women's Society of Christian Work, 166-67, 167n.35, 169-70. *see also* Ladies Society for Christian Work
Woodfin, John W., 111
World Trade Center, 232
World War I, 164-166, 167, 168, 169-71, 176, 181, 194n.62, 262
World War II, 181, 190-91, 262
Worth, Olive, 239
WPTF, 223
WRAL, 223
Wright, Alfred, 33
Wright, James, 225
Wright, Nancy Ann, 253
Wright, Orville, 157
WUNC, 223
Wyatt, Mamie, 191
Yarborough, H. H., 110n.32
YMCA, 185n.14, 190
York, Willie, 183
Young Ladies Aid Society, 145
Young, James R., 162n.16, 178
YWCA, 169, 186n.20
Zwingli, Ulrich, 2, 80